HERMAN MELVILLE
MOBY-DICK

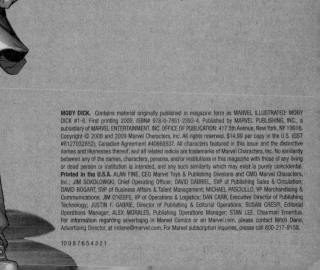

MOBY DICK. Contains material originally published in magazine form as MARVEL ILLUSTRATED: MOBY DICK #1-6. First printing 2009. ISBN# 978-0-7851-2393-4. Published by MARVEL PUBLISHING, INC., a subsidiary of MARVEL ENTERTAINMENT, INC. OFFICE OF PUBLICATION: 417 5th Avenue, New York, NY 10016. Copyright © 2008 and 2009 Marvel Characters, Inc. All rights reserved. $14.99 per copy in the U.S. (GST #R127032852); Canadian Agreement #40668537. All characters featured in this issue and the distinctive names and likenesses thereof, and all related indicia are trademarks of Marvel Characters, Inc. No similarity between any of the names, characters, persons, and/or institutions in this magazine with those of any living or dead person or institution is intended, and any such similarity which may exist is purely coincidental. **Printed in the U.S.A.** ALAN FINE, CEO Marvel Toys & Publishing Divisions and CMO Marvel Characters, Inc.; JIM SOKOLOWSKI, Chief Operating Officer; DAVID GABRIEL, SVP of Publishing Sales & Circulation; DAVID BOGART, SVP of Business Affairs & Talent Management; MICHAEL PASCIULLO, VP Merchandising & Communications; JIM O'KEEFE, VP of Operations & Logistics; DAN CARR, Executive Director of Publishing Technology; JUSTIN F. GABRIE, Director of Publishing & Editorial Operations; SUSAN CRESPI, Editorial Operations Manager; ALEX MORALES, Publishing Operations Manager; STAN LEE, Chairman Emeritus. For information regarding advertising in Marvel Comics or on Marvel.com, please contact Mitch Dane, Advertising Director, at mdane@marvel.com. For Marvel subscription inquiries, please call 800-217-9158.

10 9 8 7 6 5 4 3 2 1

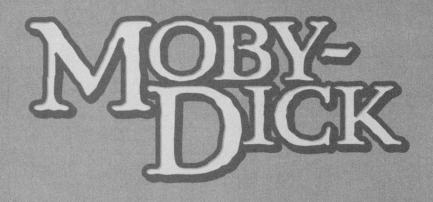

ADAPTED FROM THE NOVEL BY
HERMAN MELVILLE

Writer: **Roy Thomas**
Penciler: **Pascal Alixe**
Inker: **Victor Olazaba**
Colorist: **Sotocolor's Andrew Crossley**
Letterer: **VC's Rus Wooton**
Cover Artist: **John Watson**

Assistant Editor: **Lauren Sankovitch**
Editor: **Nicole Boose**
Senior Editor: **Ralph Macchio**

Special Thanks to Chris Allo, Jeff Suter,
Michael Lawson, Rich Ginter & Jim Nausedas

Collection Editor: **Mark D. Beazley**
Assistant Editors: **John Denning & Cory Levine**
Editor, Special Projects: **Jennifer Grünwald**
Senior Editor, Special Projects: **Jeff Youngquist**
Senior Vice President of Sales: **David Gabriel**
Production: **Jerry Kalinowski**
Book Design: **Spring Hoteling**

Editor in Chief: **Joe Quesada**
Publisher: **Dan Buckley**

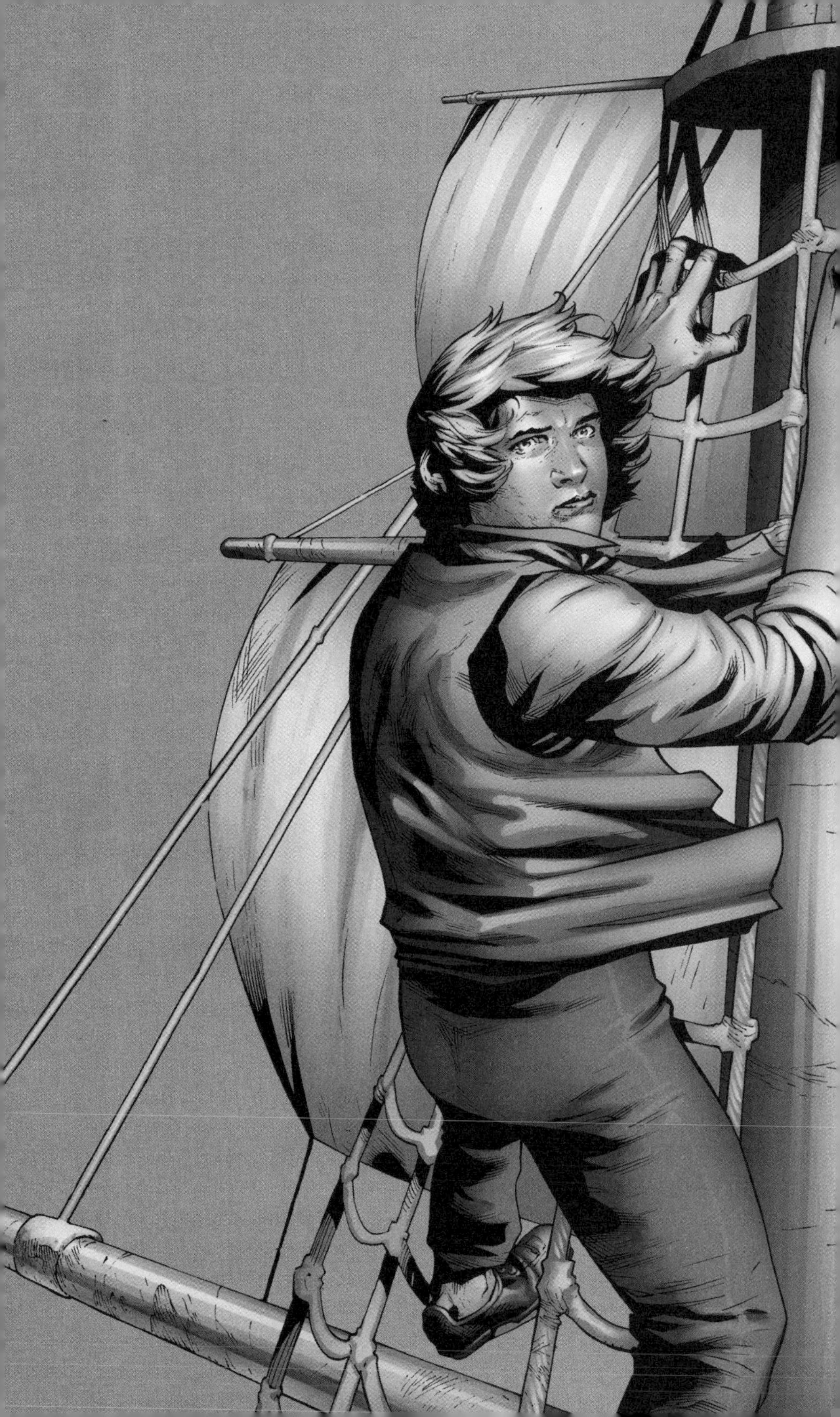

MOBY-DICK
A Personal Introduction
by Roy Thomas

The novel was a financial and critical failure in its author's lifetime.

Yet, since its rediscovery by literary critics in the 1920s, it has been anointed as a classic.

It was derided by some as ponderous, unmemorable.

Yet its first sentence—"Call me Ishmael"—is perhaps the most celebrated opening to any book ever written in America.

Most of its action takes place far—increasingly far—from the United States, and its climax occurs on the other side of the world.

Yet some would consider it the closest thing going to that wondrous will-o'-the-wisp, "the Great American Novel."

Its disastrous reception in 1851 led to the author's writing in an ever more experimental style, and finally abandoning prose entirely for poetry.

Yet today it is hailed as the pinnacle of Herman Melville's work, and has led to his earlier tales of his South Seas travels such as *Typee* and *Omoo* being celebrated and praised.

These are just a few of the paradoxes that abound in the literary life of the novel that its author christened *Moby-Dick or, The Whale*.

Including the mini-paradox that in the book's title the name of the great mammal is hyphenated, while in the text itself the name is simply "Moby Dick," no hyphen. A scholar friend of mine says this was probably due to a publishing decision more than a century and a half ago in which Melville himself had no part, and thus it has been ever since.

In the United States since the 1920s, one grows up with an awareness of *Moby-Dick* as a novel lurking "out there" somewhere, waiting to be read—or at least absorbed somehow by osmosis, because every well-educated person *should* read it.

Even if one never actually gets around to reading the book, one knows of the epic battle waged therein between the obsessed Captain Ahab (one of the most famous characters in American literature) and the great White Whale that robbed him of one of his legs.

Perhaps one has seen the film version made in the 1950s by the acclaimed director John Huston (of *Maltese Falcon* fame), with a script largely by the equally acclaimed science fiction/fantasy author Ray Bradbury, and starring Gregory Peck as a suitably driven (if perhaps a mite too handsome) Ahab. Or maybe, on some vintage-film channel, one has even stumbled across the silent-movie version, which changed the story so much that in the end even the title was changed… to *The Sea Beast.* 'Nuff said.

Two different university literature professor friends of mine have told me that, actually, it is almost impossible to get students to read this novel of perhaps 600 or so pages nowadays. Our future business and societal leaders skip directly to the Cliff's Notes or Sparknote versions, which are allegedly intended only as study guides, not as substitutes for the actual experience of reading the book. In an earlier day, a mostly younger audience might have tried to get by perusing the *Classic Comics/Classics Illustrated* adaptation, which again should simply have served as a bridge, an inspiration to seek out the original.

If so, the cheaters are mostly cheating themselves, for *Moby-Dick* is one of the most fascinating "reads" one will ever find.

I myself was first assigned to read Melville's novel in an advance freshman English class in college. By then, I'd read the *Classics Illustrated* edition, and I'd seen the color movie, with Orson Welles thundering at his parishioners from a pulpit shaped like a ship's bow, and I'd loved both. But it never occurred to me to try to avoid reading the original. After all, to my mind, comic book and movie had merely been harbingers—appetizers for the bountiful feast to come.

And that, hopefully, is what this *Marvel Illustrated* graphic novel will be, as well.

This is the first in this series that was my suggestion as a work to be adapted, as opposed to a decision made solely by others...but that's merely academic. After all, if I hadn't mentioned the possibility, is there any chance at all that *Moby-Dick* wouldn't have been chosen by the powers-that-be, and probably sooner rather than later, for inclusion? Of course not...and rightly so. I was merely eager to come to grips with the task as quickly as possible.

Not that it was an easy assignment. Not only is *Moby-Dick* a lengthy work, but it presents knotty problems that have to be solved.

Chief among them is the fact that, as is well known, quite a few of its chapters, especially in the middle section, are not really "fiction" at all in the usual sense of the word. Instead, Melville used the voice of his narrator, young Ishmael, to present a virtually encyclopedic view of whaling in all its aspects...partly based on the author's own youthful experiences, and partly upon bookish learning. In the end, I decided it was best to concentrate pretty much solely on the storyline itself—heaven knows, there's plenty of that!—but that didn't stop me, while re-reading the novel, from reveling in those chapter-long asides and gleaning an occasional tidbit from them that could be sandwiched into the story proper.

Another problem I hadn't foreseen: One of the most rewarding aspects of the novel is the friendship that speedily develops between Ishmael and the South Seas islander Queequeg. The much-tattooed harpooner has a colorfully primitive kind of speech, based on a rudimentary knowledge of English... at least, he does in the novel's first few chapters. After that, for some reason, his words are almost never directly quoted; instead, Ishmael merely sums up, in proper syntax, what Queequeg has said. I managed to give Queequeg a bit more actual dialogue, trying hard to keep it in harmony with his words in the early chapters.

In addition, the editors and I made what I like to think is the defensible decision to play up the three-days pursuit of Moby-Dick. This chase, its violent tragedy, and its brief aftermath comprise only the final three of the novel's 135 chapters (plus the one-page epilogue)...but these become virtually the final one-third of the adaptation.

And, to go from the big picture to the small detail: Which leg *did* Ahab lose to the whale on the previous voyage, anyway? Amazingly, in all those pages after pages, Melville never says! Most pictorial images over the past 150-plus years have made it the right leg that was replaced with one of ivory. We went with tradition.

I hope and believe that readers of this *Marvel Illustrated* graphic novel will revel, as I did, in the lush art of Pascal Alixe, who had to balance the twin tasks of keeping a mostly ship-bound story visually interesting for page after page...with the larger-than-life clash, in the latter pages, between tiny men and gargantuan whale. This, aided by the inking of Victor Olazaba, our hardworking artist accomplished admirably. And John Watson's covers became a wondrous, dramatically decorated stage curtain, which was to be opened upon the drama within.

For myself: this was the third time in my life that I have read and savored *Moby-Dick*. If I'm lucky, it won't be the last.

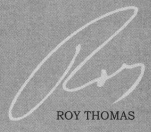

ROY THOMAS

Roy Thomas began his award-winning career as a writer and editor in 1965, working with Stan Lee in the early days of the Marvel Age of Comics, scripting key runs of The X-Men, The Avengers, Dr. Strange, Fantastic Four, The Amazing Spider-Man, *and other titles, later becoming the original long-running writer/editor of Marvel's* Conan *magazines.*

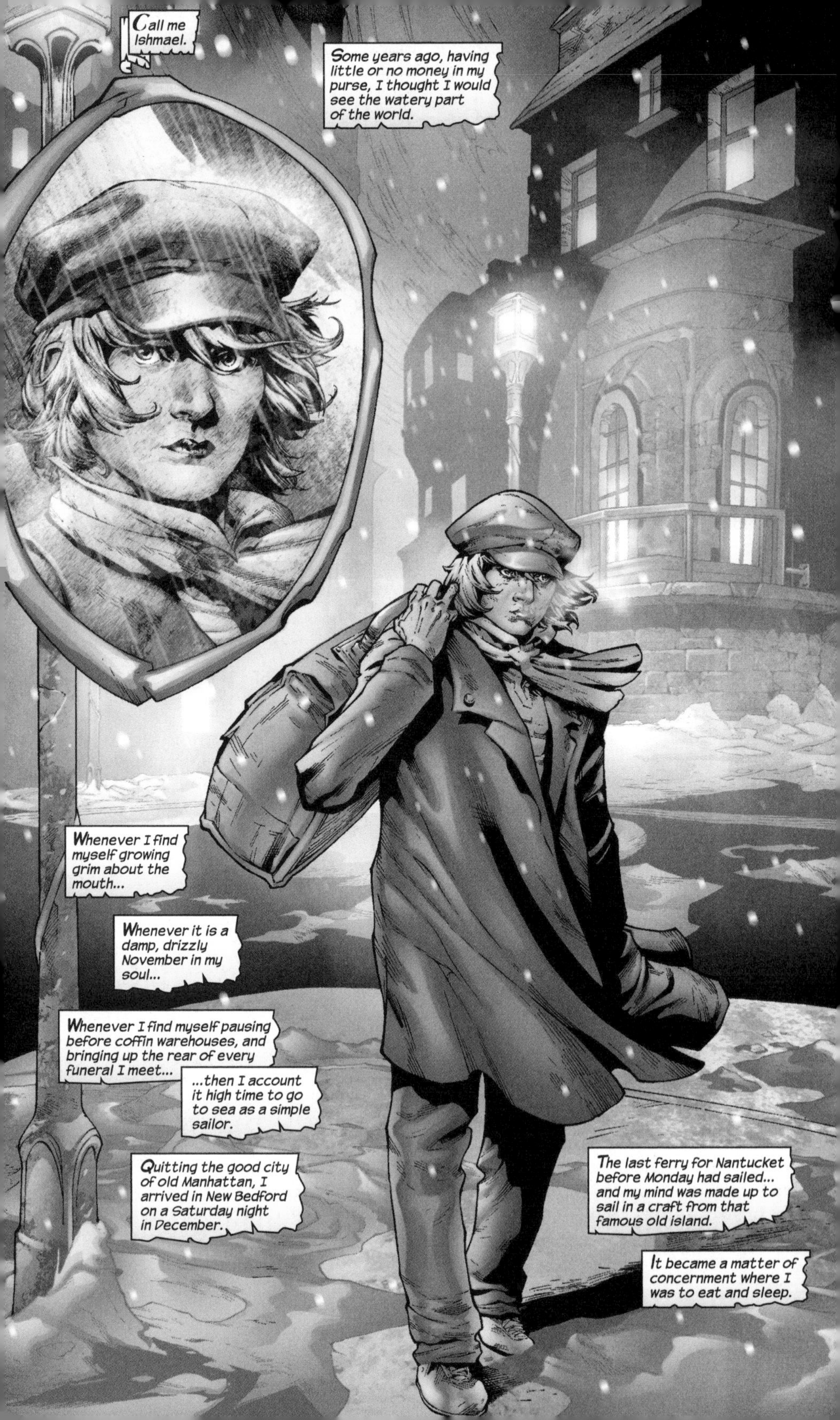
Call me Ishmael.
Some years ago, having little or no money in my purse, I thought I would see the watery part of the world.
Whenever I find myself growing grim about the mouth...
Whenever it is a damp, drizzly November in my soul...
Whenever I find myself pausing before coffin warehouses, and bringing up the rear of every funeral I meet...
...then I account it high time to go to sea as a simple sailor.
Quitting the good city of old Manhattan, I arrived in New Bedford on a Saturday night in December.
The last ferry for Nantucket before Monday had sailed... and my mind was made up to sail in a craft from that famous old island.
It became a matter of concernment where I was to eat and sleep.

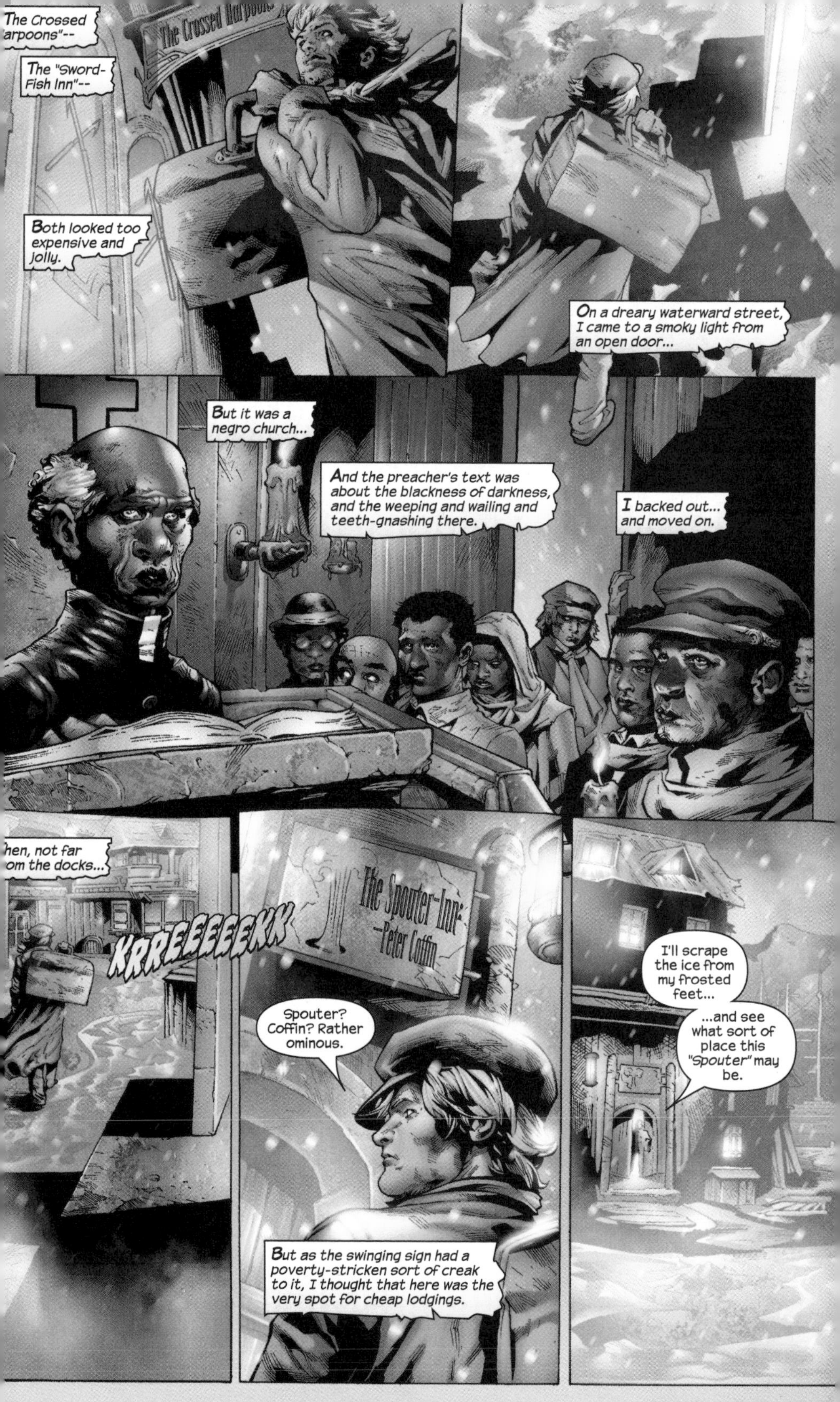
The Crossed
arpoons"--
The "Sword-Fish Inn"--
Both looked too expensive and jolly.
The Crossed Harpoons
On a dreary waterward street, I came to a smoky light from an open door...
But it was a negro church...
And the preacher's text was about the blackness of darkness, and the weeping and wailing and teeth-gnashing there.
I backed out... and moved on.
hen, not far
om the docks...
KRREEEEEEKK
The Spouter-Inn: —Peter Coffin
Spouter? Coffin? Rather ominous.
But as the swinging sign had a poverty-stricken sort of creak to it, I thought that here was the very spot for cheap lodgings.
I'll scrape the ice from my frosted feet...
...and see what sort of place this "Spouter" may be.

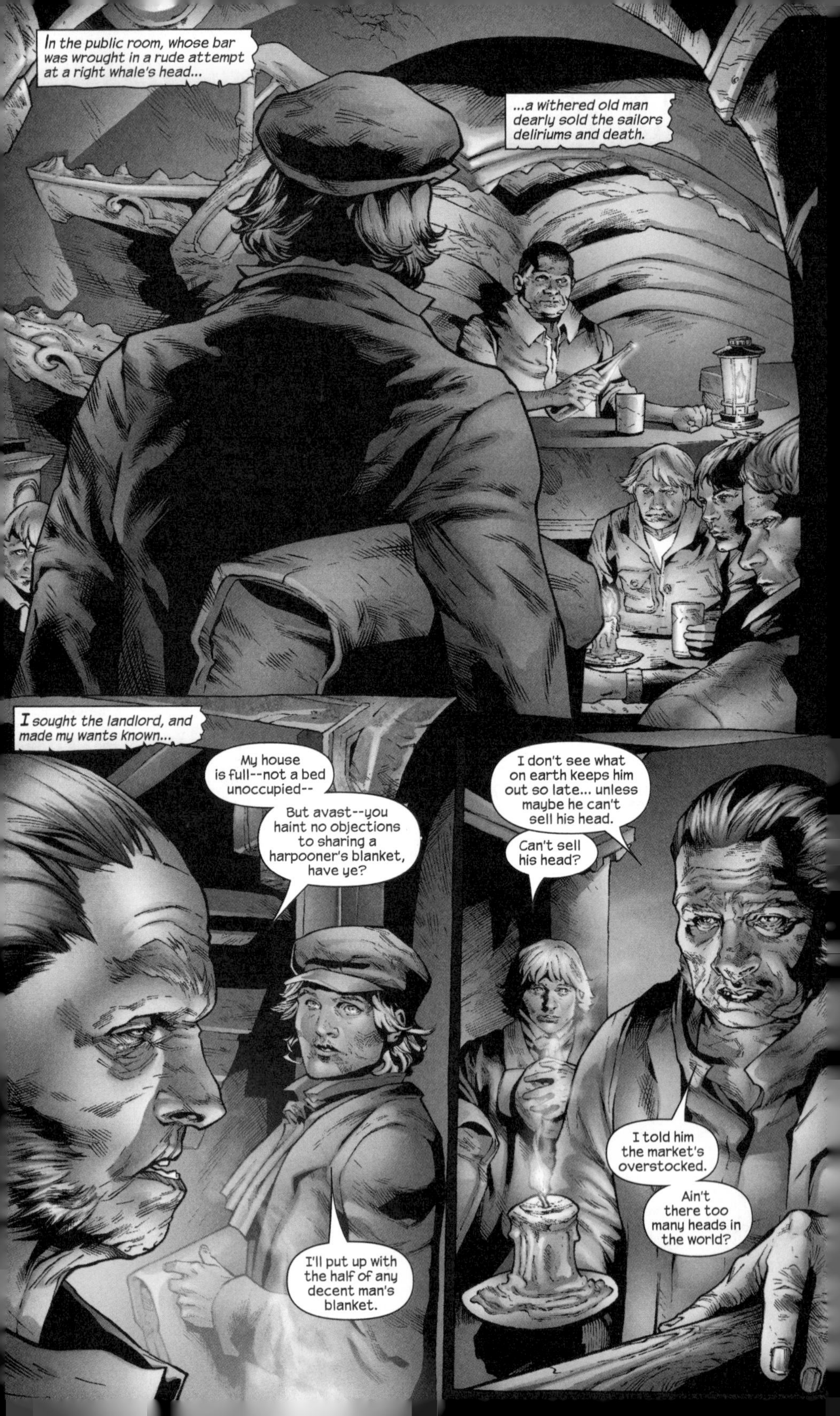
In the public room, whose bar was wrought in a rude attempt at a right whale's head...
...a withered old man dearly sold the sailors deliriums and death.
I sought the landlord, and made my wants known...
My house is full--not a bed unoccupied--
But avast--you haint no objections to sharing a harpooner's blanket, have ye?
I'll put up with the half of any decent man's blanket.
I don't see what on earth keeps him out so late... unless maybe he can't sell his head.
Can't sell his head?
I told him the market's overstocked.
Ain't there too many heads in the world?

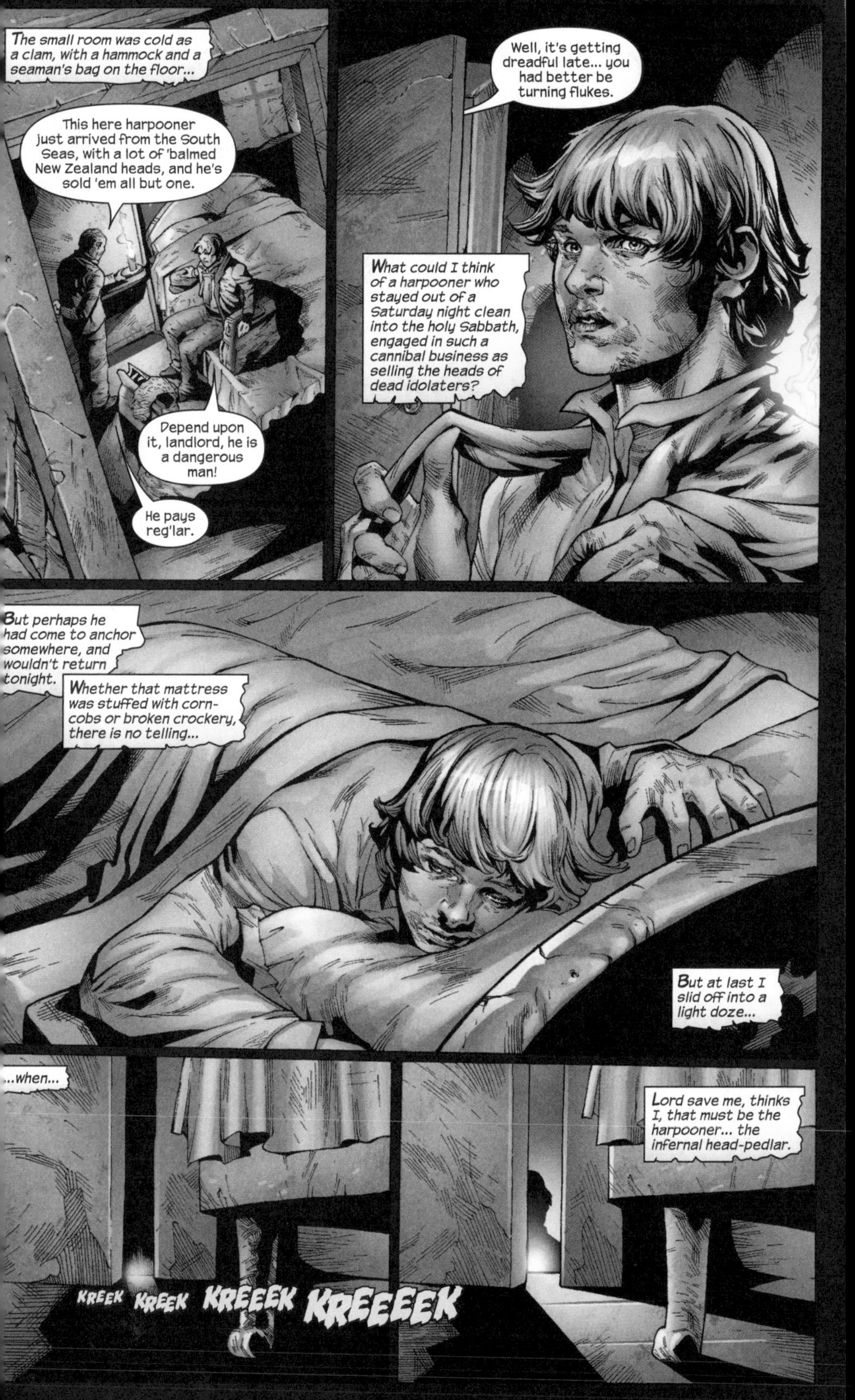
The small room was cold as a clam, with a hammock and a seaman's bag on the floor...
This here harpooner just arrived from the South Seas, with a lot of 'balmed New Zealand heads, and he's sold 'em all but one.
Depend upon it, landlord, he is a dangerous man!
He pays reg'lar.
Well, it's getting dreadful late... you had better be turning flukes.
What could I think of a harpooner who stayed out of a Saturday night clean into the holy Sabbath, engaged in such a cannibal business as selling the heads of dead idolaters?
But perhaps he had come to anchor somewhere, and wouldn't return tonight.
Whether that mattress was stuffed with corn-cobs or broken crockery, there is no telling...
But at last I slid off into a light doze...
...when...
Lord save me, thinks I, that must be the harpooner... the infernal head-pedlar.
KREEK KREEK KREEEK KREEEEEK

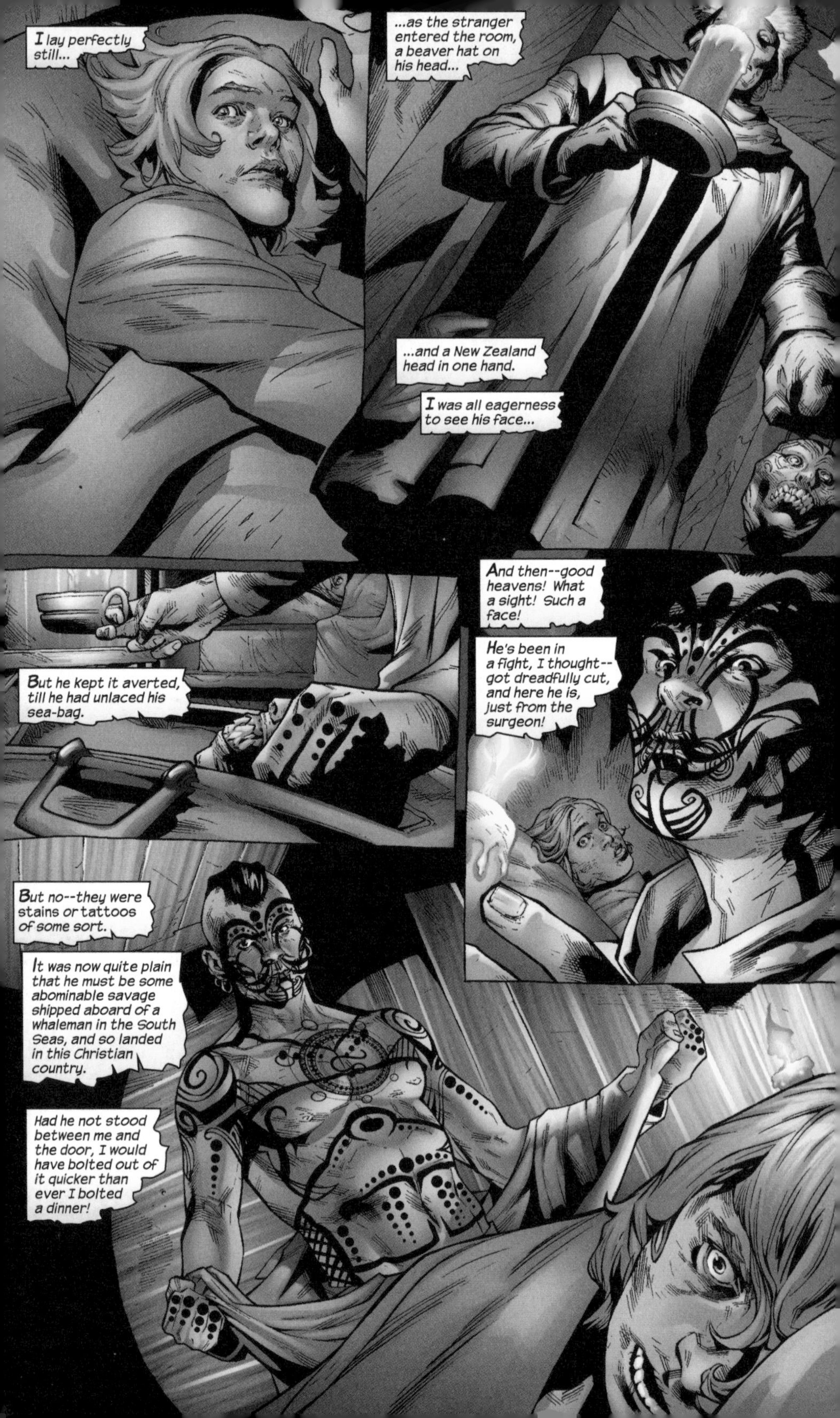
I lay perfectly still...
...as the stranger entered the room, a beaver hat on his head...
...and a New Zealand head in one hand.
I was all eagerness to see his face...
But he kept it averted, till he had unlaced his sea-bag.
And then--good heavens! What a sight! Such a face!
He's been in a fight, I thought--got dreadfully cut, and here he is, just from the surgeon!
But no--they were stains or tattoos of some sort.
It was now quite plain that he must be some abominable savage shipped aboard of a whaleman in the South Seas, and so landed in this Christian country.
Had he not stood between me and the door, I would have bolted out of it quicker than ever I bolted a dinner!

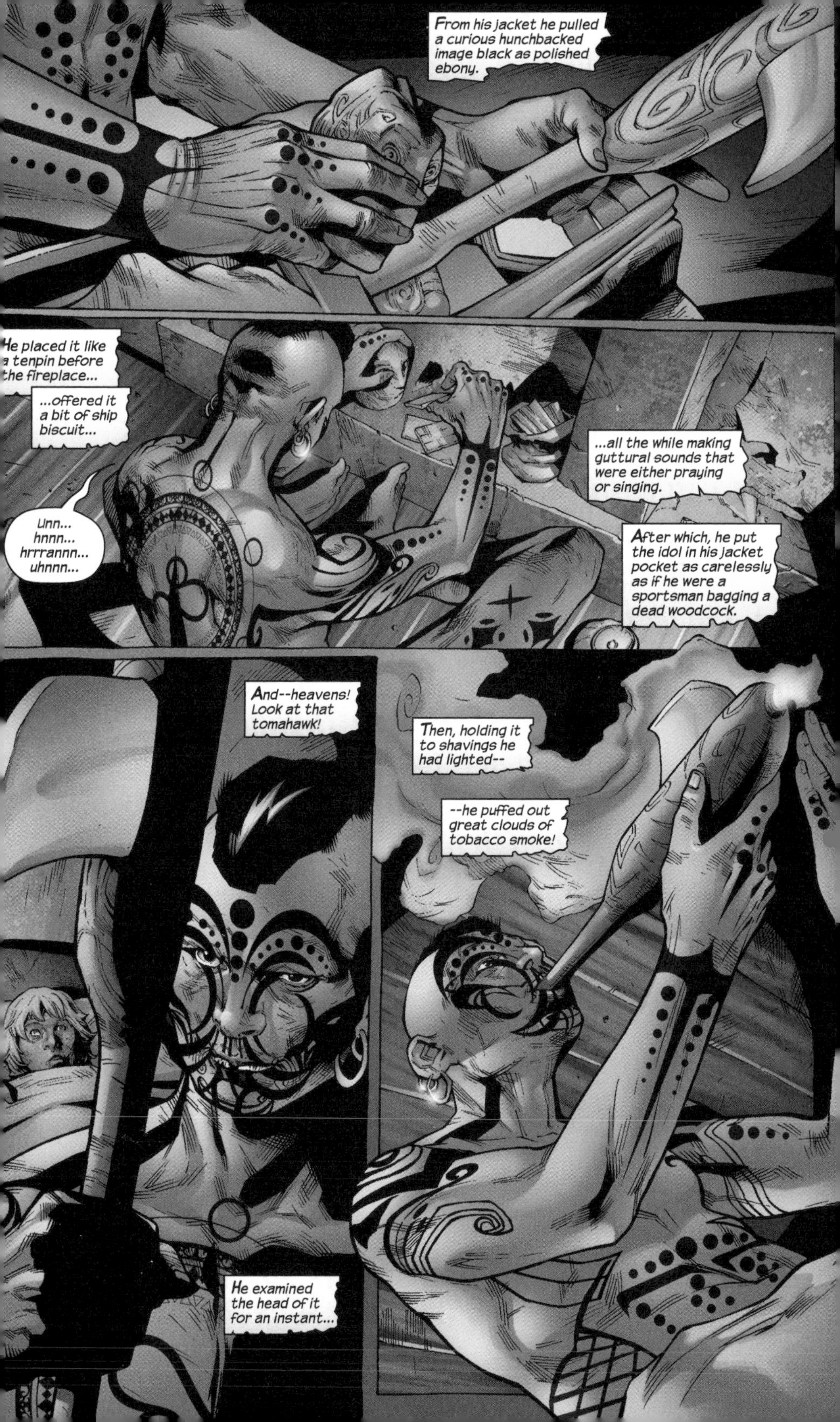
From his jacket he pulled a curious hunchbacked image black as polished ebony.
He placed it like a tenpin before the fireplace...
...offered it a bit of ship biscuit...
Unn... hnnn... hrrrannn... uhnnn...
...all the while making guttural sounds that were either praying or singing.
After which, he put the idol in his jacket pocket as carelessly as if he were a sportsman bagging a dead woodcock.
And--heavens! Look at that tomahawk!
He examined the head of it for an instant...
Then, holding it to shavings he had lighted--
--he puffed out great clouds of tobacco smoke!

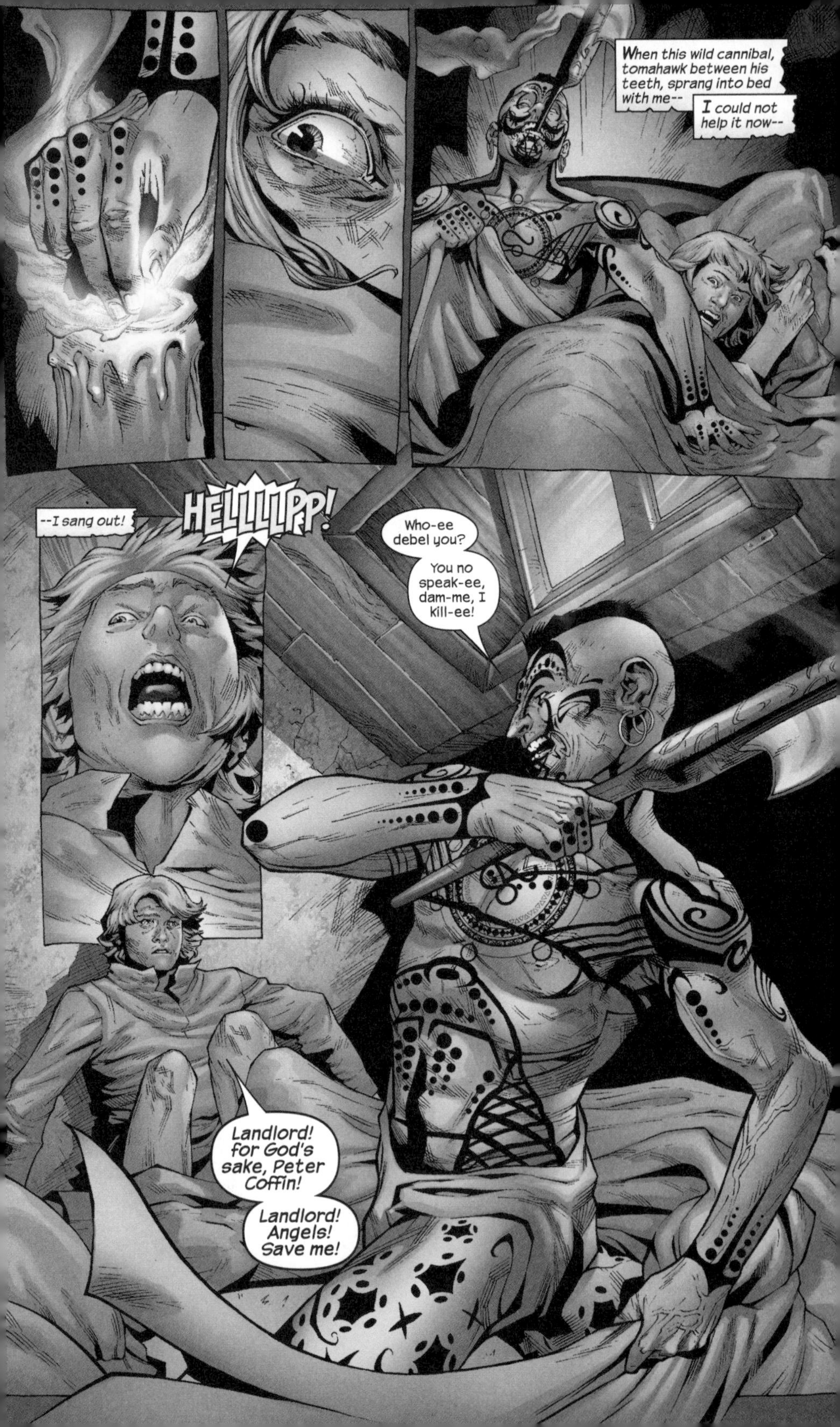
When this wild cannibal, tomahawk between his teeth, sprang into bed with me--
I could not help it now--
--I sang out!
HELLLLLPP!
Who-ee debel you?
You no speak-ee, dam-me, I kill-ee!
Landlord! for God's sake, Peter Coffin!
Landlord! Angels! Save me!

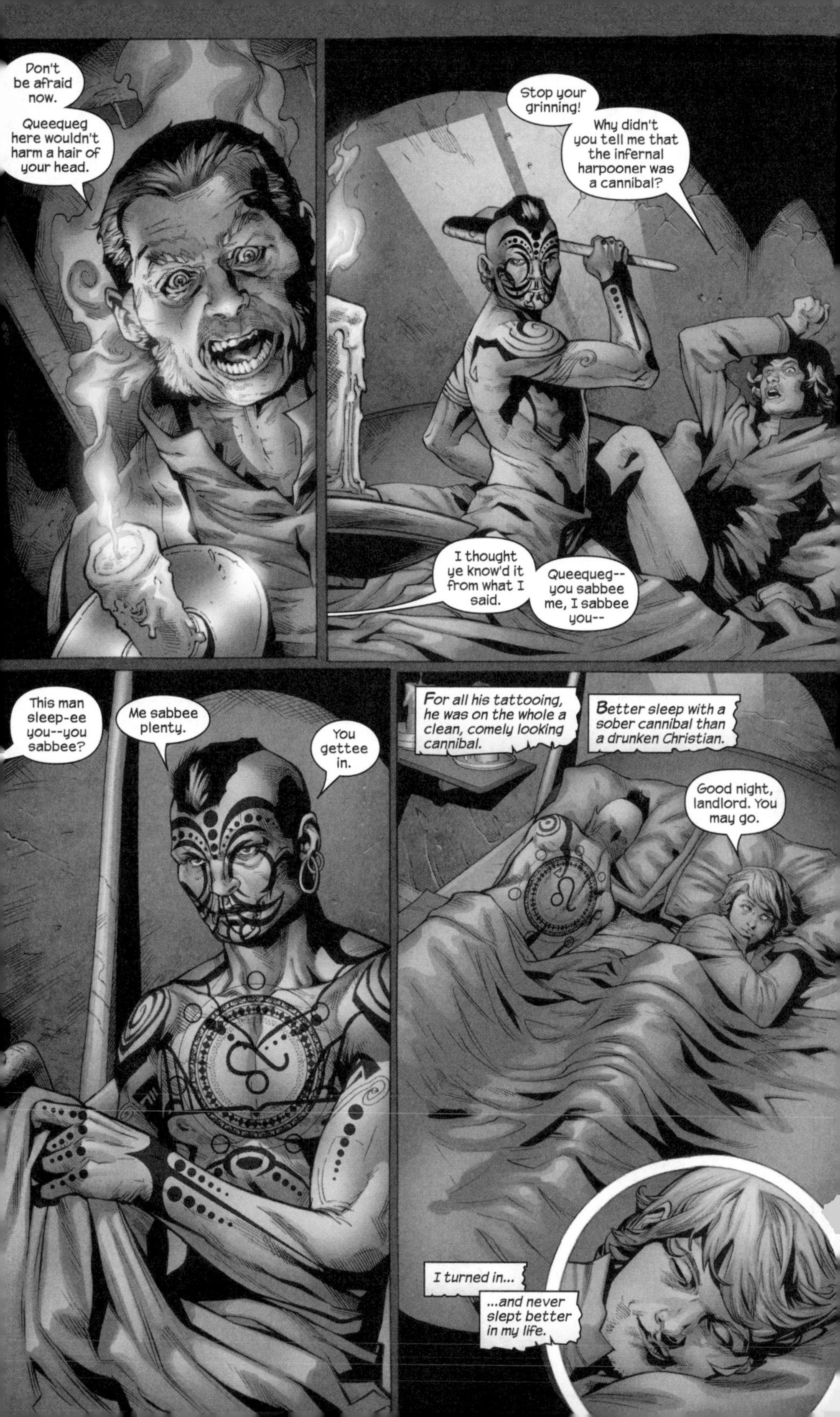
Don't be afraid now.
Queequeg here wouldn't harm a hair of your head.
Stop your grinning!
Why didn't you tell me that the infernal harpooner was a cannibal?
I thought ye know'd it from what I said.
Queequeg--you sabbee me, I sabbee you--
This man sleep-ee you--you sabbee?
Me sabbee plenty.
You gettee in.
For all his tattooing, he was on the whole a clean, comely looking cannibal.
Better sleep with a sober cannibal than a drunken Christian.
Good night, landlord. You may go.
I turned in...
...and never slept better in my life.

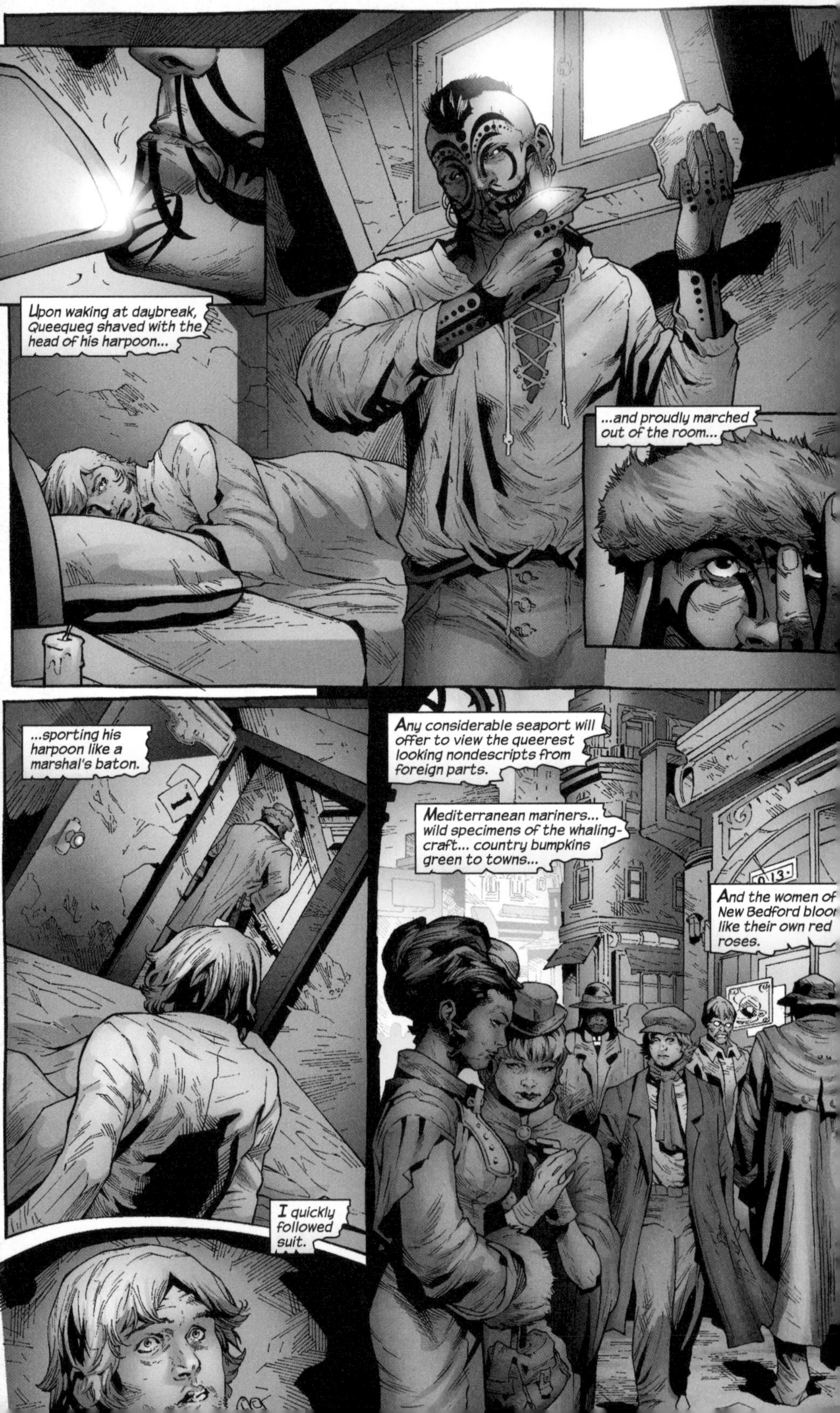
Upon waking at daybreak, Queequeg shaved with the head of his harpoon...
...and proudly marched out of the room...
...sporting his harpoon like a marshal's baton.
I quickly followed suit.
Any considerable seaport will offer to view the queerest looking nondescripts from foreign parts.
Mediterranean mariners... wild specimens of the whaling-craft... country bumpkins green to towns...
And the women of New Bedford bloo like their own red roses.

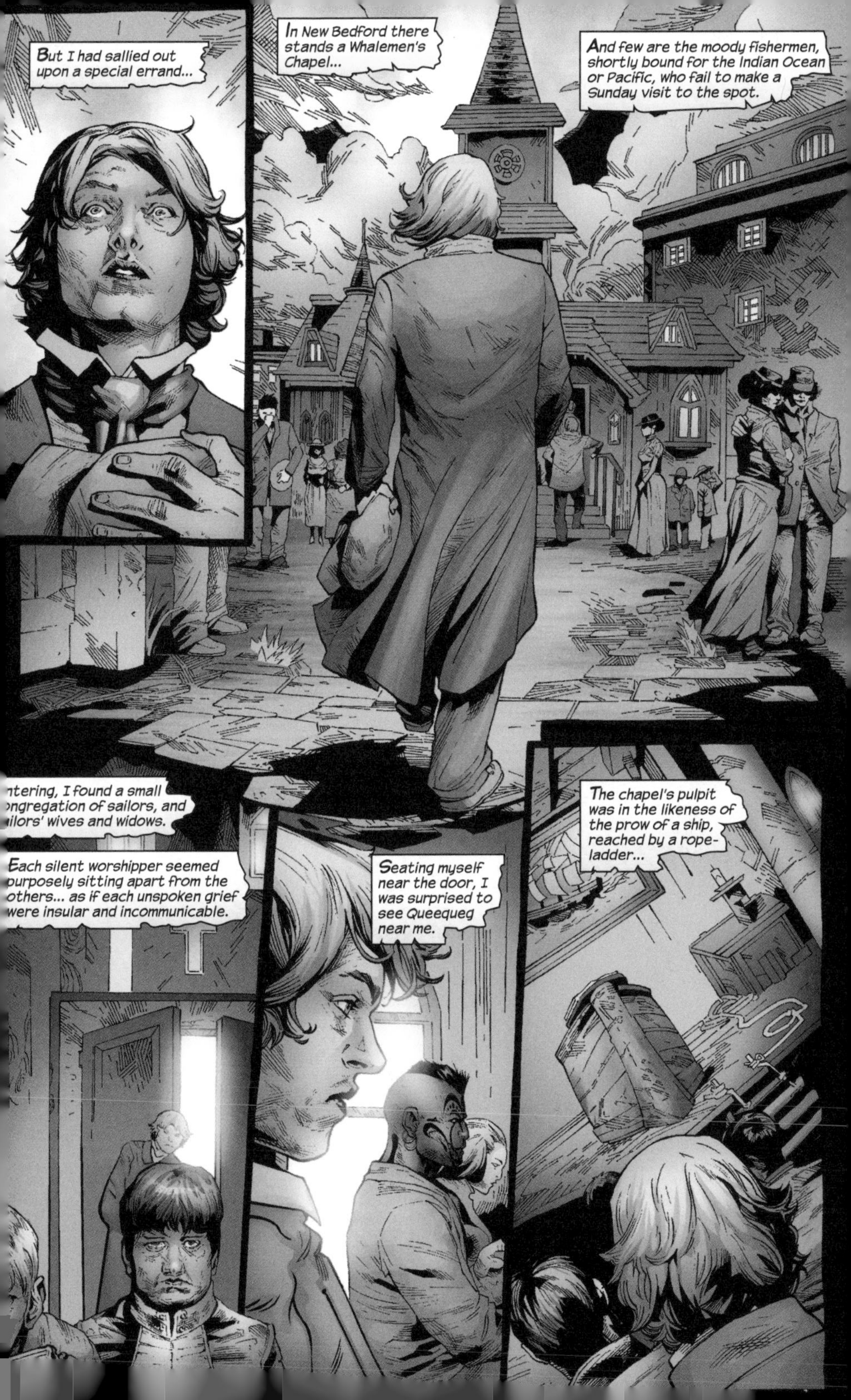
But I had sallied out upon a special errand...
In New Bedford there stands a Whalemen's Chapel...
And few are the moody fishermen, shortly bound for the Indian Ocean or Pacific, who fail to make a Sunday visit to the spot.
ntering, I found a small ongregation of sailors, and ilors' wives and widows.
Each silent worshipper seemed purposely sitting apart from the others... as if each unspoken grief were insular and incommunicable.
Seating myself near the door, I was surprised to see Queequeg near me.
The chapel's pulpit was in the likeness of the prow of a ship, reached by a rope-ladder...

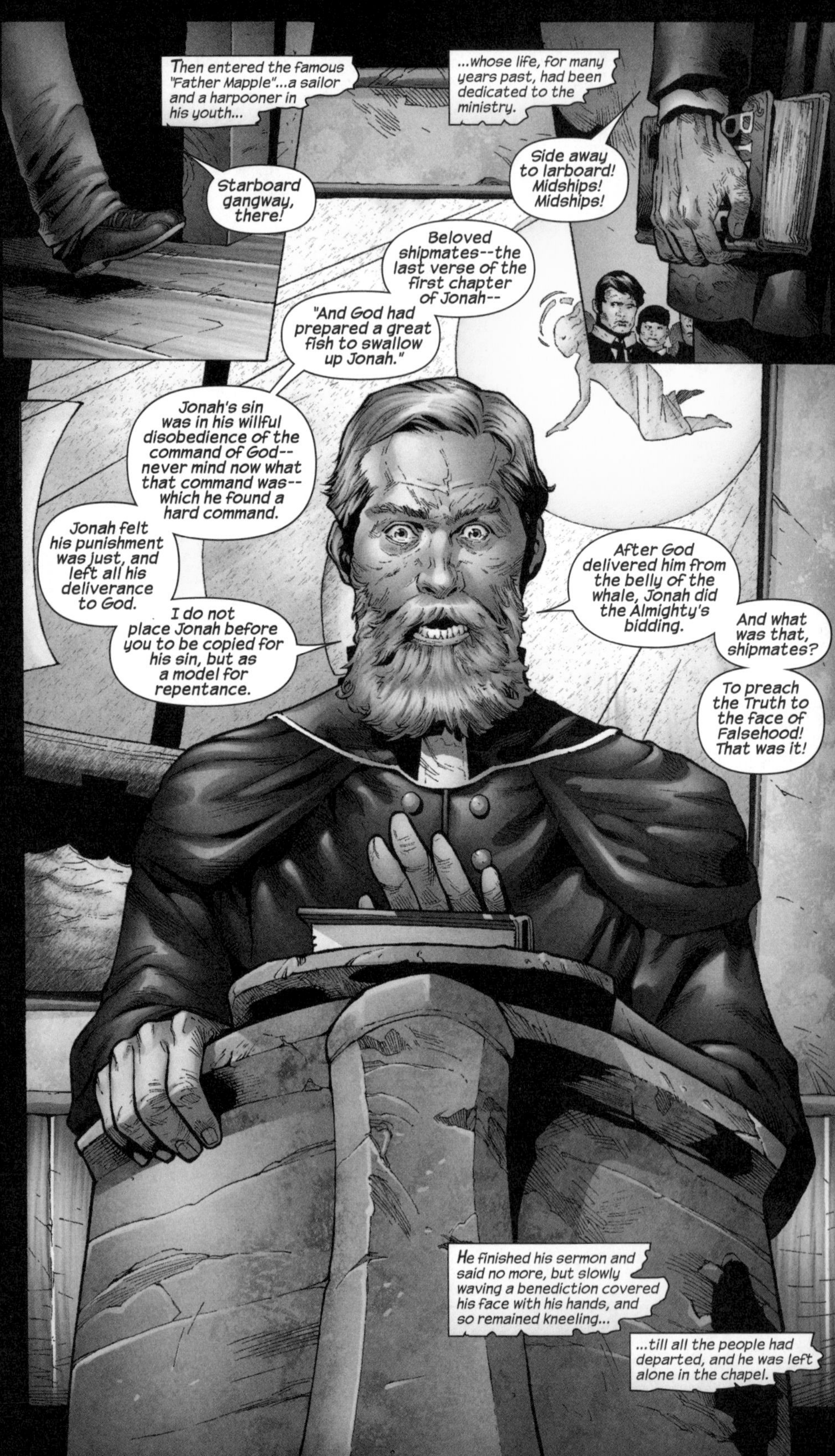

Then entered the famous "Father Mapple"...a sailor and a harpooner in his youth...
...whose life, for many years past, had been dedicated to the ministry.
Starboard gangway, there!
Side away to larboard! Midships! Midships!
Beloved shipmates--the last verse of the first chapter of Jonah--
"And God had prepared a great fish to swallow up Jonah."
Jonah's sin was in his willful disobedience of the command of God--never mind now what that command was--which he found a hard command.
Jonah felt his punishment was just, and left all his deliverance to God.
I do not place Jonah before you to be copied for his sin, but as a model for repentance.
After God delivered him from the belly of the whale, Jonah did the Almighty's bidding.
And what was that, shipmates?
To preach the Truth to the face of Falsehood! That was it!
He finished his sermon and said no more, but slowly waving a benediction covered his face with his hands, and so remained kneeling...
...till all the people had departed, and he was left alone in the chapel.

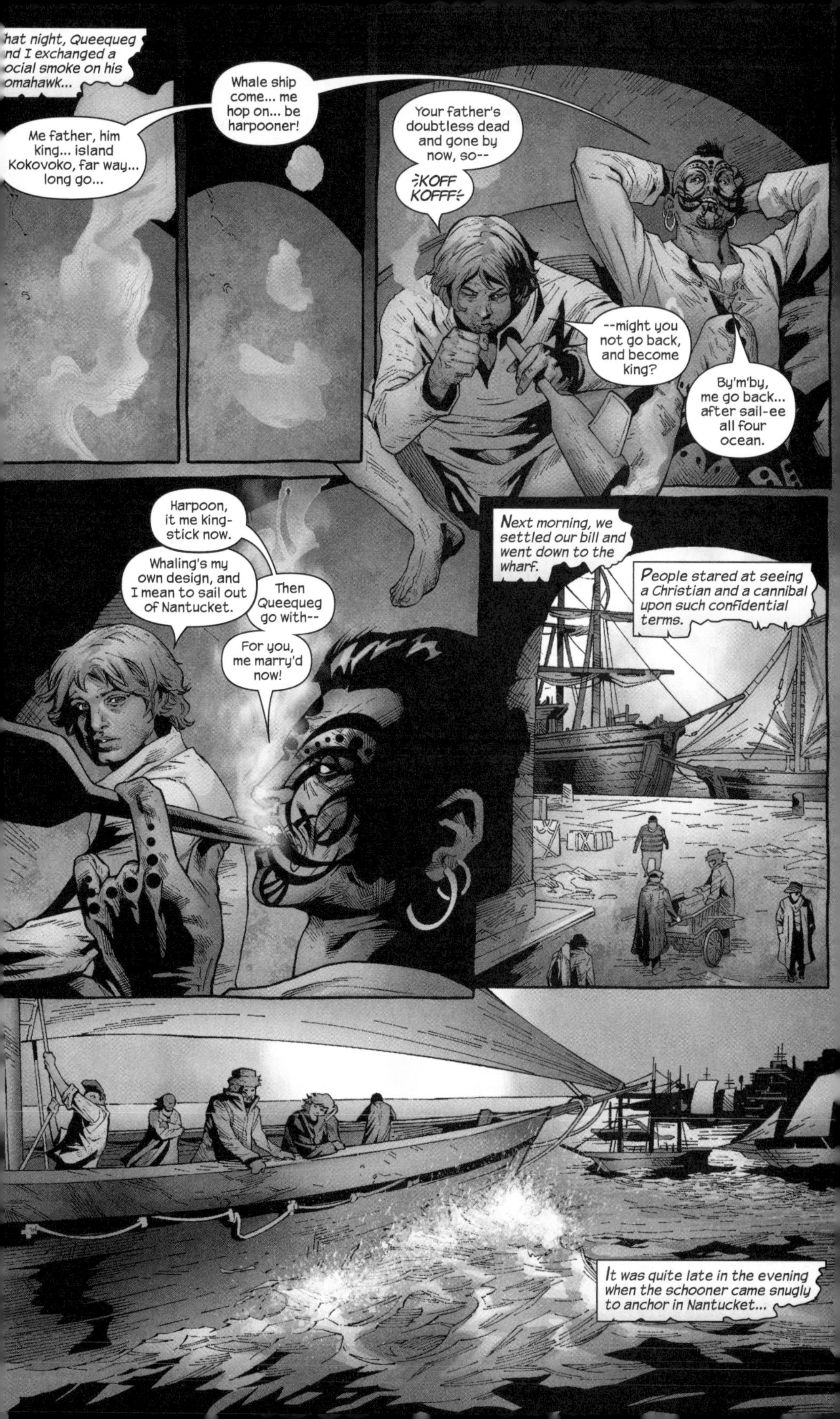
hat night, Queequeg
nd I exchanged a
ocial smoke on his
omahawk...
Me father, him king... island Kokovoko, far way... long go...
Whale ship come... me hop on... be harpooner!
Your father's doubtless dead and gone by now, so--
KOFF KOFFF
--might you not go back, and become king?
By'm'by, me go back... after sail-ee all four ocean.
Harpoon, it me king-stick now.
Whaling's my own design, and I mean to sail out of Nantucket.
Then Queequeg go with--
For you, me marry'd now!
Next morning, we settled our bill and went down to the wharf.
People stared at seeing a Christian and a cannibal upon such confidential terms.
It was quite late in the evening when the schooner came snugly to anchor in Nantucket...

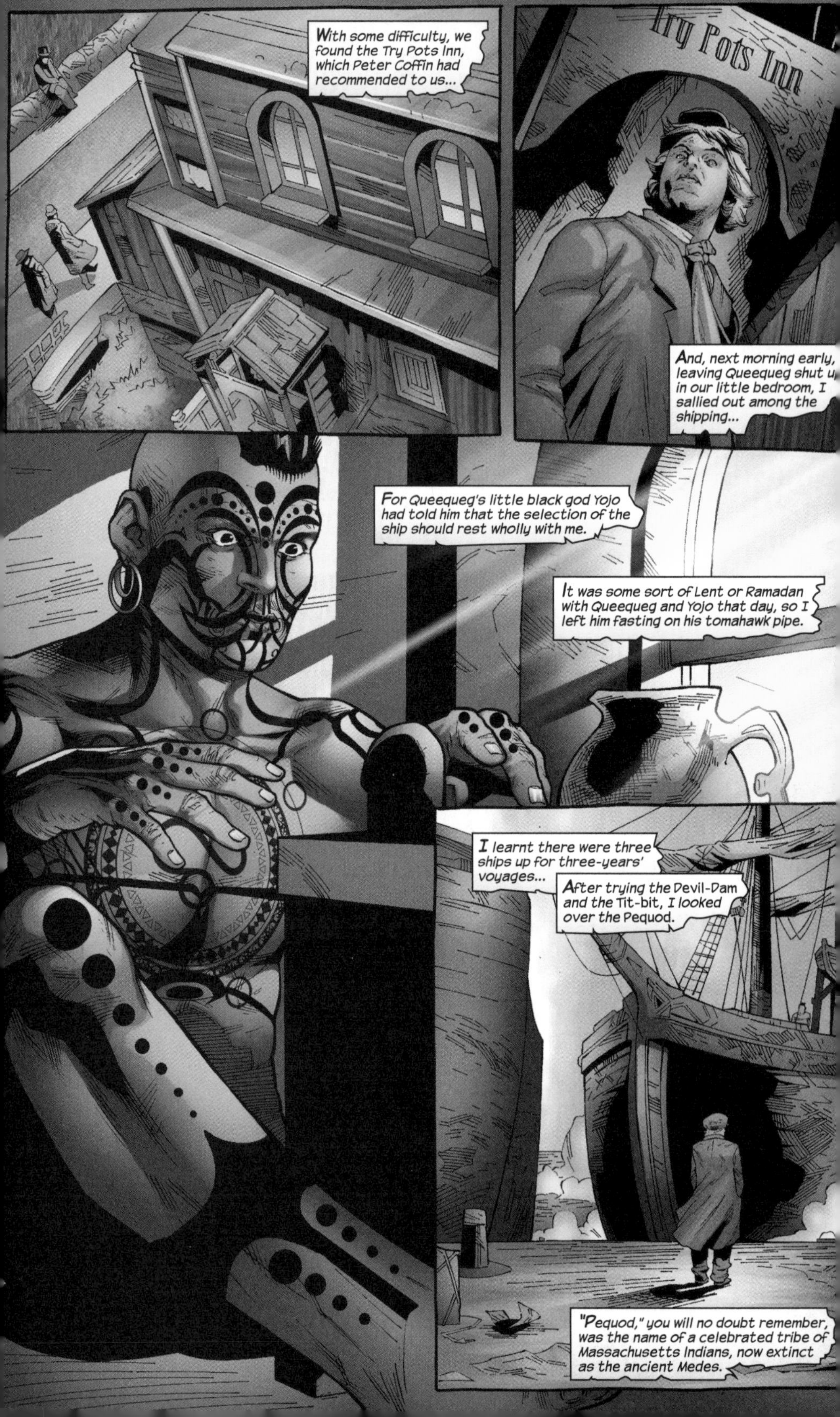
With some difficulty, we found the Try Pots Inn, which Peter Coffin had recommended to us...
Try Pots Inn
And, next morning early, leaving Queequeg shut u in our little bedroom, I sallied out among the shipping...
For Queequeg's little black god Yojo had told him that the selection of the ship should rest wholly with me.
It was some sort of Lent or Ramadan with Queequeg and Yojo that day, so I left him fasting on his tomahawk pipe.
I learnt there were three ships up for three-years' voyages...
After trying the Devil-Dam and the Tit-bit, I looked over the Pequod.
"Pequod," you will no doubt remember, was the name of a celebrated tribe of Massachusetts Indians, now extinct as the ancient Medes.

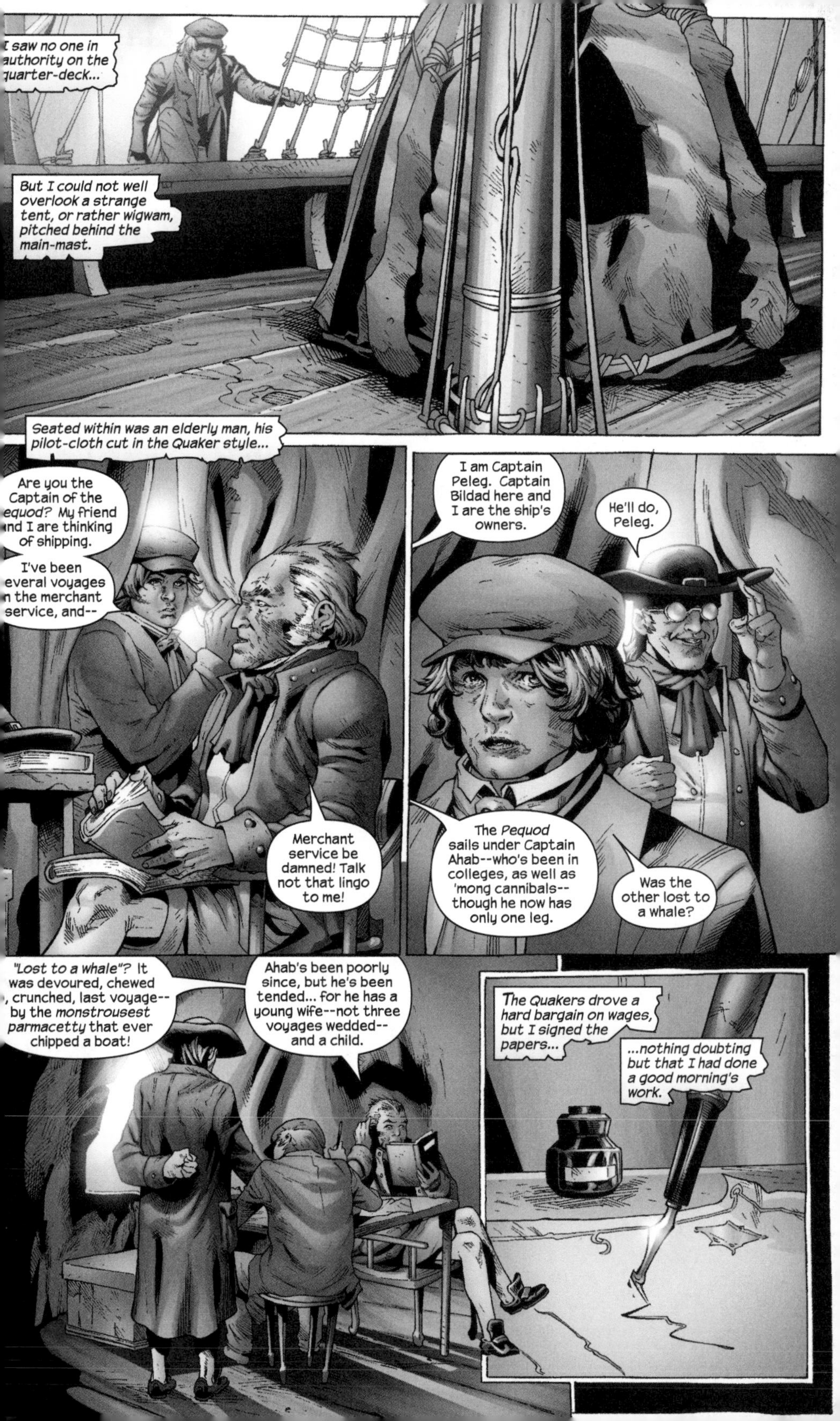
I saw no one in authority on the quarter-deck...
But I could not well overlook a strange tent, or rather wigwam, pitched behind the main-mast.
Seated within was an elderly man, his pilot-cloth cut in the Quaker style...
Are you the Captain of the Pequod? My friend and I are thinking of shipping.
I've been several voyages in the merchant service, and--
Merchant service be damned! Talk not that lingo to me!
I am Captain Peleg. Captain Bildad here and I are the ship's owners.
He'll do, Peleg.
The Pequod sails under Captain Ahab--who's been in colleges, as well as 'mong cannibals--though he now has only one leg.
Was the other lost to a whale?
"Lost to a whale"? It was devoured, chewed, crunched, last voyage--by the monstrousest parmacetty that ever chipped a boat!
Ahab's been poorly since, but he's been tended... for he has a young wife--not three voyages wedded--and a child.
The Quakers drove a hard bargain on wages, but I signed the papers...
...nothing doubting but that I had done a good morning's work.

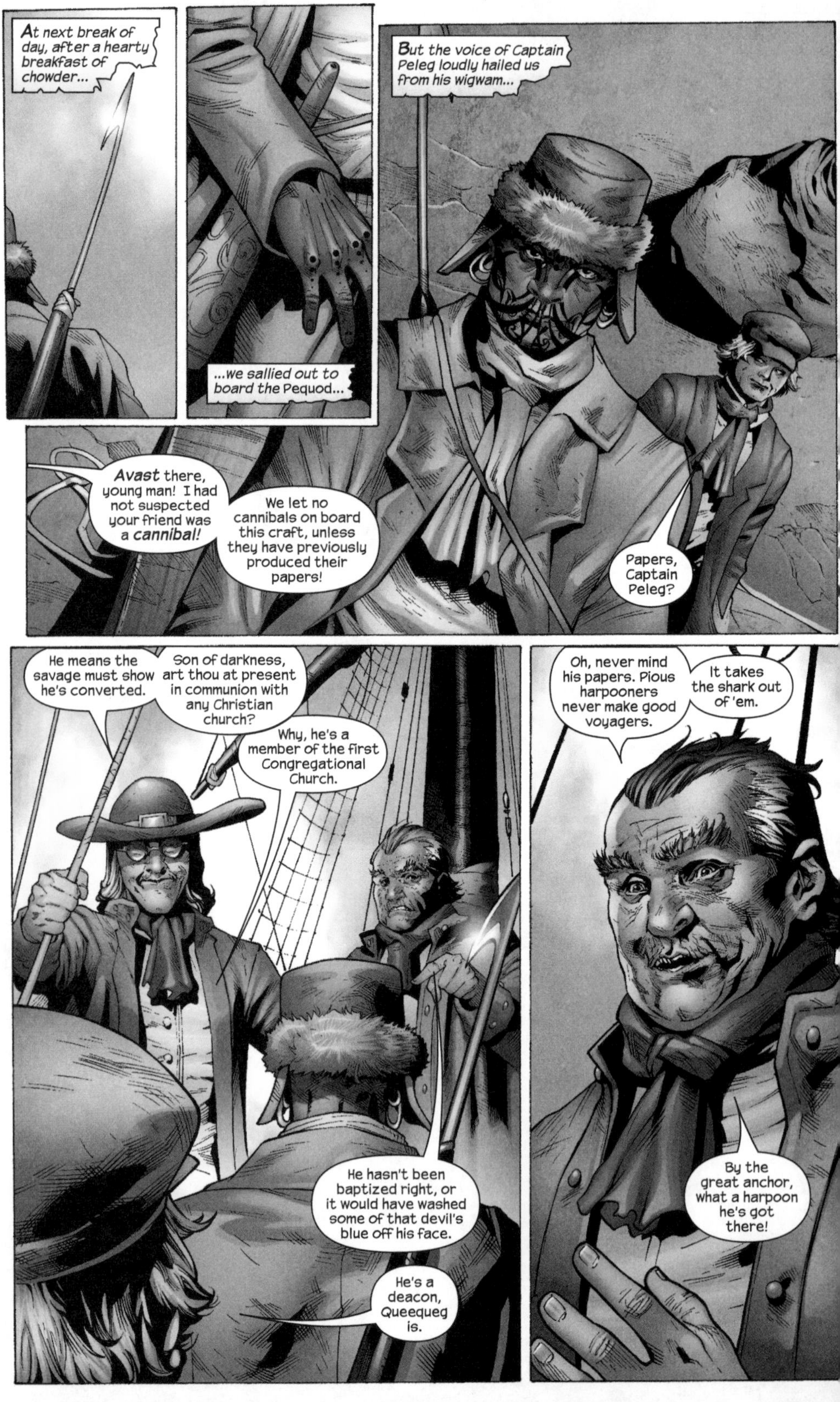
At next break of day, after a hearty breakfast of chowder...
...we sallied out to board the Pequod...
But the voice of Captain Peleg loudly hailed us from his wigwam...
Avast there, young man! I had not suspected your friend was a cannibal!
We let no cannibals on board this craft, unless they have previously produced their papers!
Papers, Captain Peleg?
He means the savage must show he's converted.
Son of darkness, art thou at present in communion with any Christian church?
Why, he's a member of the first Congregational Church.
He hasn't been baptized right, or it would have washed some of that devil's blue off his face.
He's a deacon, Queequeg is.
Oh, never mind his papers. Pious harpooners never make good voyagers.
It takes the shark out of 'em.
By the great anchor, what a harpoon he's got there!

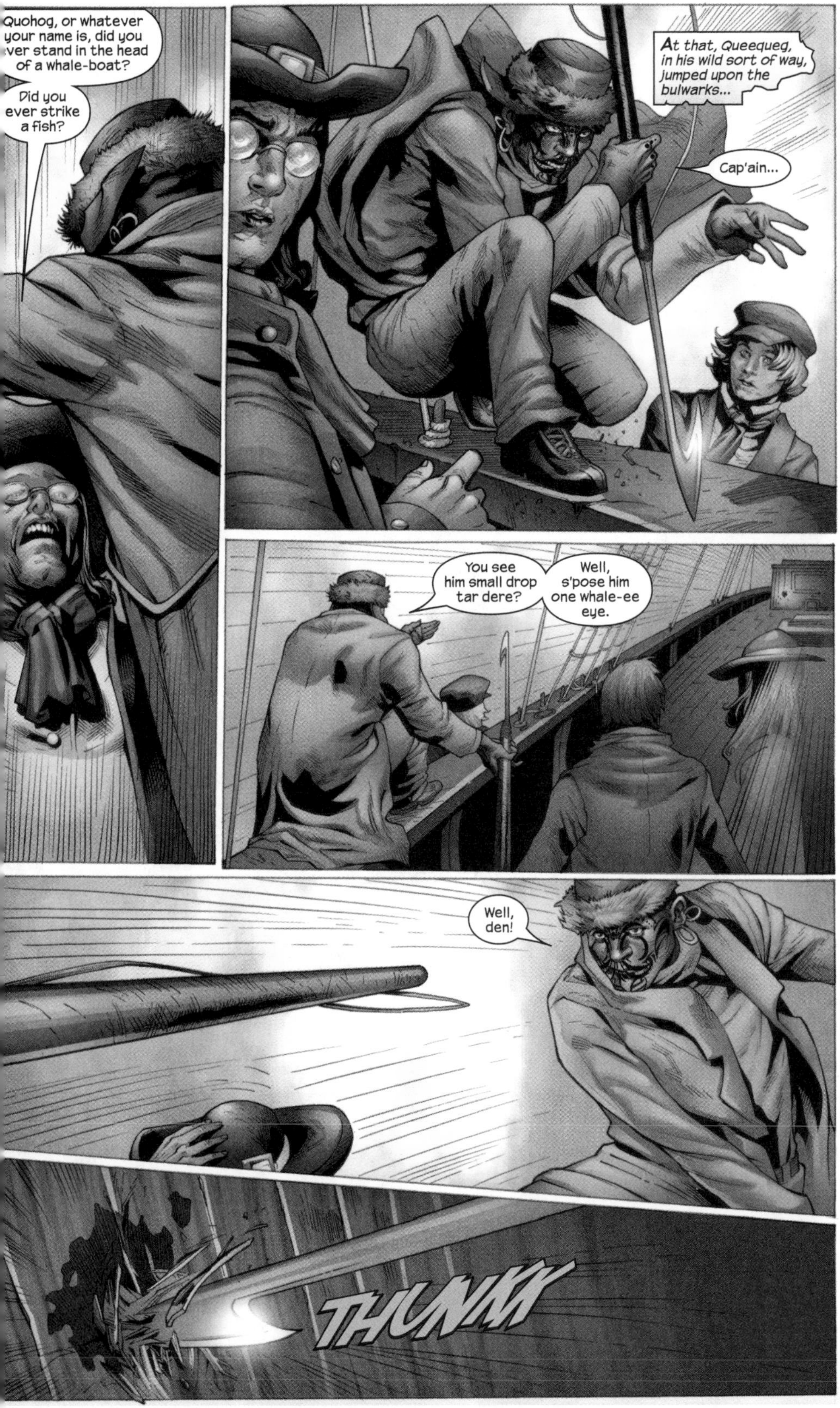
Quohog, or whatever your name is, did you ever stand in the head of a whale-boat?
Did you ever strike a fish?
At that, Queequeg, in his wild sort of way, jumped upon the bulwarks...
Cap'ain...
You see him small drop tar dere?
Well, s'pose him one whale-ee eye.
Well, den!
THUNK

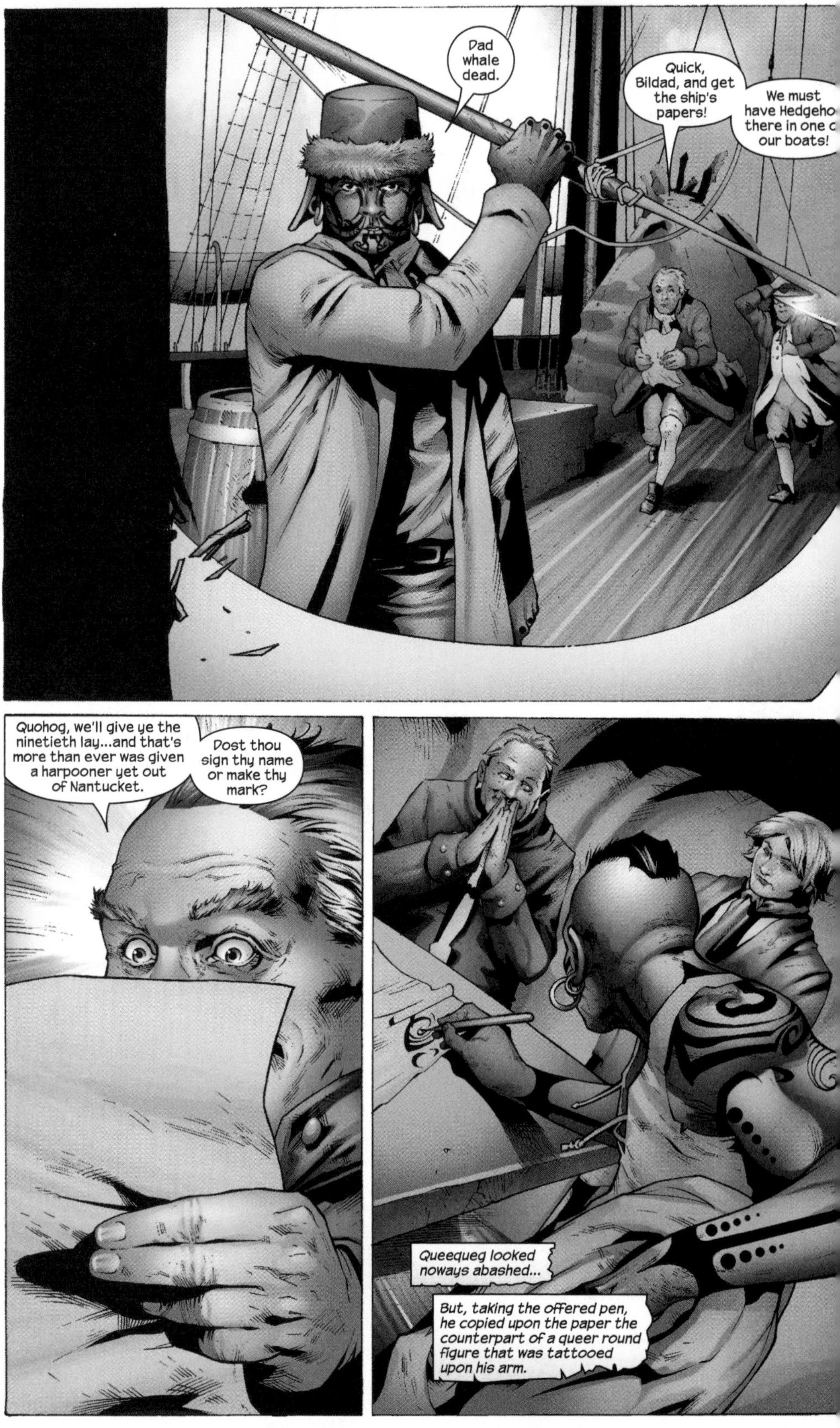

Dad whale dead.
Quick, Bildad, and get the ship's papers!
We must have Hedgeho there in one o our boats!
Quohog, we'll give ye the ninetieth lay...and that's more than ever was given a harpooner yet out of Nantucket.
Dost thou sign thy name or make thy mark?
Queequeg looked noways abashed...
But, taking the offered pen, he copied upon the paper the counterpart of a queer round figure that was tattooed upon his arm.

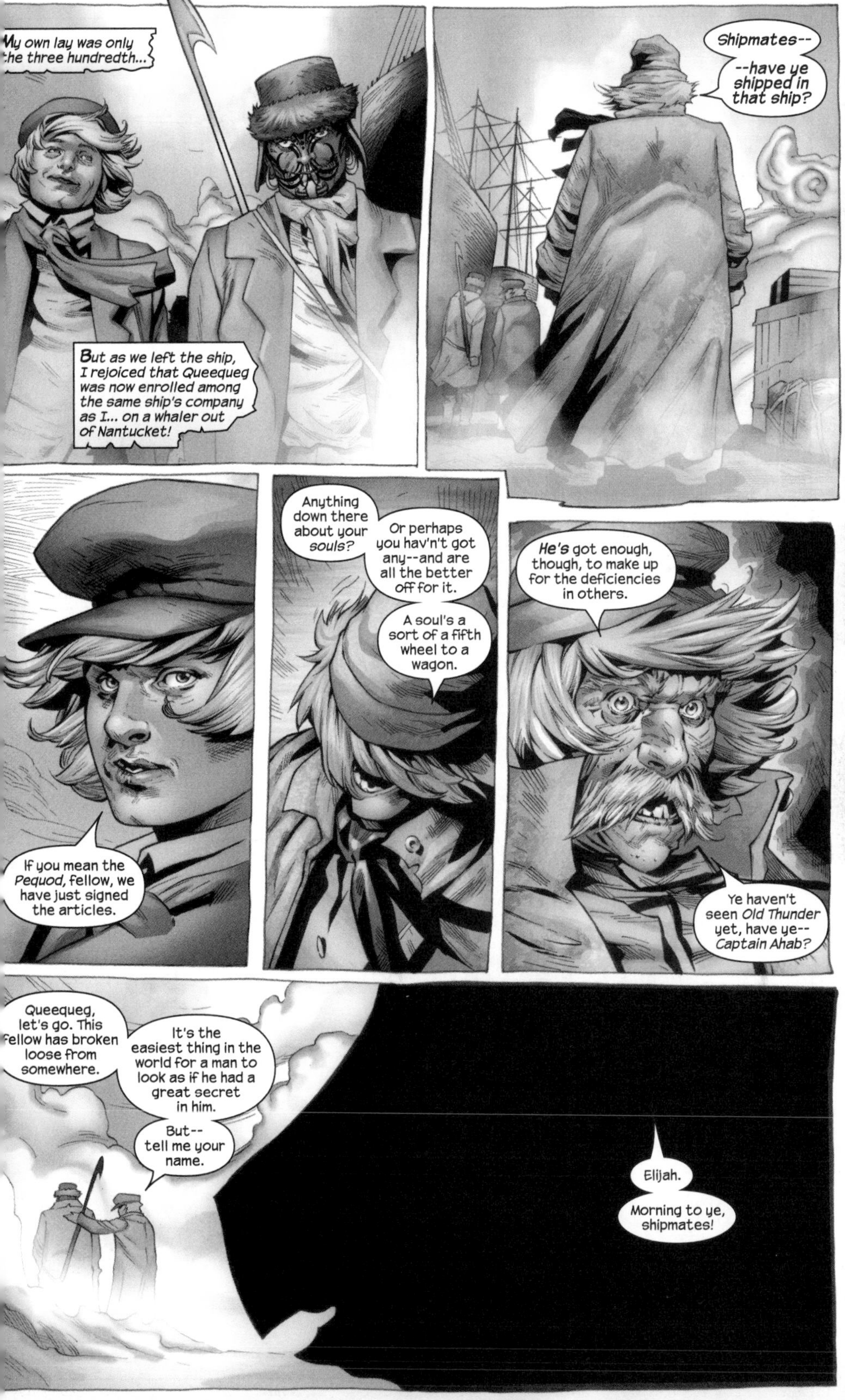
My own lay was only the three hundredth...
But as we left the ship, I rejoiced that Queequeg was now enrolled among the same ship's company as I... on a whaler out of Nantucket!
Shipmates--
--have ye shipped in that ship?
If you mean the Pequod, fellow, we have just signed the articles.
Anything down there about your souls?
Or perhaps you hav'n't got any--and are all the better off for it.
A soul's a sort of a fifth wheel to a wagon.
He's got enough, though, to make up for the deficiencies in others.
Ye haven't seen Old Thunder yet, have ye-- Captain Ahab?
Queequeg, let's go. This fellow has broken loose from somewhere.
It's the easiest thing in the world for a man to look as if he had a great secret in him.
But-- tell me your name.
Elijah.
Morning to ye, shipmates!

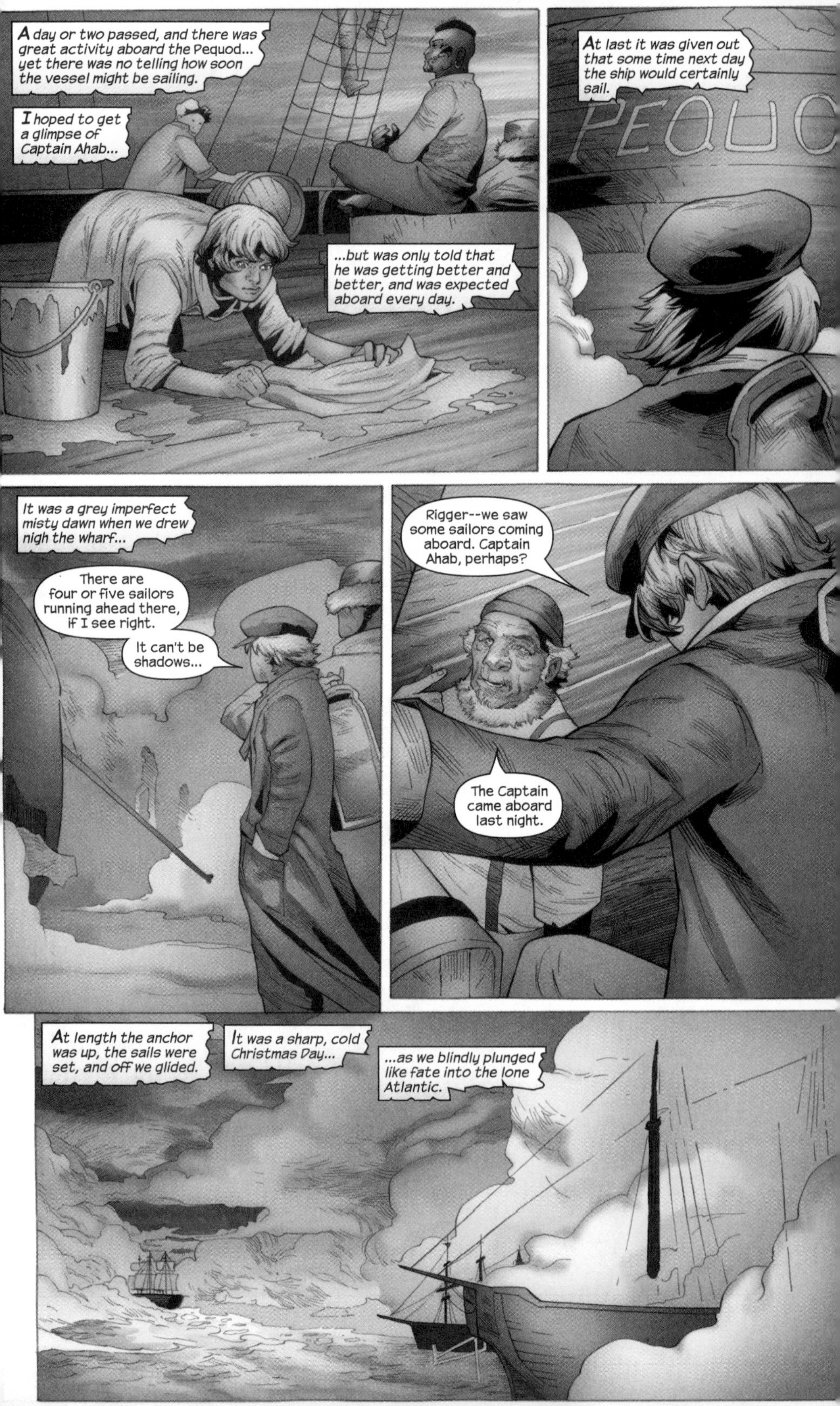

A day or two passed, and there was great activity aboard the Pequod... yet there was no telling how soon the vessel might be sailing.
I hoped to get a glimpse of Captain Ahab...
...but was only told that he was getting better and better, and was expected aboard every day.
At last it was given out that some time next day the ship would certainly sail.
PEQUO
It was a grey imperfect misty dawn when we drew nigh the wharf...
There are four or five sailors running ahead there, if I see right.
It can't be shadows...
Rigger--we saw some sailors coming aboard. Captain Ahab, perhaps?
The Captain came aboard last night.
At length the anchor was up, the sails were set, and off we glided.
It was a sharp, cold Christmas Day...
...as we blindly plunged like fate into the lone Atlantic.

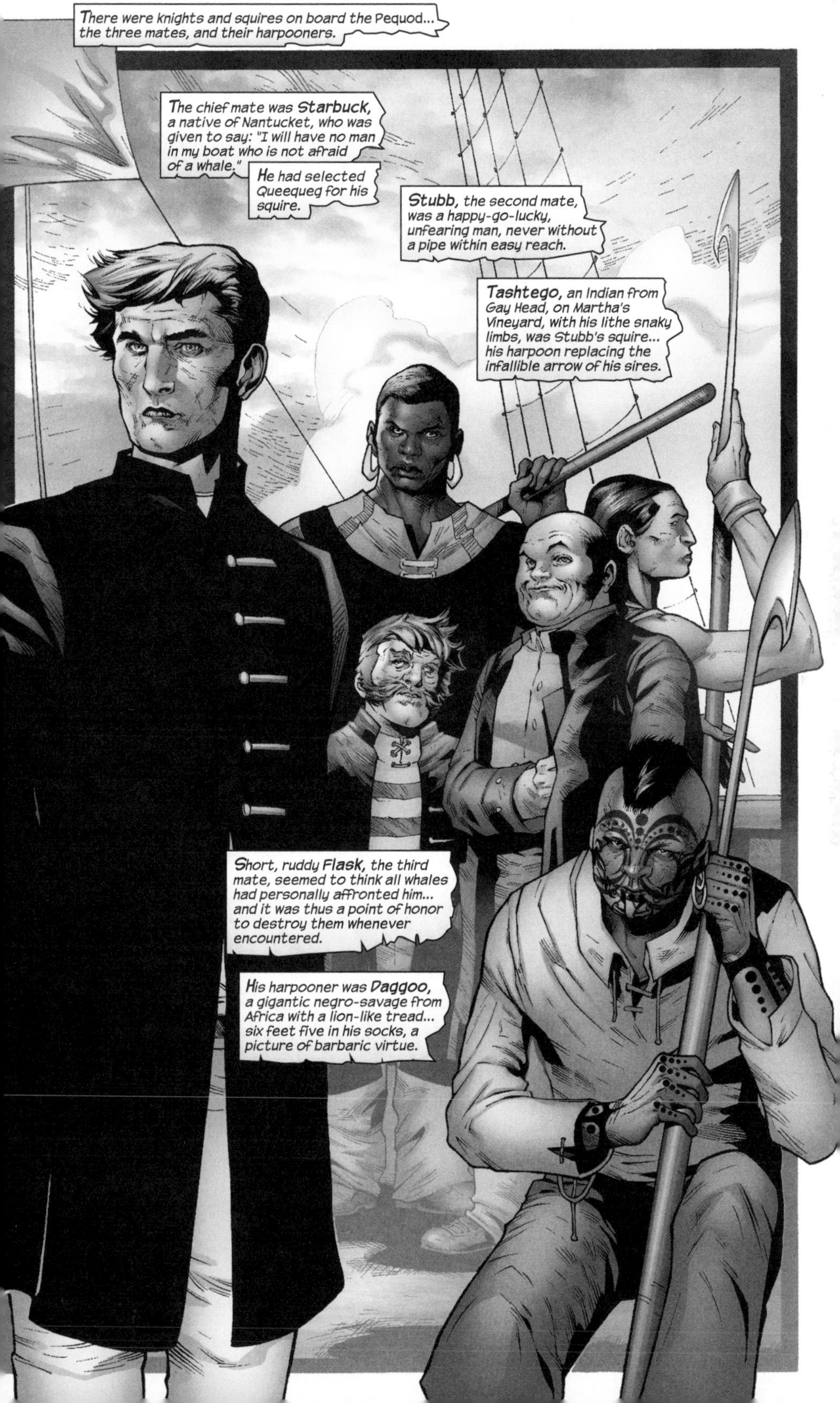
There were knights and squires on board the Pequod... the three mates, and their harpooners.
The chief mate was Starbuck, a native of Nantucket, who was given to say: "I will have no man in my boat who is not afraid of a whale."
He had selected Queequeg for his squire.
Stubb, the second mate, was a happy-go-lucky, unfearing man, never without a pipe within easy reach.
Tashtego, an Indian from Gay Head, on Martha's Vineyard, with his lithe snaky limbs, was Stubb's squire... his harpoon replacing the infallible arrow of his sires.
Short, ruddy Flask, the third mate, seemed to think all whales had personally affronted him... and it was thus a point of honor to destroy them whenever encountered.
His harpooner was Daggoo, a gigantic negro-savage from Africa with a lion-like tread... six feet five in his socks, a picture of barbaric virtue.

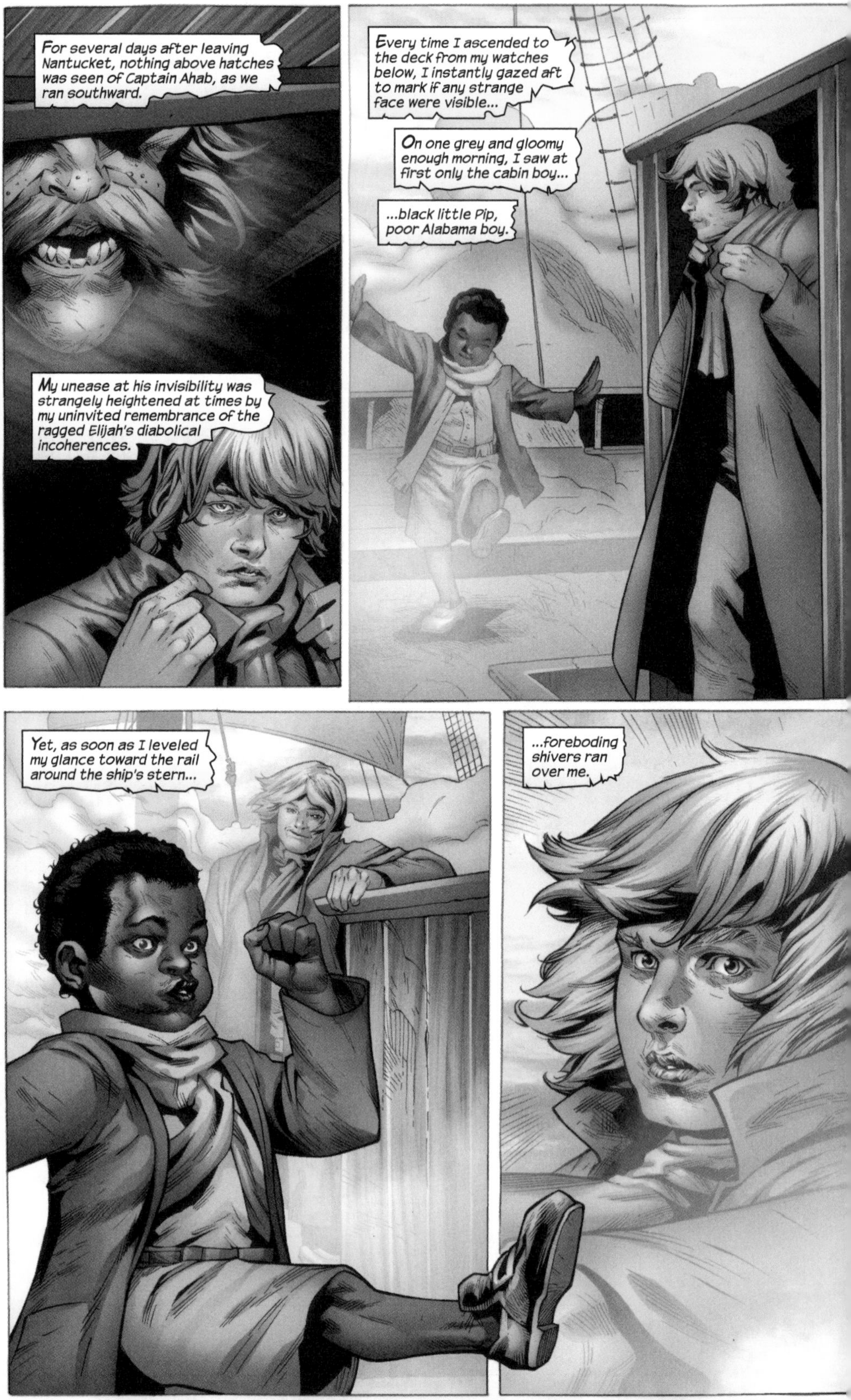
For several days after leaving Nantucket, nothing above hatches was seen of Captain Ahab, as we ran southward.
My unease at his invisibility was strangely heightened at times by my uninvited remembrance of the ragged Elijah's diabolical incoherences.
Every time I ascended to the deck from my watches below, I instantly gazed aft to mark if any strange face were visible...
On one grey and gloomy enough morning, I saw at first only the cabin boy...
...black little Pip, poor Alabama boy.
Yet, as soon as I leveled my glance toward the rail around the ship's stern...
...foreboding shivers ran over me.

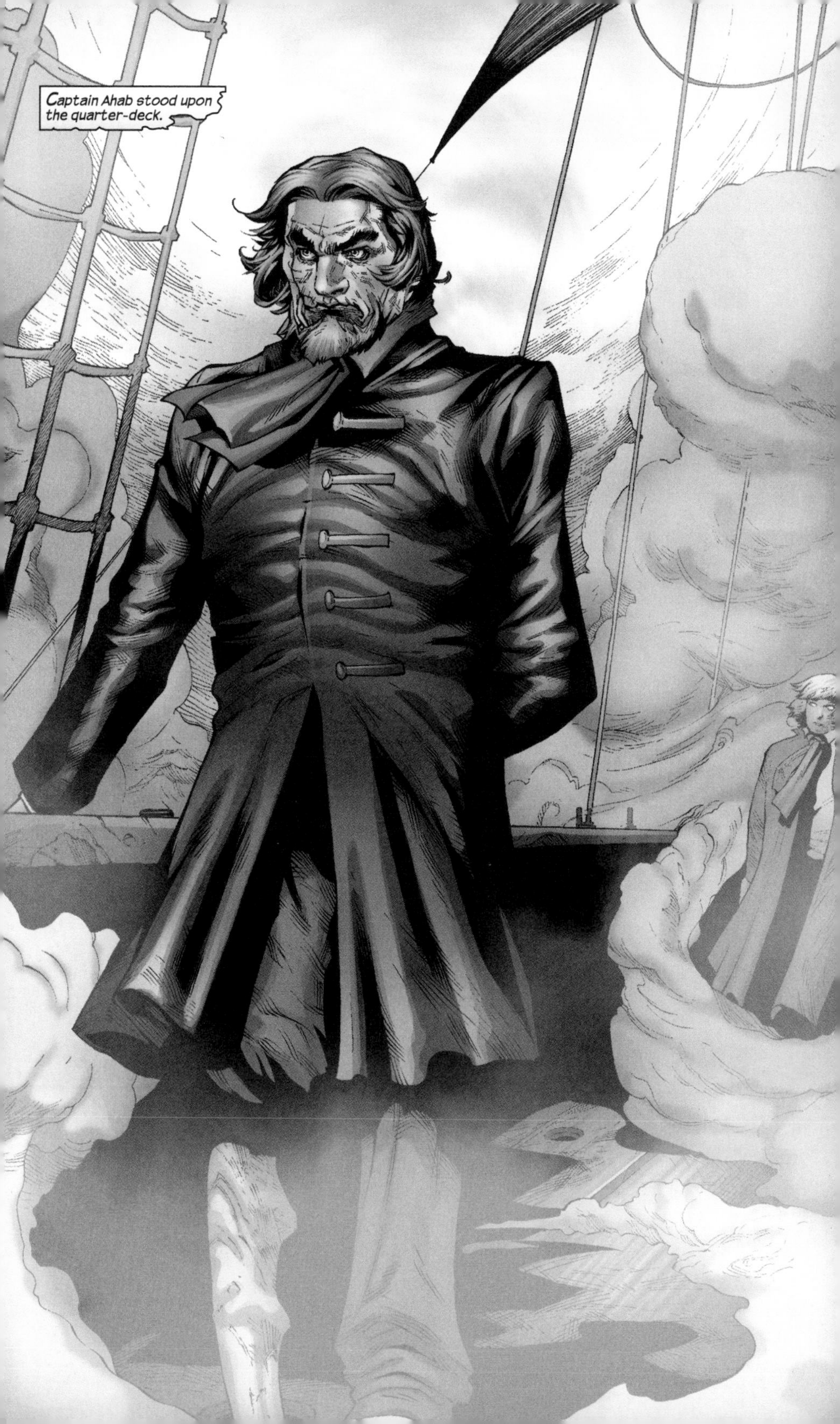
Captain Ahab stood upon the quarter-deck.

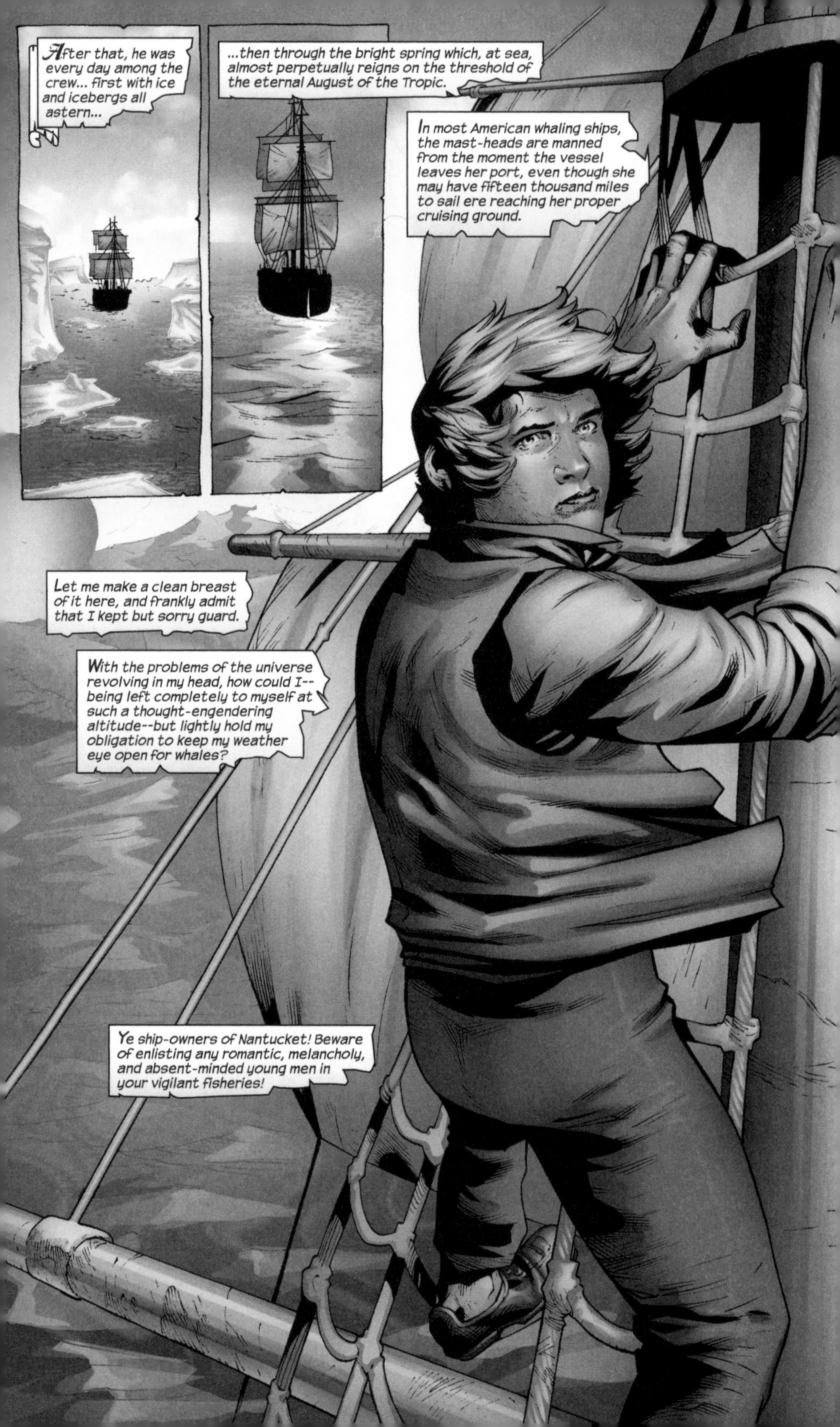
After that, he was every day among the crew... first with ice and icebergs all astern...
...then through the bright spring which, at sea, almost perpetually reigns on the threshold of the eternal August of the Tropic.
In most American whaling ships, the mast-heads are manned from the moment the vessel leaves her port, even though she may have fifteen thousand miles to sail ere reaching her proper cruising ground.
Let me make a clean breast of it here, and frankly admit that I kept but sorry guard.
With the problems of the universe revolving in my head, how could I--being left completely to myself at such a thought-engendering altitude--but lightly hold my obligation to keep my weather eye open for whales?
Ye ship-owners of Nantucket! Beware of enlisting any romantic, melancholy, and absent-minded young men in your vigilant fisheries!

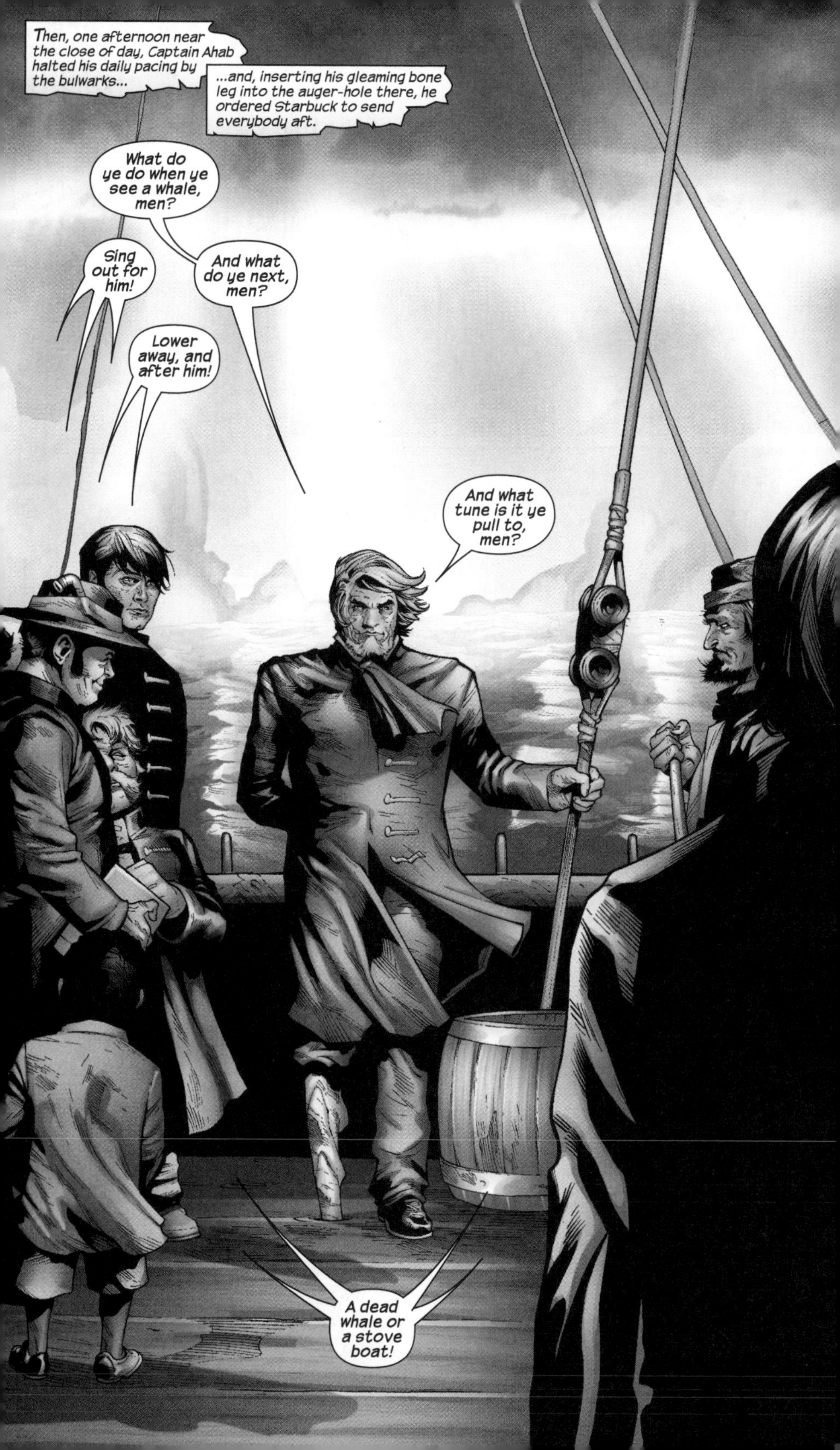
Then, one afternoon near the close of day, Captain Ahab halted his daily pacing by the bulwarks...
...and, inserting his gleaming bone leg into the auger-hole there, he ordered Starbuck to send everybody aft.
What do ye do when ye see a whale, men?
Sing out for him!
And what do ye next, men?
Lower away, and after him!
And what tune is it ye pull to, men?
A dead whale or a stove boat!

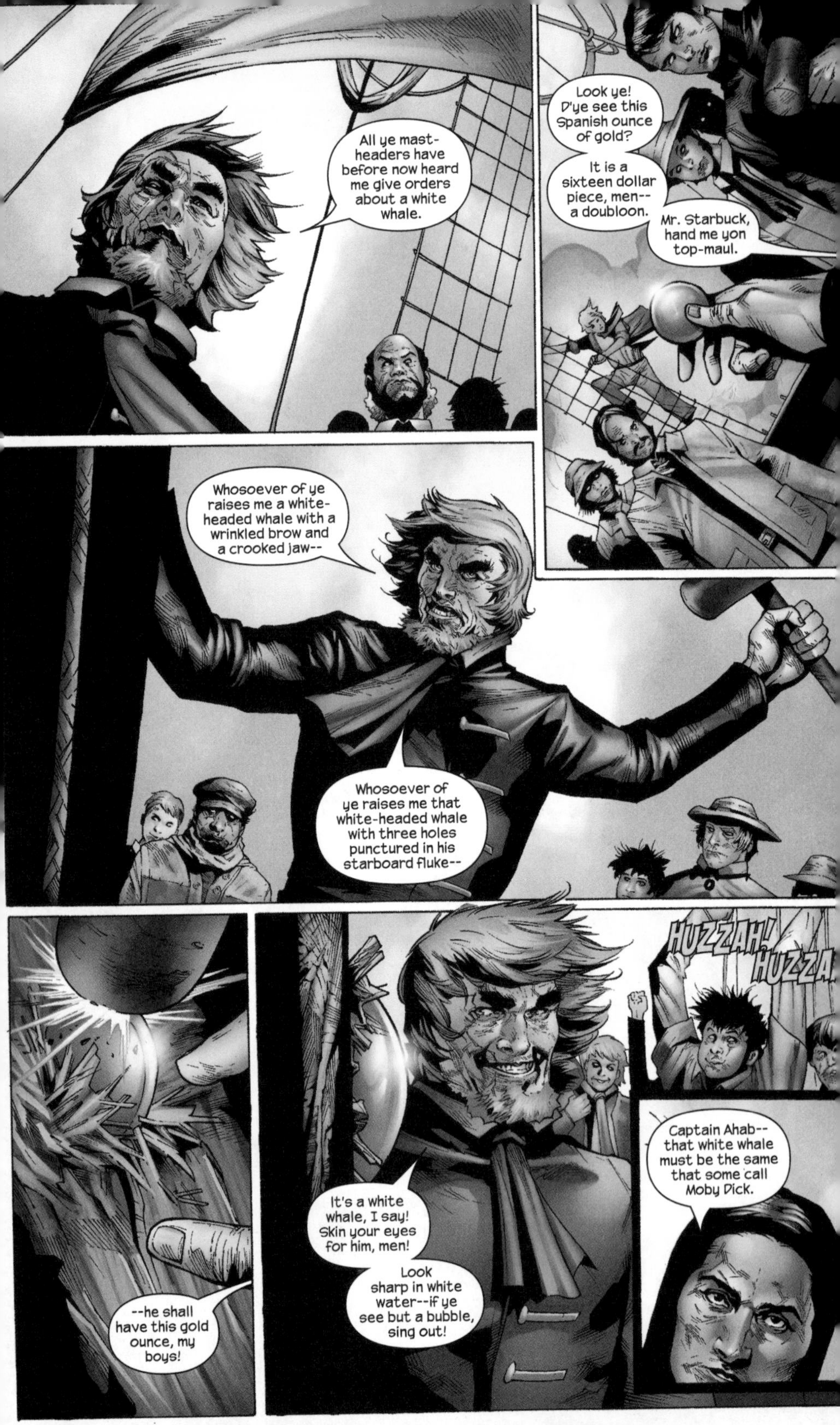
All ye mast-headers have before now heard me give orders about a white whale.
Look ye! D'ye see this Spanish ounce of gold?
It is a sixteen dollar piece, men--a doubloon.
Mr. Starbuck, hand me yon top-maul.
Whosoever of ye raises me a white-headed whale with a wrinkled brow and a crooked jaw--
Whosoever of ye raises me that white-headed whale with three holes punctured in his starboard fluke--
--he shall have this gold ounce, my boys!
HUZZAH! HUZZA
It's a white whale, I say! Skin your eyes for him, men!
Look sharp in white water--if ye see but a bubble, sing out!
Captain Ahab--that white whale must be the same that some call Moby Dick.

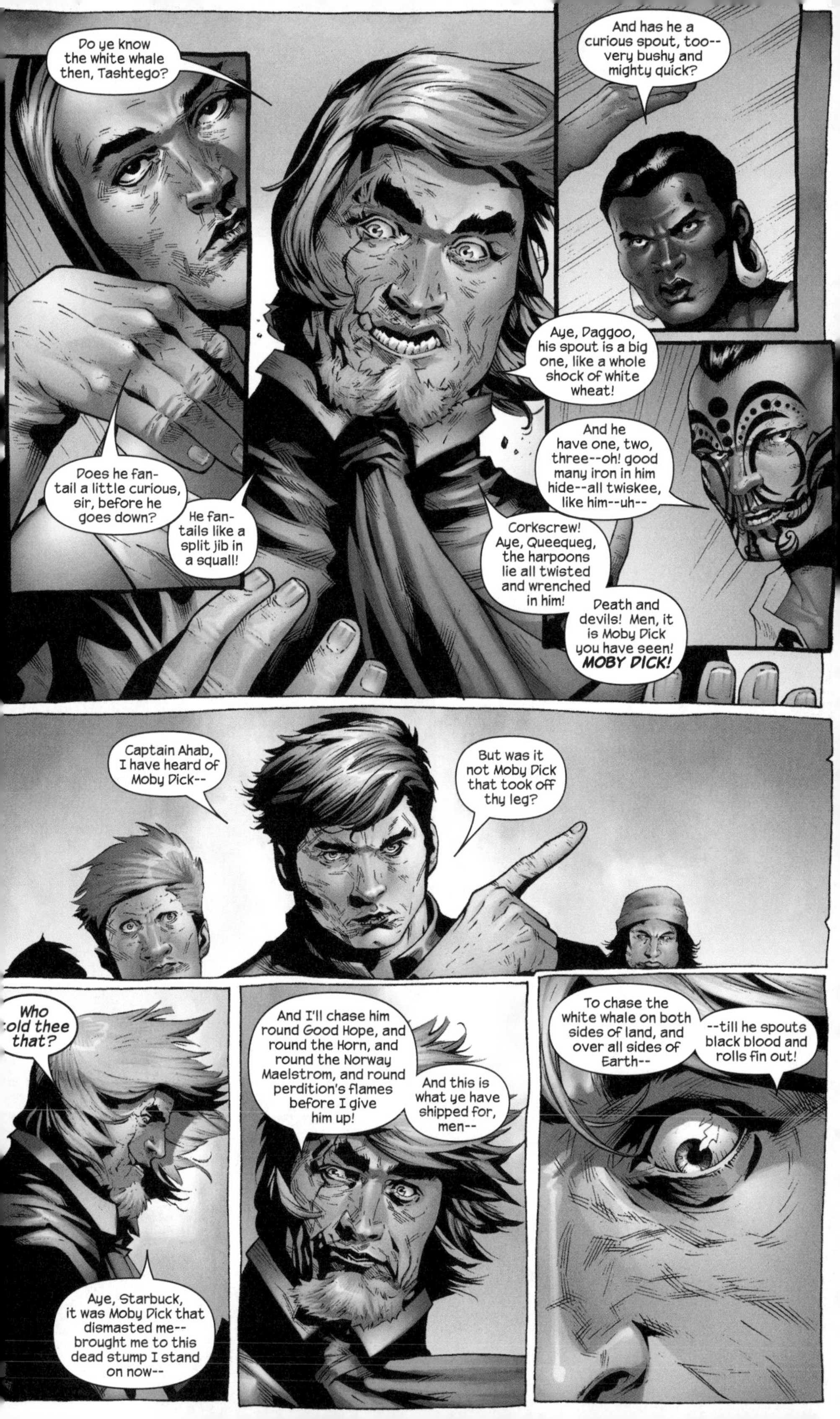
Do ye know the white whale then, Tashtego?
And has he a curious spout, too--very bushy and mighty quick?
Aye, Daggoo, his spout is a big one, like a whole shock of white wheat!
And he have one, two, three--oh! good many iron in him hide--all twiskee, like him--uh--
Does he fan-tail a little curious, sir, before he goes down?
He fan-tails like a split jib in a squall!
Corkscrew! Aye, Queequeg, the harpoons lie all twisted and wrenched in him!
Death and devils! Men, it is Moby Dick you have seen! MOBY DICK!
Captain Ahab, I have heard of Moby Dick--
But was it not Moby Dick that took off thy leg?
Who told thee that?
Aye, Starbuck, it was Moby Dick that dismasted me--brought me to this dead stump I stand on now--
And I'll chase him round Good Hope, and round the Horn, and round the Norway Maelstrom, and round perdition's flames before I give him up!
And this is what ye have shipped for, men--
To chase the white whale on both sides of land, and over all sides of Earth--
--till he spouts black blood and rolls fin out!

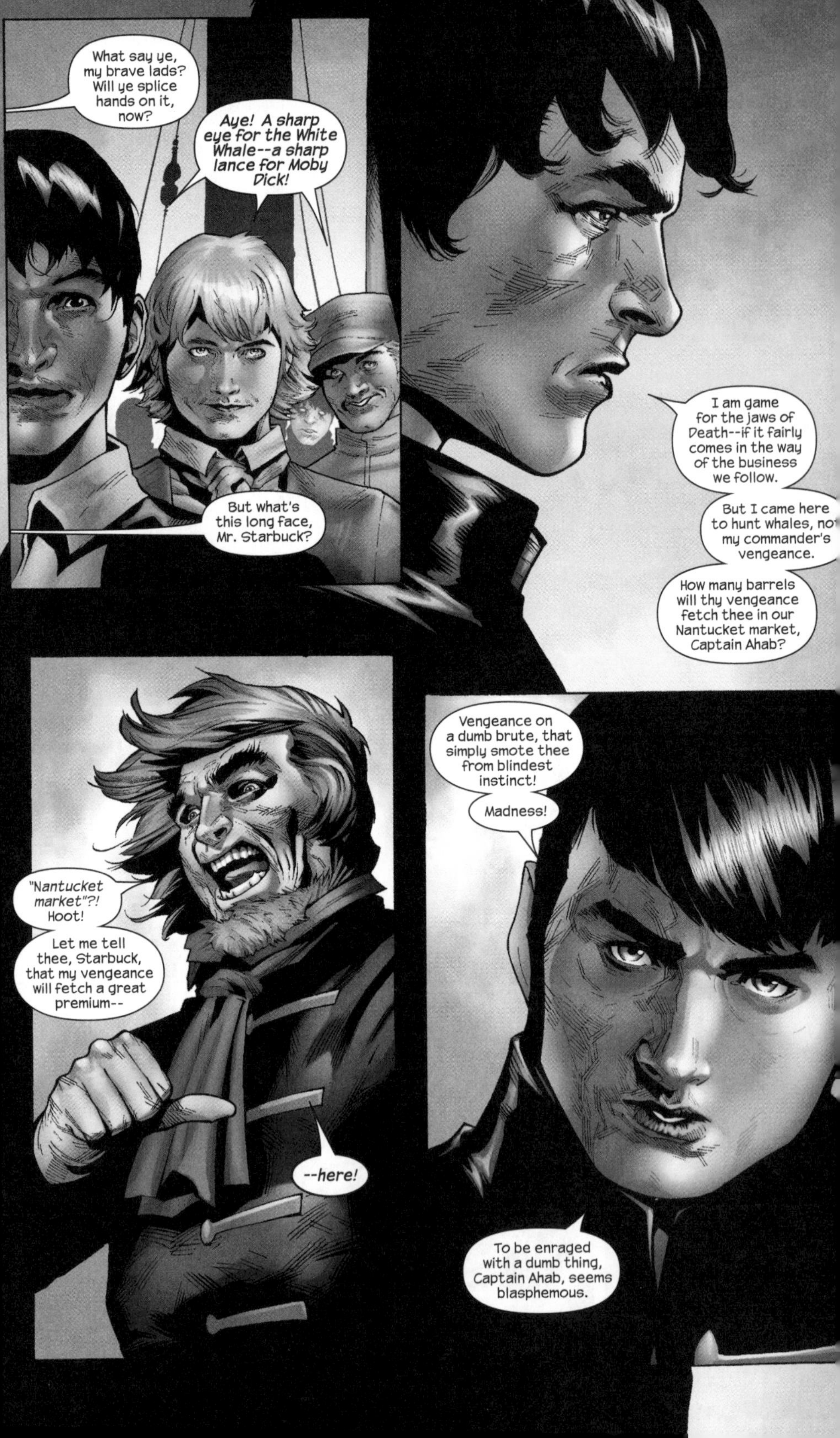
What say ye, my brave lads? Will ye splice hands on it, now?
Aye! A sharp eye for the White Whale--a sharp lance for Moby Dick!
But what's this long face, Mr. Starbuck?
I am game for the jaws of Death--if it fairly comes in the way of the business we follow.
But I came here to hunt whales, not my commander's vengeance.
How many barrels will thy vengeance fetch thee in our Nantucket market, Captain Ahab?
"Nantucket market"?! Hoot!
Let me tell thee, Starbuck, that my vengeance will fetch a great premium--
--here!
Vengeance on a dumb brute, that simply smote thee from blindest instinct!
Madness!
To be enraged with a dumb thing, Captain Ahab, seems blasphemous.

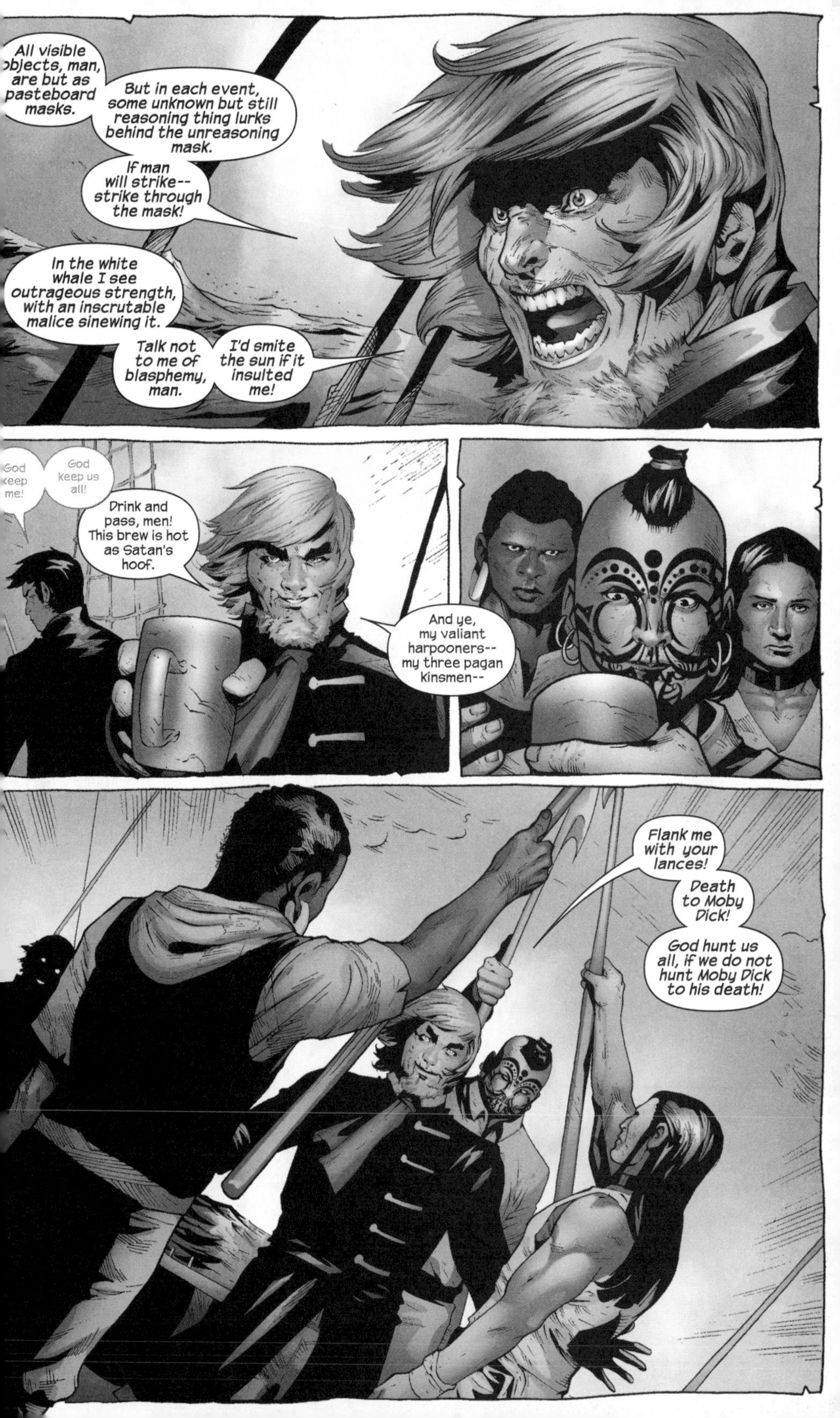
All visible objects, man, are but as pasteboard masks.
But in each event, some unknown but still reasoning thing lurks behind the unreasoning mask.
If man will strike--strike through the mask!
In the white whale I see outrageous strength, with an inscrutable malice sinewing it.
Talk not to me of blasphemy, man.
I'd smite the sun if it insulted me!
God keep me!
God keep us all!
Drink and pass, men! This brew is hot as Satan's hoof.
And ye, my valiant harpooners--my three pagan kinsmen--
Flank me with your lances!
Death to Moby Dick!
God hunt us all, if we do not hunt Moby Dick to his death!

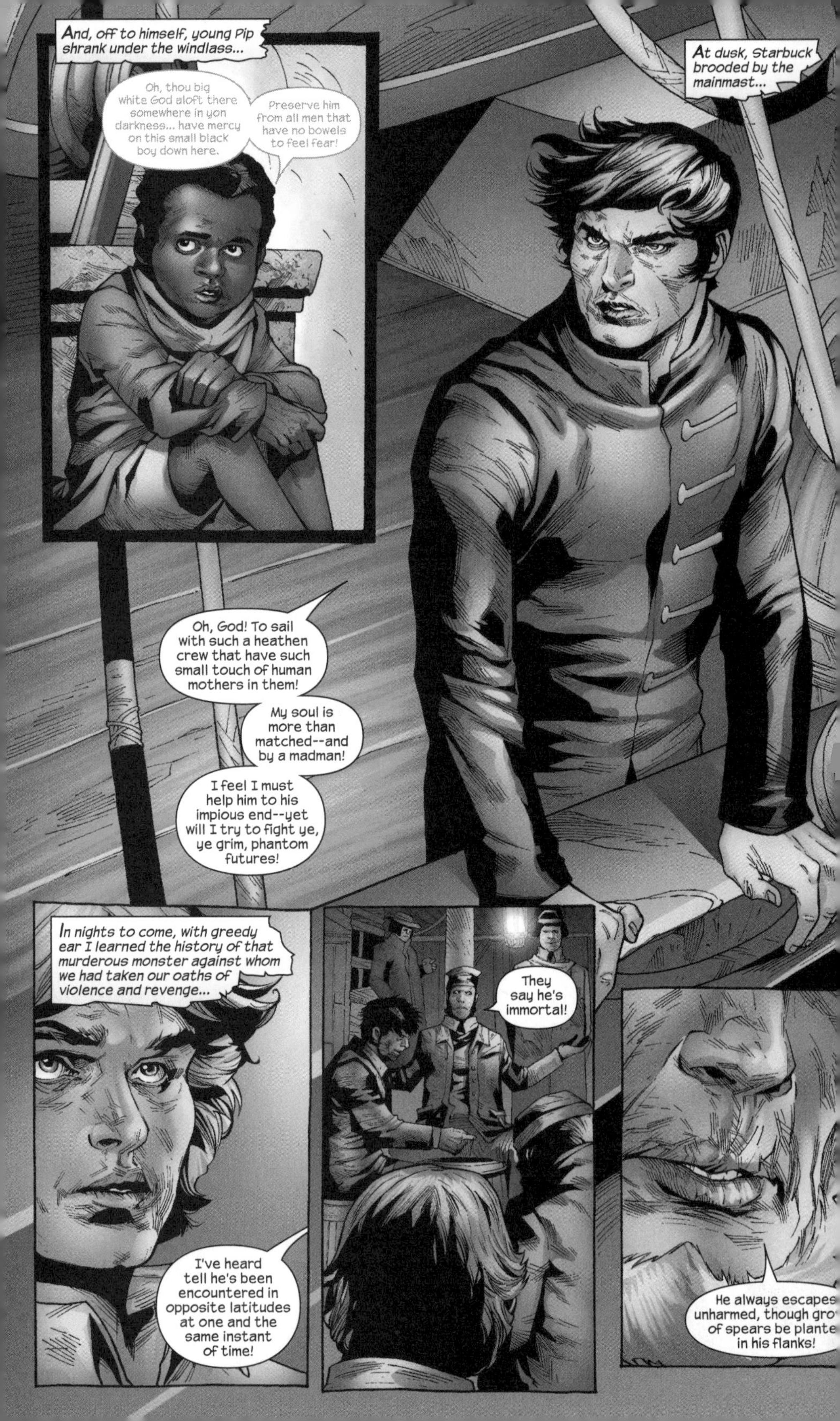
And, off to himself, young Pip shrank under the windlass...
Oh, thou big white God aloft there somewhere in yon darkness... have mercy on this small black boy down here.
Preserve him from all men that have no bowels to feel fear!
At dusk, Starbuck brooded by the mainmast...
Oh, God! To sail with such a heathen crew that have such small touch of human mothers in them!
My soul is more than matched--and by a madman!
I feel I must help him to his impious end--yet will I try to fight ye, ye grim, phantom futures!
In nights to come, with greedy ear I learned the history of that murderous monster against whom we had taken our oaths of violence and revenge...
I've heard tell he's been encountered in opposite latitudes at one and the same instant of time!
They say he's immortal!
He always escapes unharmed, though gro of spears be plante in his flanks!

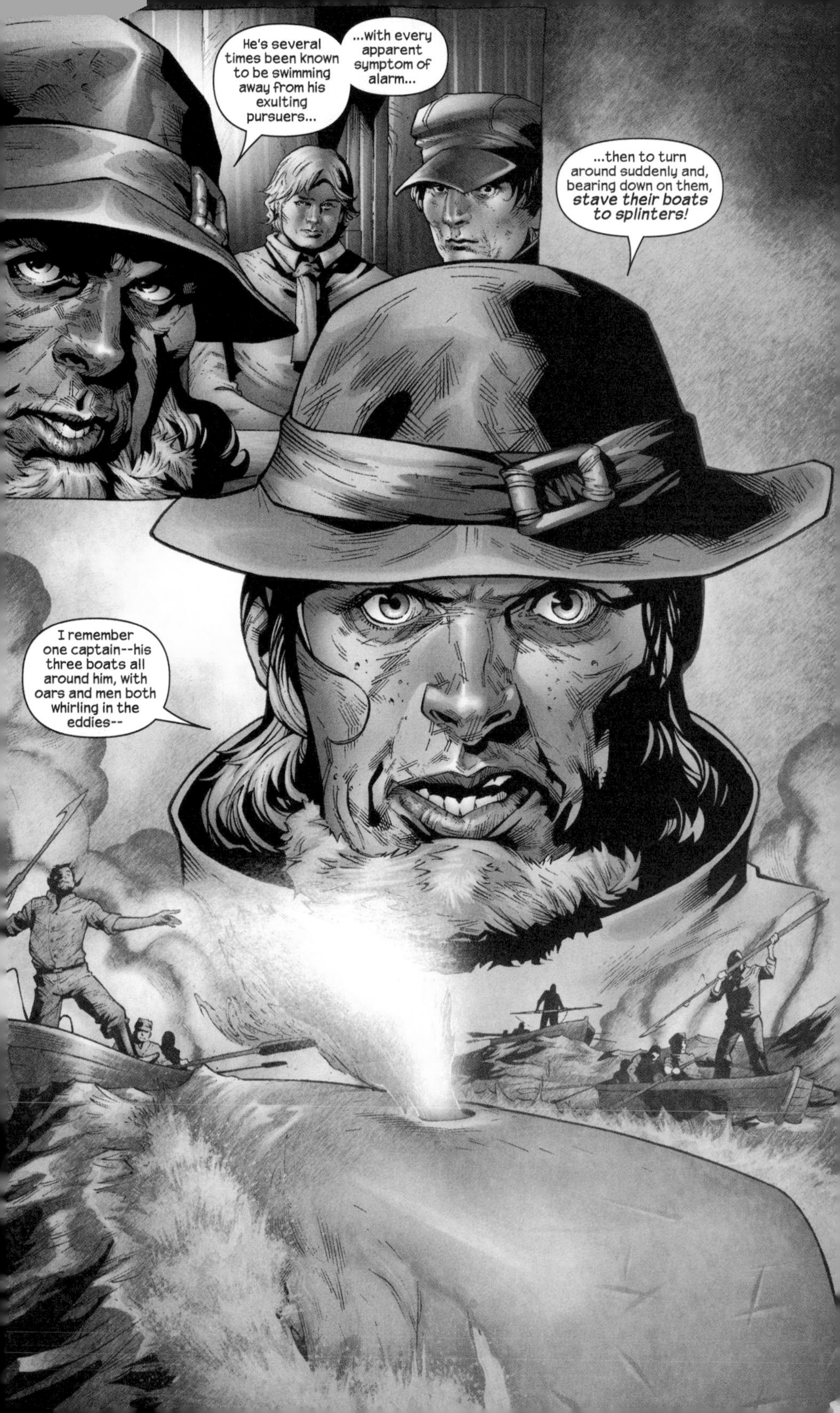
He's several times been known to be swimming away from his exulting pursuers...
...with every apparent symptom of alarm...
...then to turn around suddenly and, bearing down on them, *stave their boats to splinters!*
I remember one captain--his three boats all around him, with oars and men both whirling in the eddies--

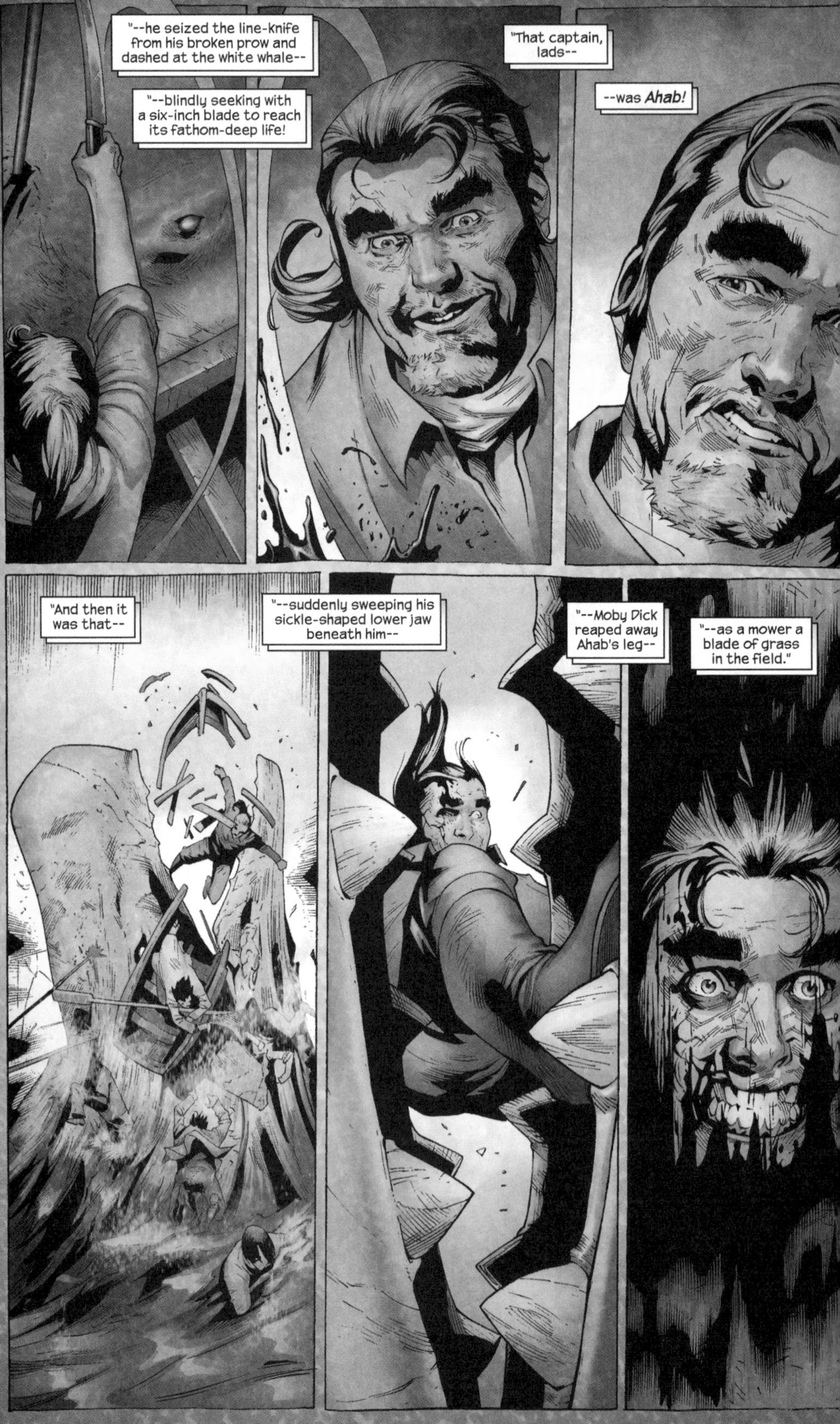
"--he seized the line-knife from his broken prow and dashed at the white whale--
"--blindly seeking with a six-inch blade to reach its fathom-deep life!
"That captain, lads--
--was *Ahab!*
"And then it was that--
"--suddenly sweeping his sickle-shaped lower jaw beneath him--
"--Moby Dick reaped away Ahab's leg--
"--as a mower a blade of grass in the field."

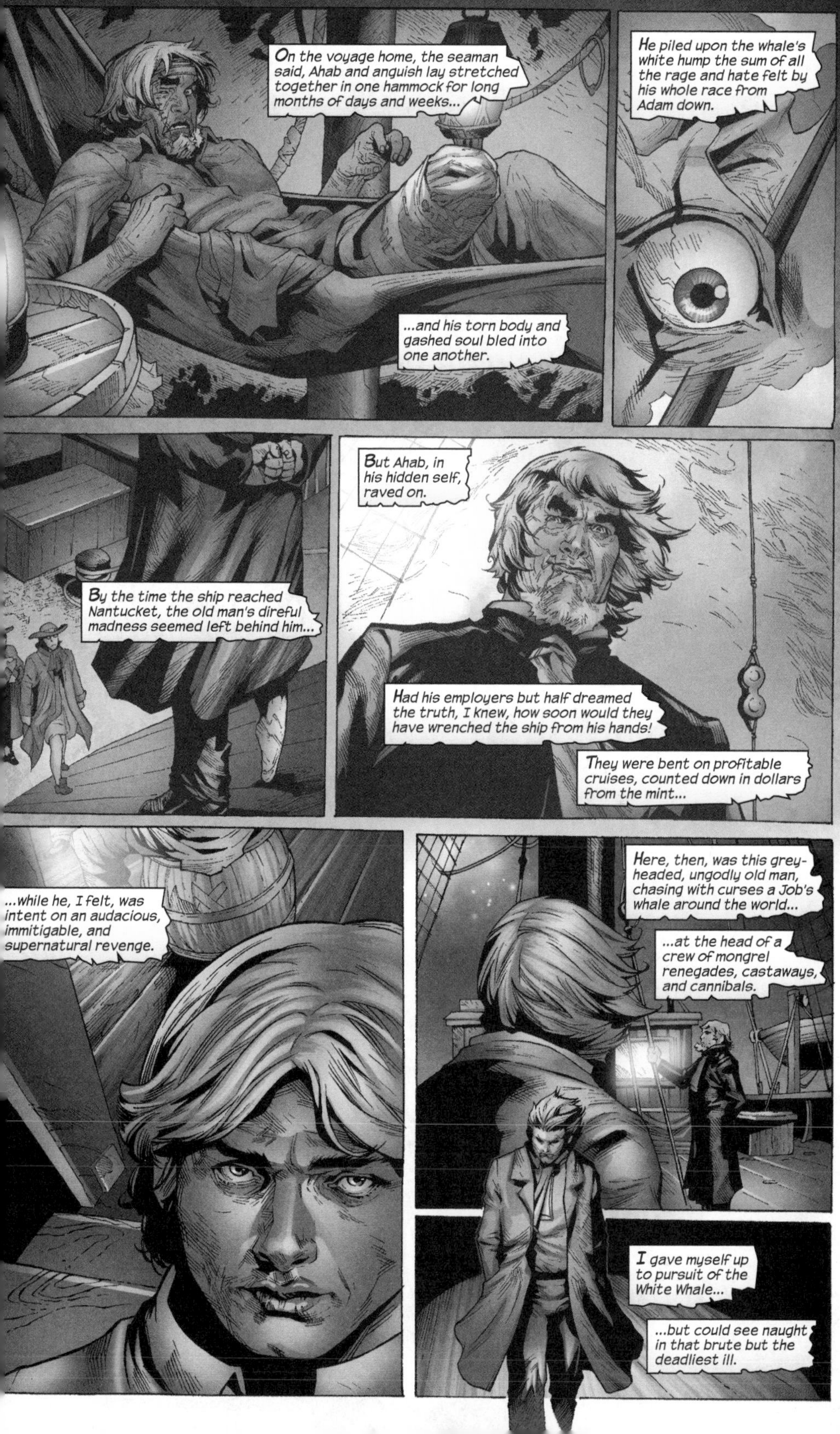

On the voyage home, the seaman said, Ahab and anguish lay stretched together in one hammock for long months of days and weeks...
...and his torn body and gashed soul bled into one another.
He piled upon the whale's white hump the sum of all the rage and hate felt by his whole race from Adam down.
By the time the ship reached Nantucket, the old man's direful madness seemed left behind him...
But Ahab, in his hidden self, raved on.
Had his employers but half dreamed the truth, I knew, how soon would they have wrenched the ship from his hands!
They were bent on profitable cruises, counted down in dollars from the mint...
...while he, I felt, was intent on an audacious, immitigable, and supernatural revenge.
Here, then, was this grey-headed, ungodly old man, chasing with curses a Job's whale around the world...
...at the head of a crew of mongrel renegades, castaways, and cannibals.
I gave myself up to pursuit of the White Whale...
...but could see naught in that brute but the deadliest ill.

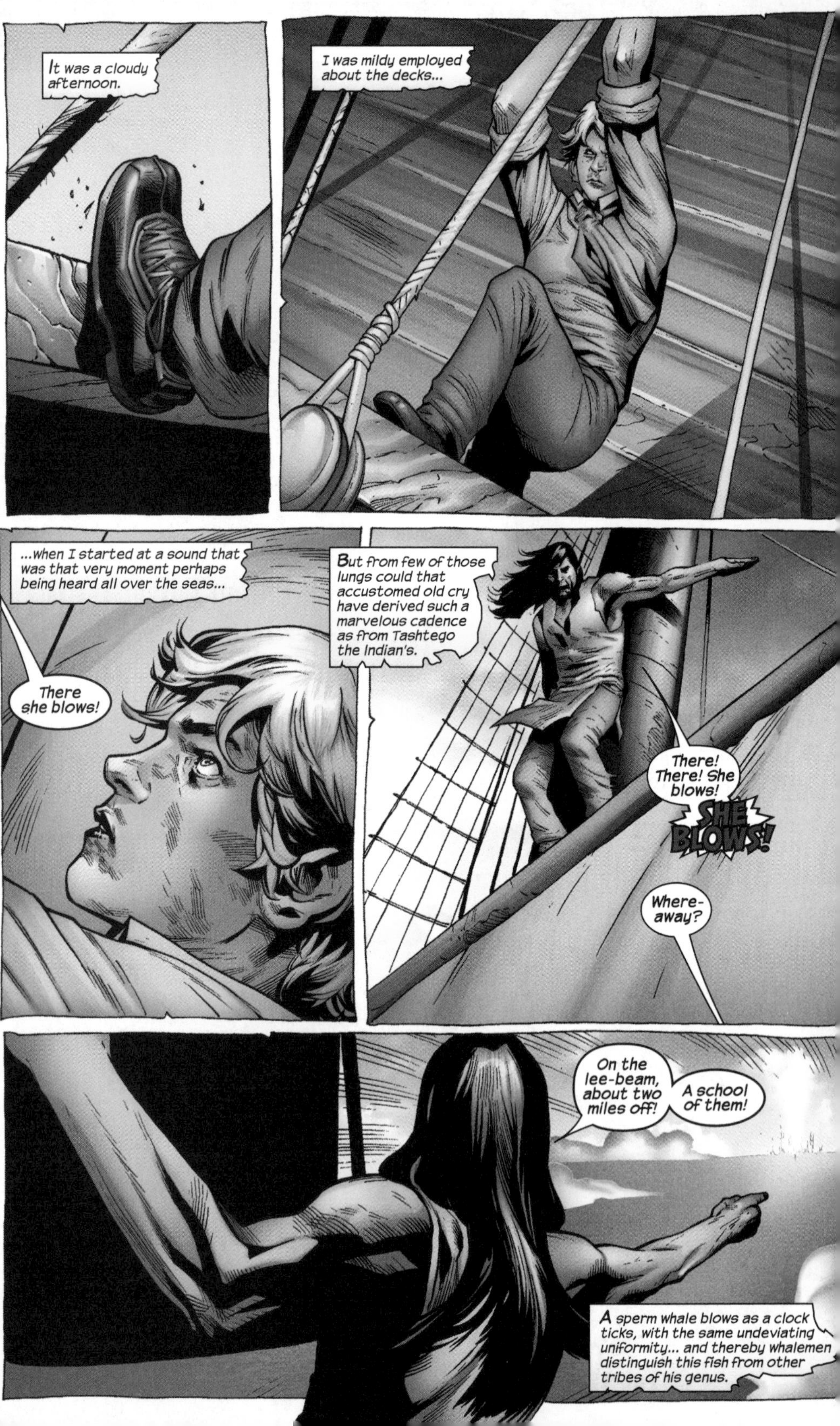

It was a cloudy afternoon.
I was mildy employed about the decks...
...when I started at a sound that was that very moment perhaps being heard all over the seas...
There she blows!
But from few of those lungs could that accustomed old cry have derived such a marvelous cadence as from Tashtego the Indian's.
There! There! She blows!
SHE BLOWS!
Where-away?
On the lee-beam, about two miles off!
A school of them!
A sperm whale blows as a clock ticks, with the same undeviating uniformity... and thereby whalemen distinguish this fish from other tribes of his genus.

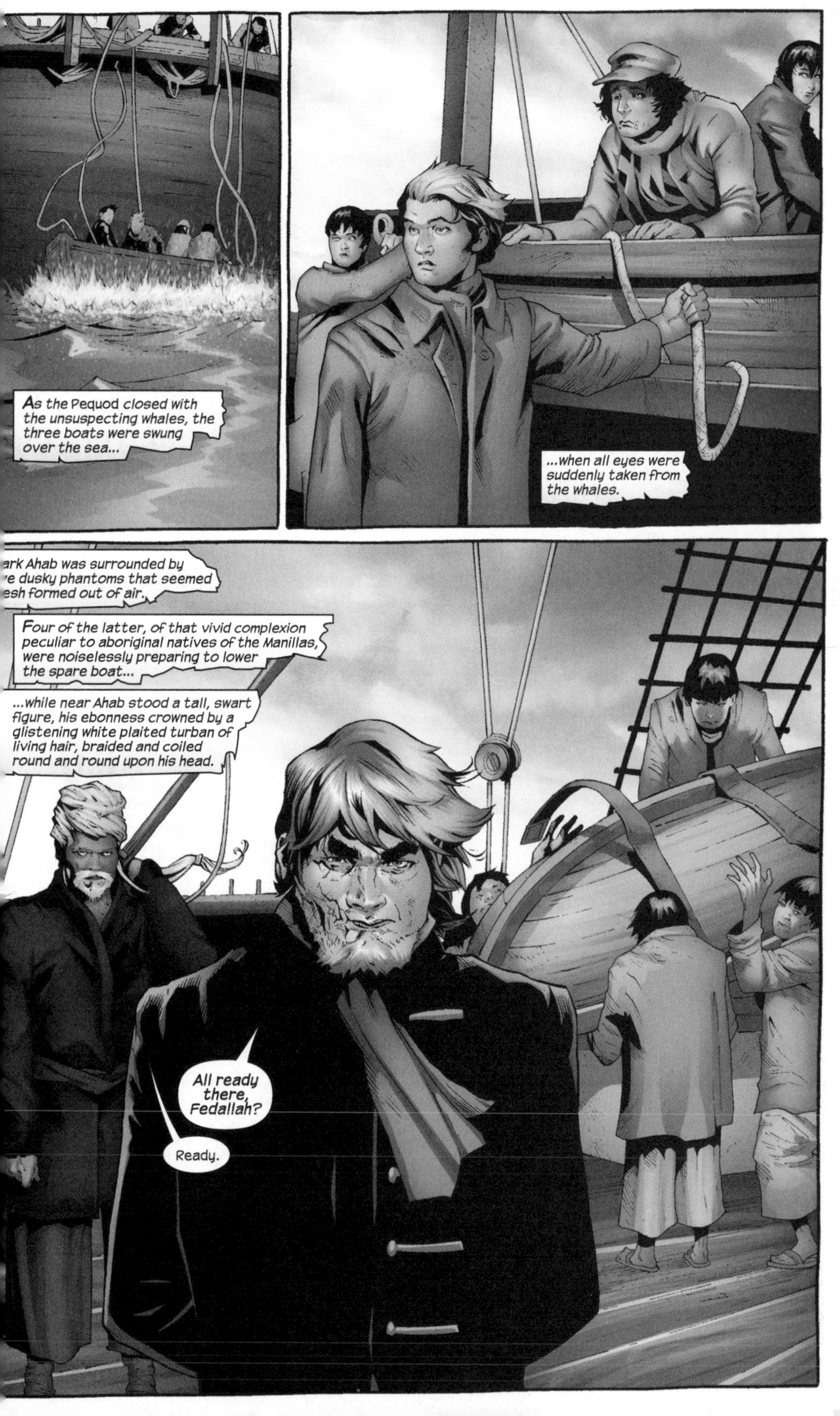
As the Pequod closed with the unsuspecting whales, the three boats were swung over the sea...
...when all eyes were suddenly taken from the whales.
ark Ahab was surrounded by
e dusky phantoms that seemed
esh formed out of air.
Four of the latter, of that vivid complexion peculiar to aboriginal natives of the Manillas, were noiselessly preparing to lower the spare boat...
...while near Ahab stood a tall, swart figure, his ebonness crowned by a glistening white plaited turban of living hair, braided and coiled round and round upon his head.
All ready there, Fedallah?
Ready.

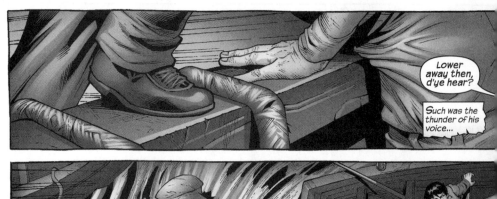

Lower away then, d'ye hear?

Such was the thunder of his voice...

...that, spite of their amazement, the three other boats dropped into the sea...

...and the men sprang over the rail.

But hardly had they pulled out from under the ship's lee, into a sea rough with swells...

...when a fourth keel pulled under the stern, with the five strangers rowing Ahab.

Starbuck-- Stubb--Flask spread yourselves widely!

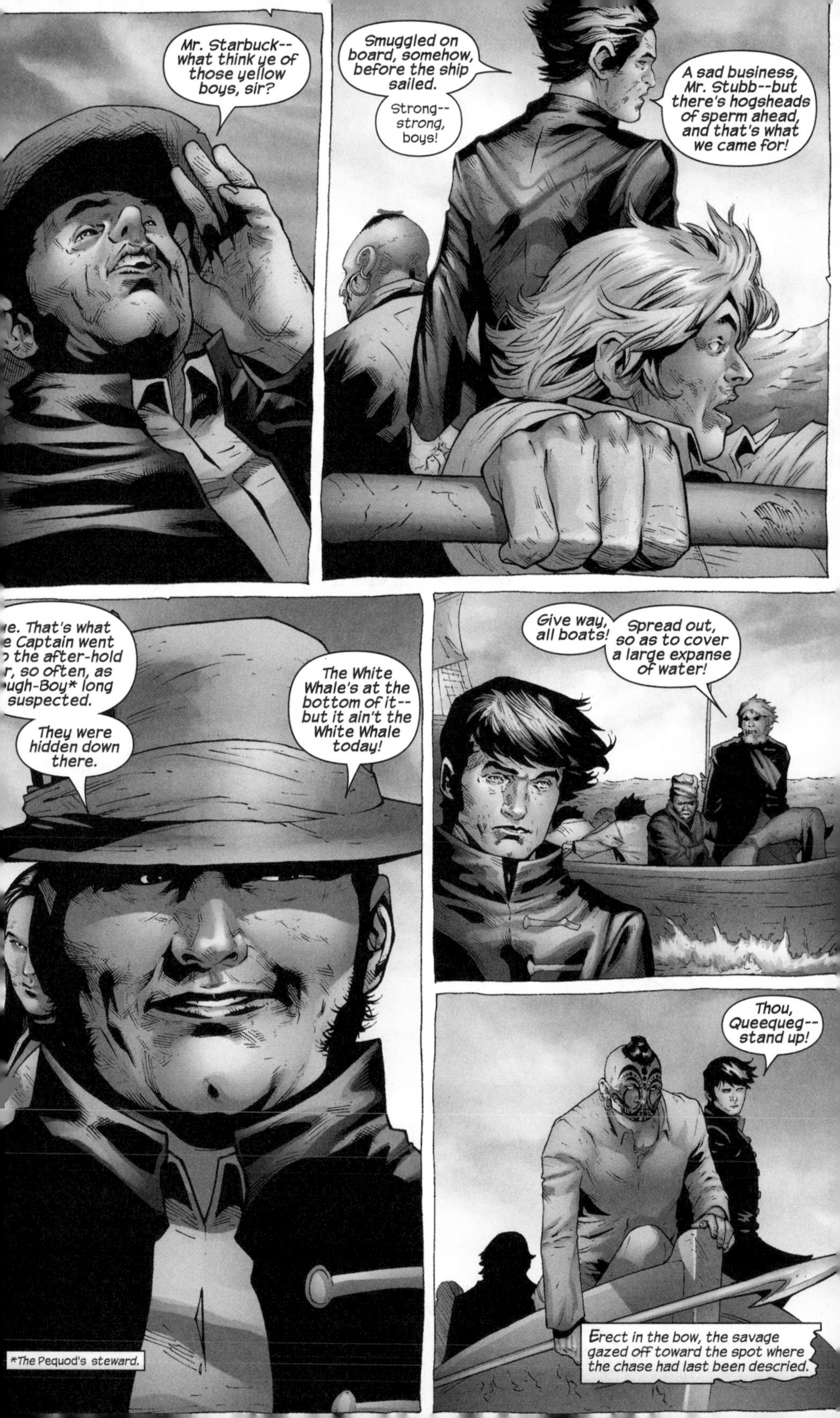

Mr. Starbuck--what think ye of those yellow boys, sir?
Smuggled on board, somehow, before the ship sailed.
Strong--strong, boys!
A sad business, Mr. Stubb--but there's hogsheads of sperm ahead, and that's what we came for!
e. That's what e Captain went o the after-hold r, so often, as ugh-Boy* long suspected.
They were hidden down there.
The White Whale's at the bottom of it--but it ain't the White Whale today!
*The Pequod's steward.
Give way, all boats!
Spread out, so as to cover a large expanse of water!
Thou, Queequeg--stand up!
Erect in the bow, the savage gazed off toward the spot where the chase had last been descried.

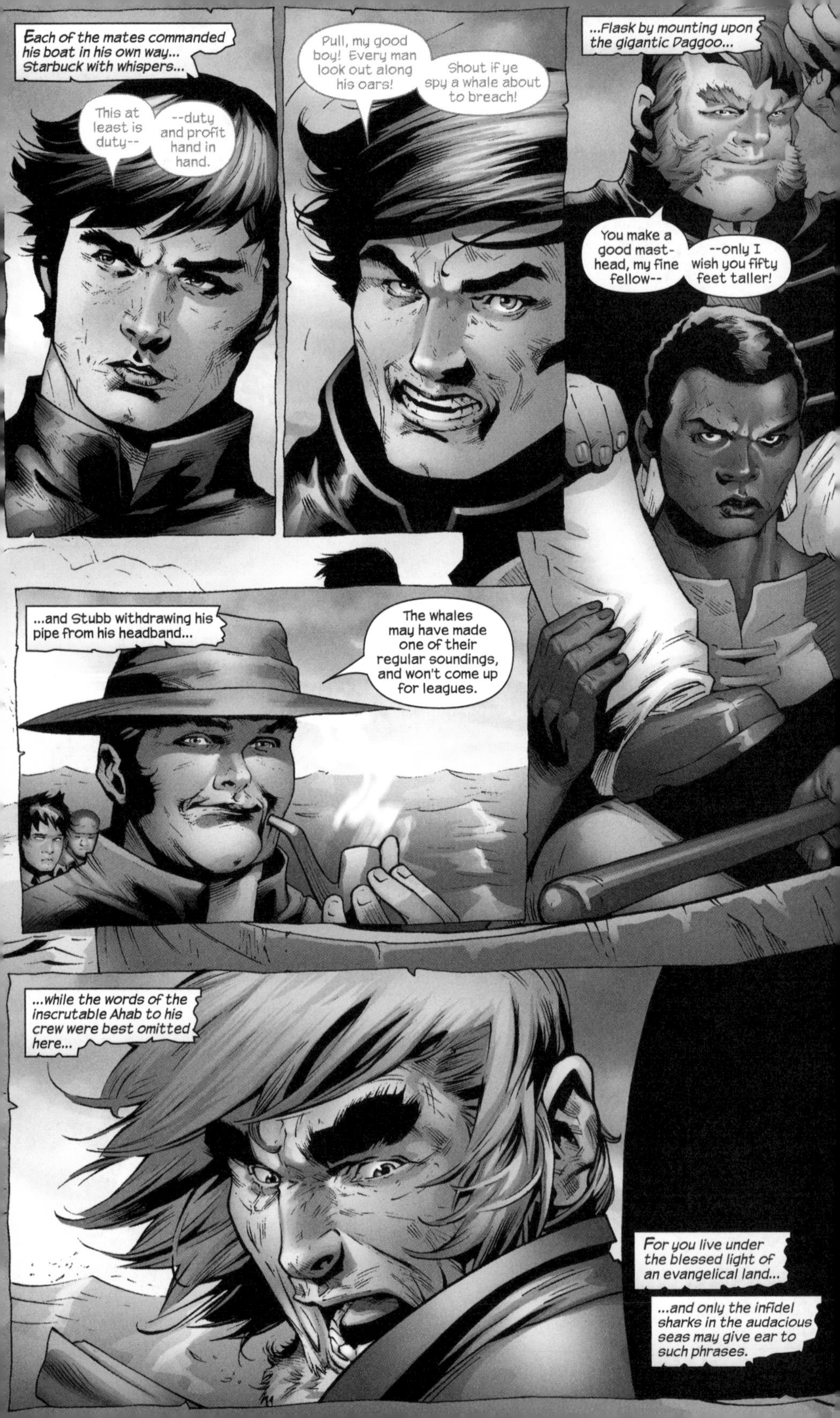

Each of the mates commanded his boat in his own way... Starbuck with whispers...
This at least is duty--
--duty and profit hand in hand.
Pull, my good boy! Every man look out along his oars!
Shout if ye spy a whale about to breach!
...Flask by mounting upon the gigantic Daggoo...
You make a good mast-head, my fine fellow--
--only I wish you fifty feet taller!
...and Stubb withdrawing his pipe from his headband...
The whales may have made one of their regular soundings, and won't come up for leagues.
...while the words of the inscrutable Ahab to his crew were best omitted here...
For you live under the blessed light of an evangelical land...
...and only the infidel sharks in the audacious seas may give ear to such phrases.

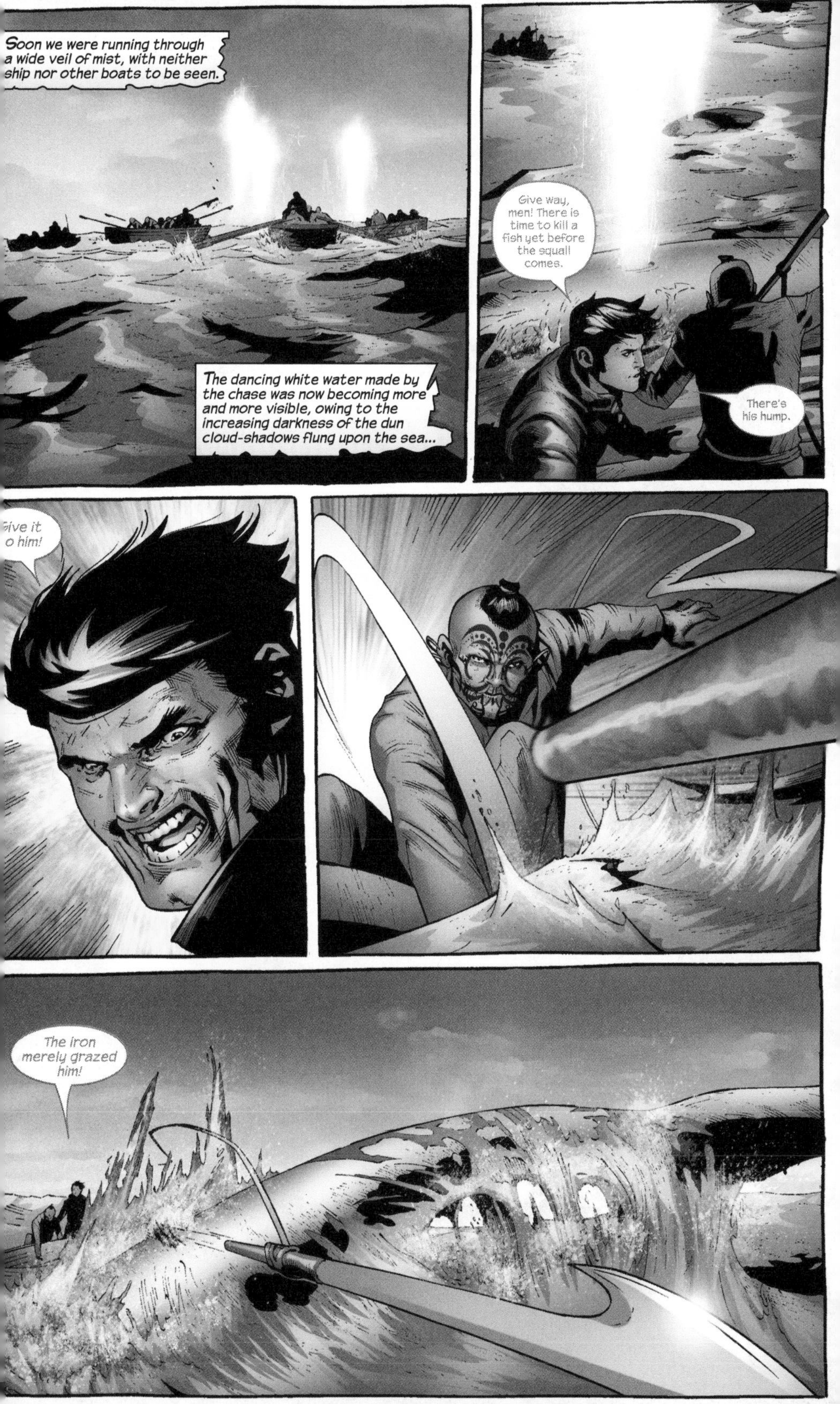
Soon we were running through a wide veil of mist, with neither ship nor other boats to be seen.
The dancing white water made by the chase was now becoming more and more visible, owing to the increasing darkness of the dun cloud-shadows flung upon the sea...
Give way, men! There is time to kill a fish yet before the squall comes.
There's his hump.
ive it o him!
The iron merely grazed him!

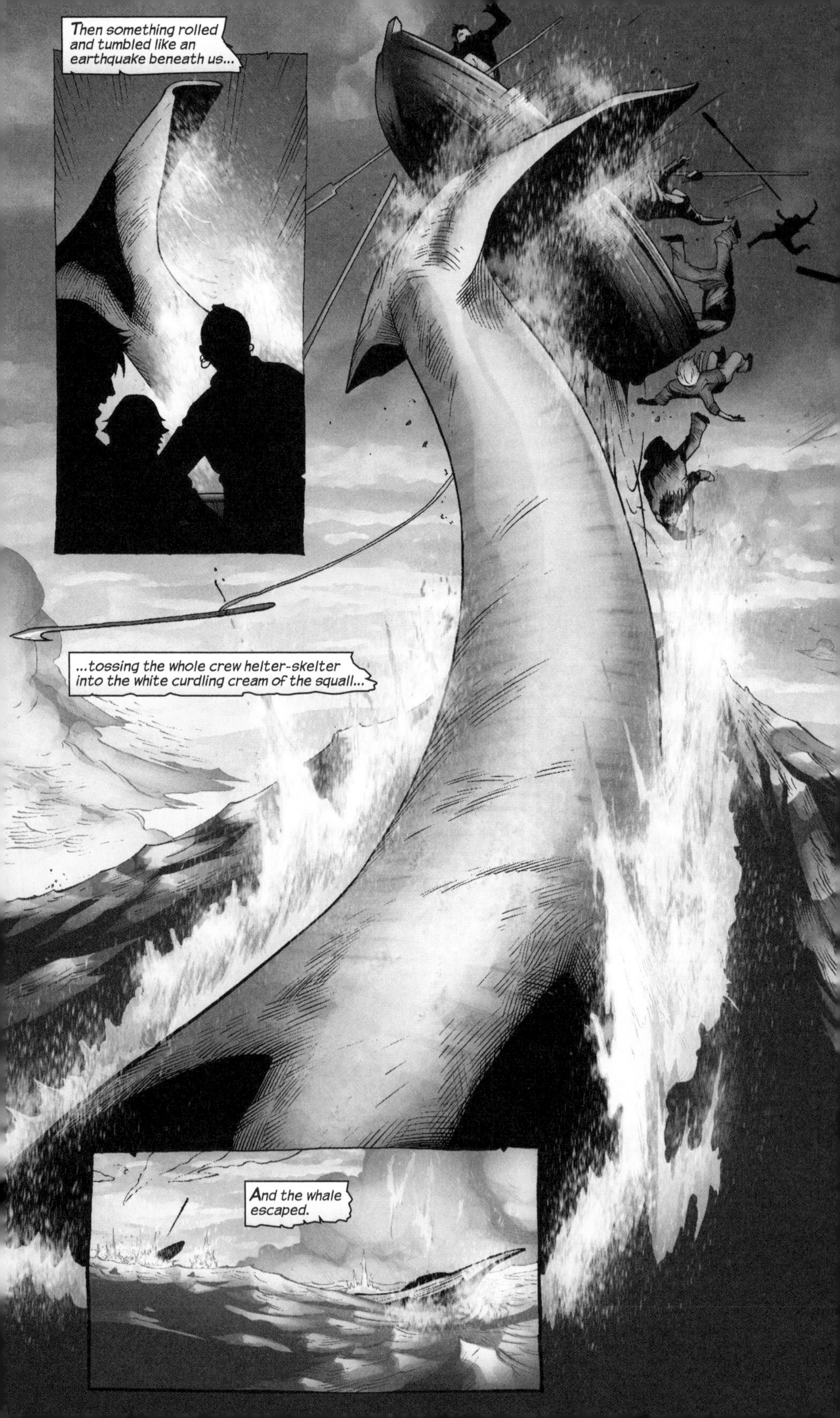
Then something rolled and tumbled like an earthquake beneath us...
...tossing the whole crew helter-skelter into the white curdling cream of the squall...
And the whale escaped.

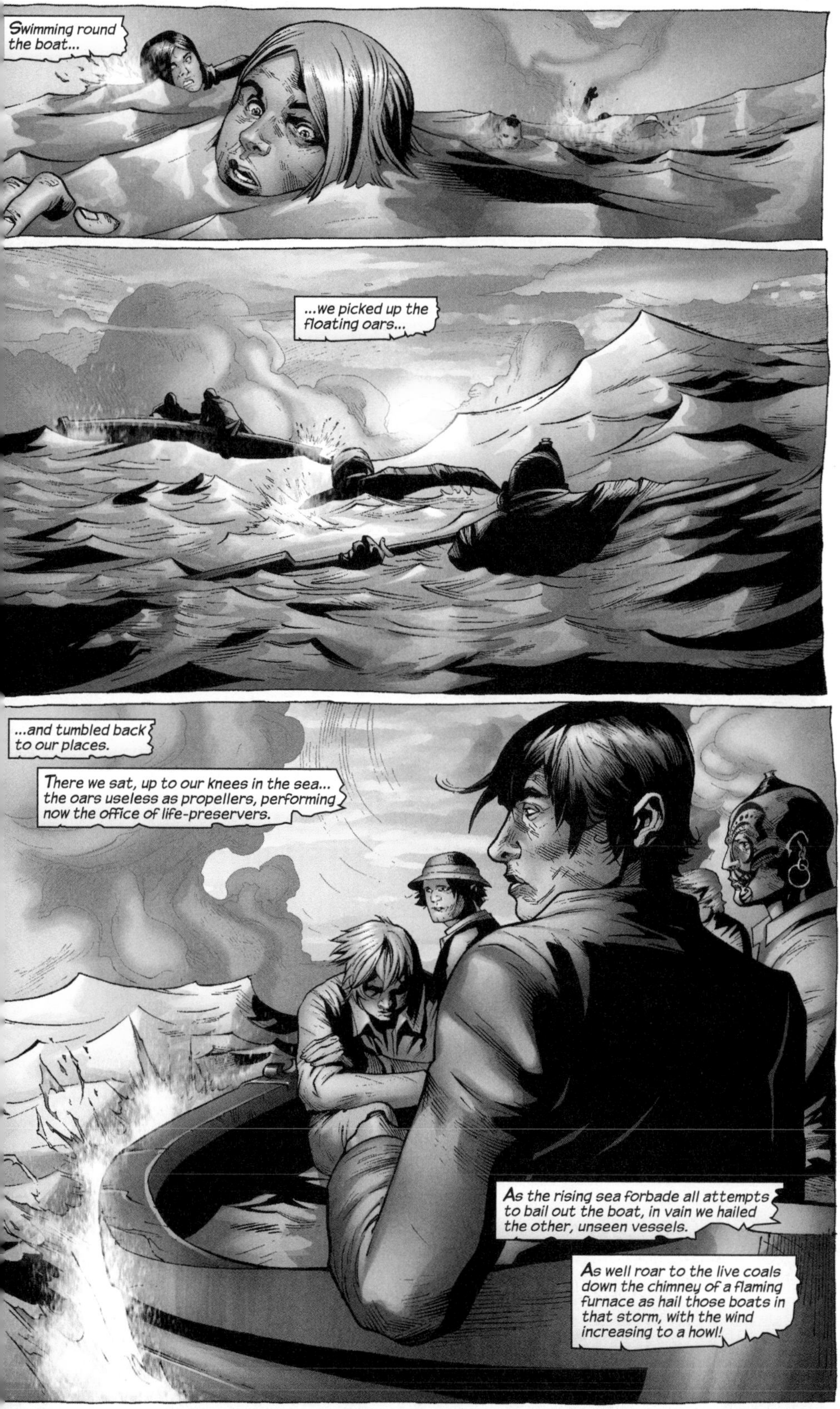
Swimming round the boat...
...we picked up the floating oars...
...and tumbled back to our places.
There we sat, up to our knees in the sea... the oars useless as propellers, performing now the office of life-preservers.
As the rising sea forbade all attempts to bail out the boat, in vain we hailed the other, unseen vessels.
As well roar to the live coals down the chimney of a flaming furnace as hail those boats in that storm, with the wind increasing to a howl!

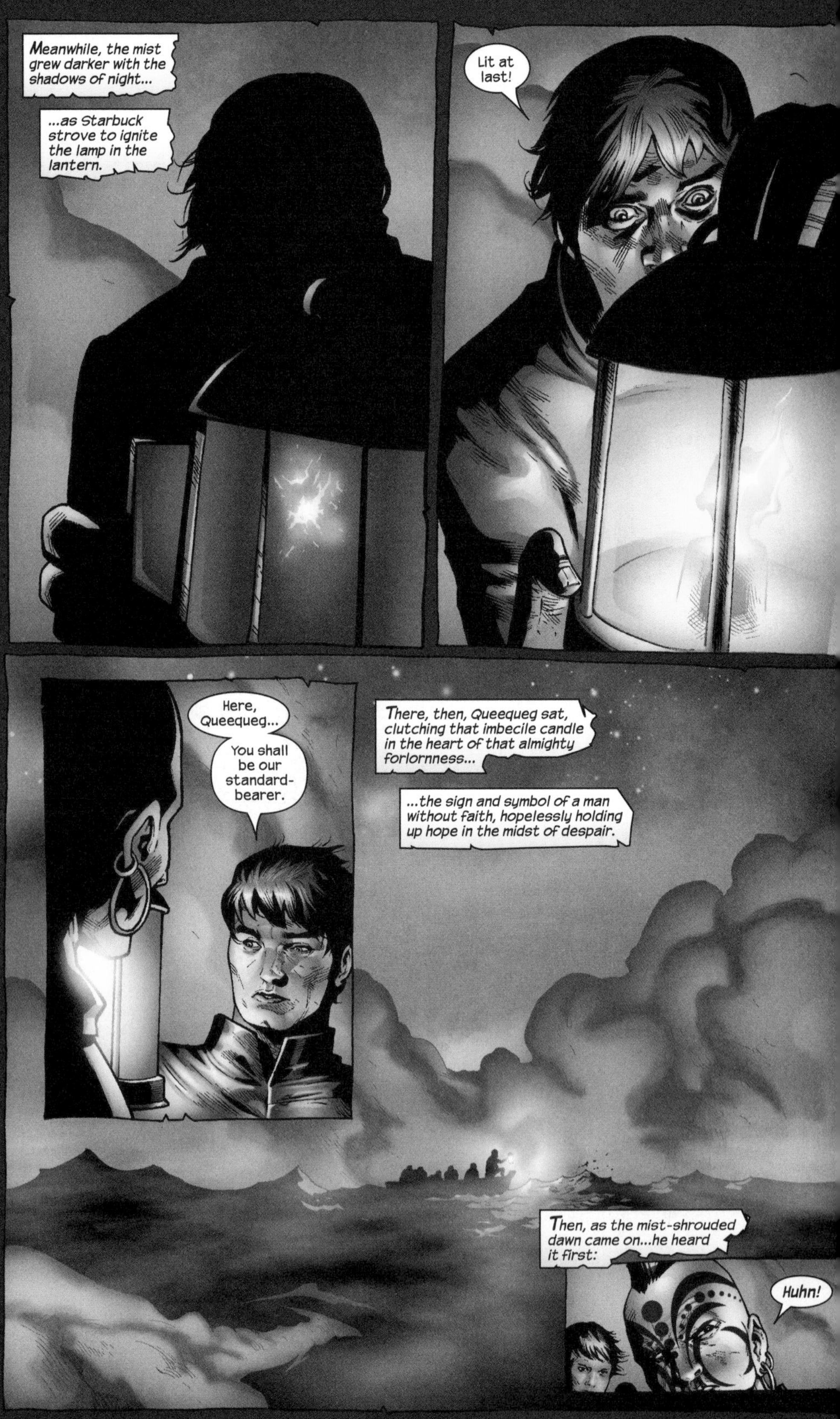
Meanwhile, the mist grew darker with the shadows of night...
...as Starbuck strove to ignite the lamp in the lantern.
Lit at last!
Here, Queequeg...
You shall be our standard-bearer.
There, then, Queequeg sat, clutching that imbecile candle in the heart of that almighty forlornness...
...the sign and symbol of a man without faith, hopelessly holding up hope in the midst of despair.
Then, as the mist-shrouded dawn came on...he heard it first:
Huhn!

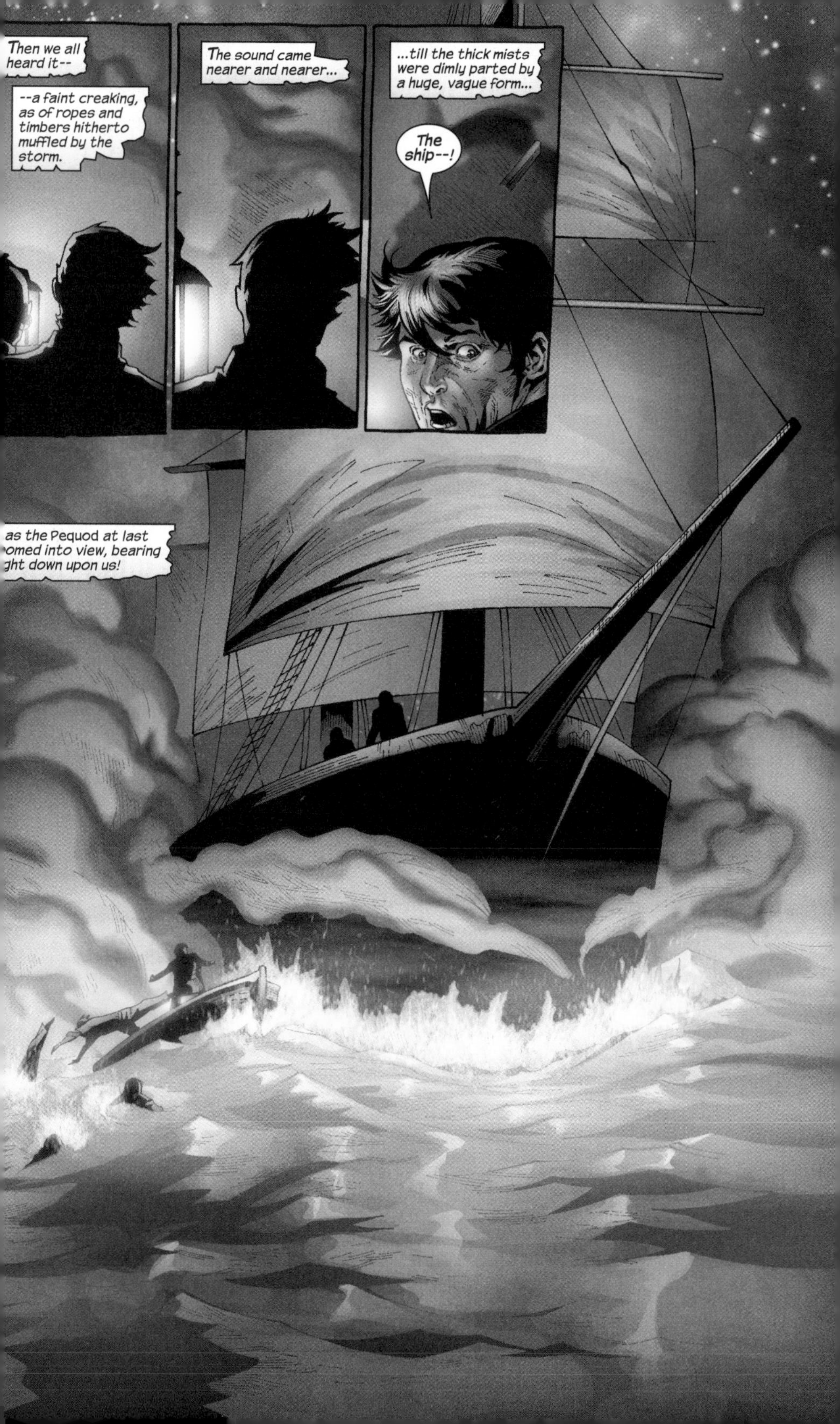
Then we all heard it--
--a faint creaking, as of ropes and timbers hitherto muffled by the storm.
The sound came nearer and nearer...
...till the thick mists were dimly parted by a huge, vague form...
The ship--!
as the Pequod at last
omed into view, bearing
ght down upon us!

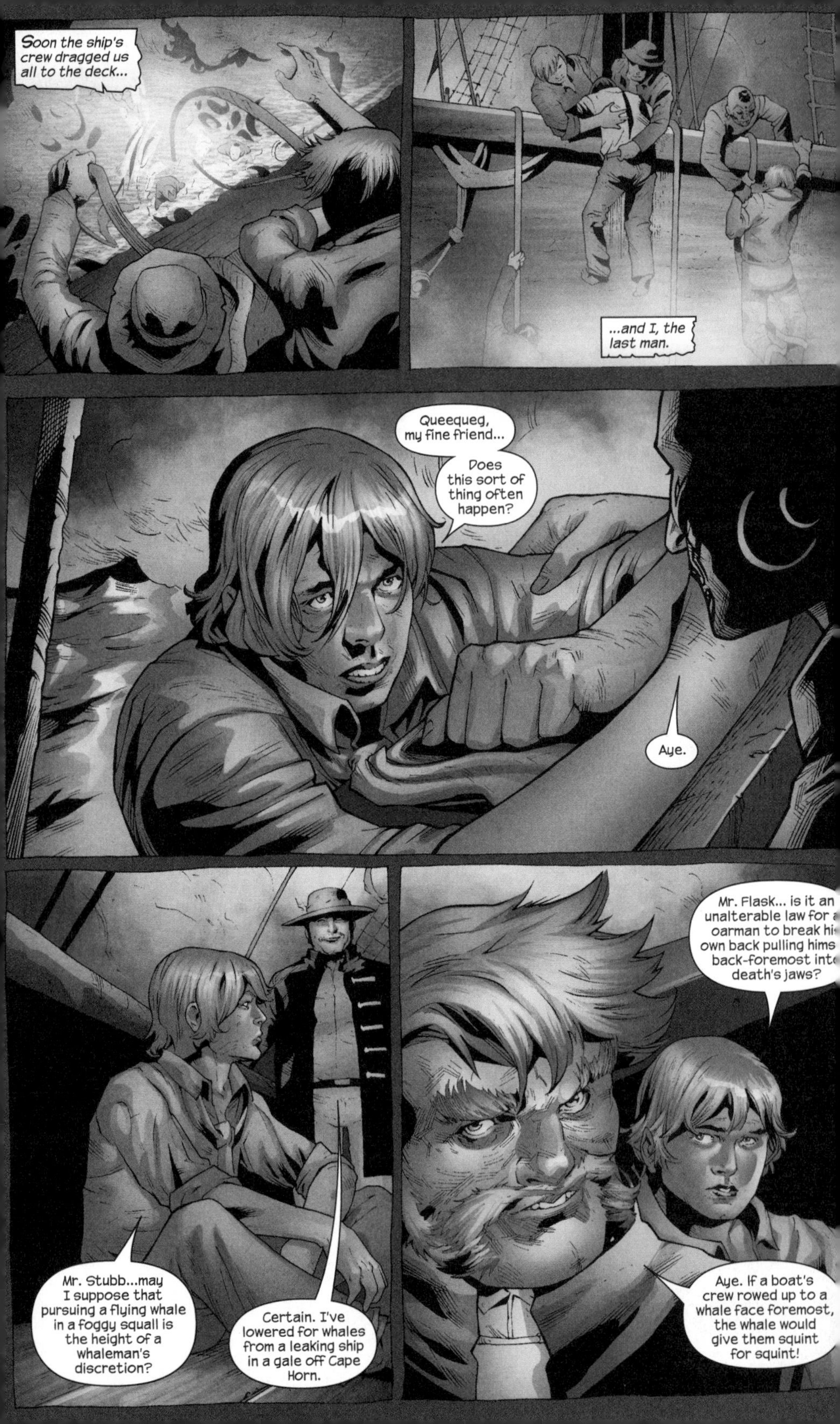

Soon the ship's crew dragged us all to the deck...
...and I, the last man.
Queequeg, my fine friend...
Does this sort of thing often happen?
Aye.
Mr. Stubb...may I suppose that pursuing a flying whale in a foggy squall is the height of a whaleman's discretion?
Certain. I've lowered for whales from a leaking ship in a gale off Cape Horn.
Mr. Flask... is it an unalterable law for a oarman to break his own back pulling hims back-foremost into death's jaws?
Aye. If a boat's crew rowed up to a whale face foremost, the whale would give them squint for squint!

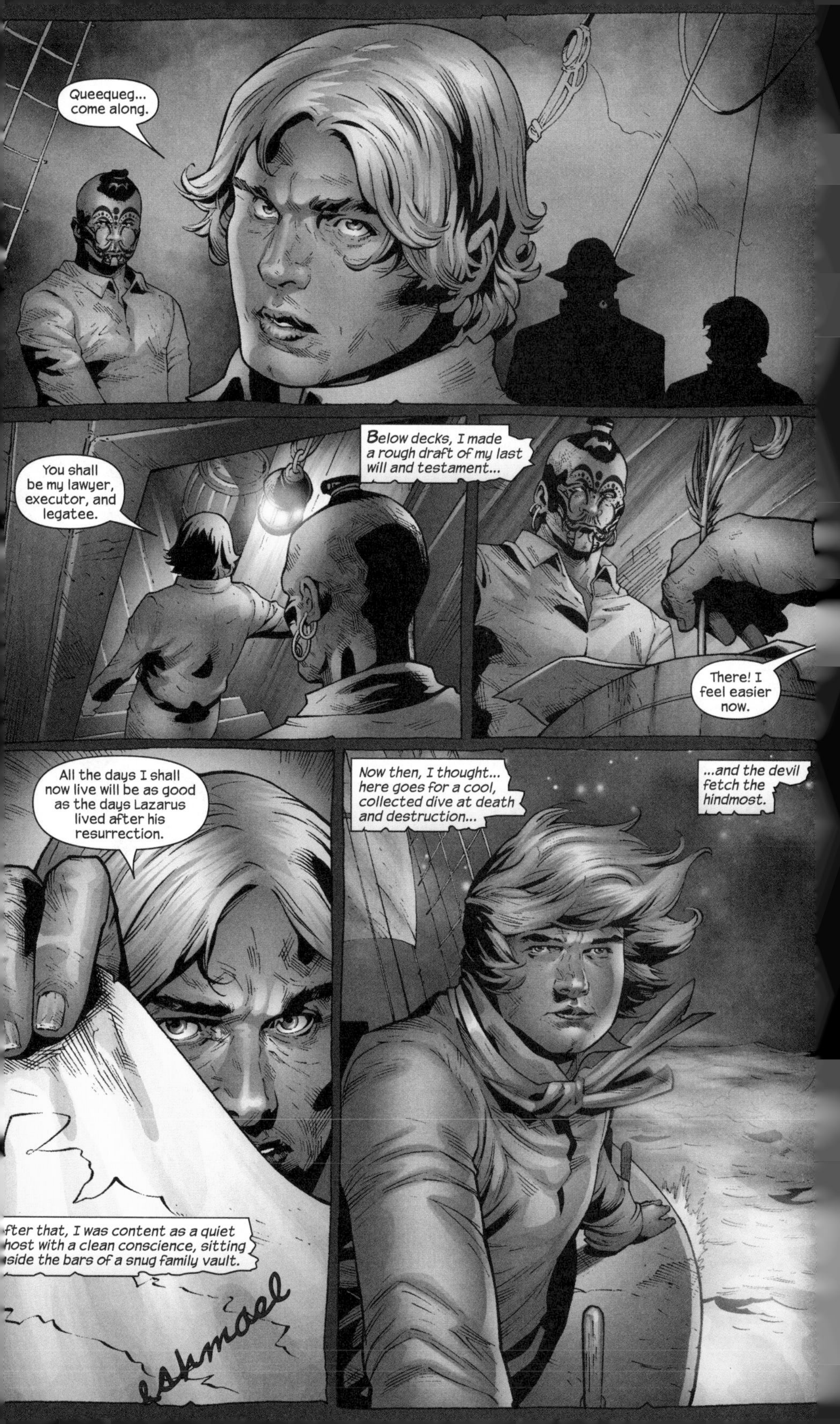
Queequeg... come along.
You shall be my lawyer, executor, and legatee.
Below decks, I made a rough draft of my last will and testament...
There! I feel easier now.
All the days I shall now live will be as good as the days Lazarus lived after his resurrection.
fter that, I was content as a quiet host with a clean conscience, sitting side the bars of a snug family vault.
Now then, I thought... here goes for a cool, collected dive at death and destruction...
...and the devil fetch the hindmost.

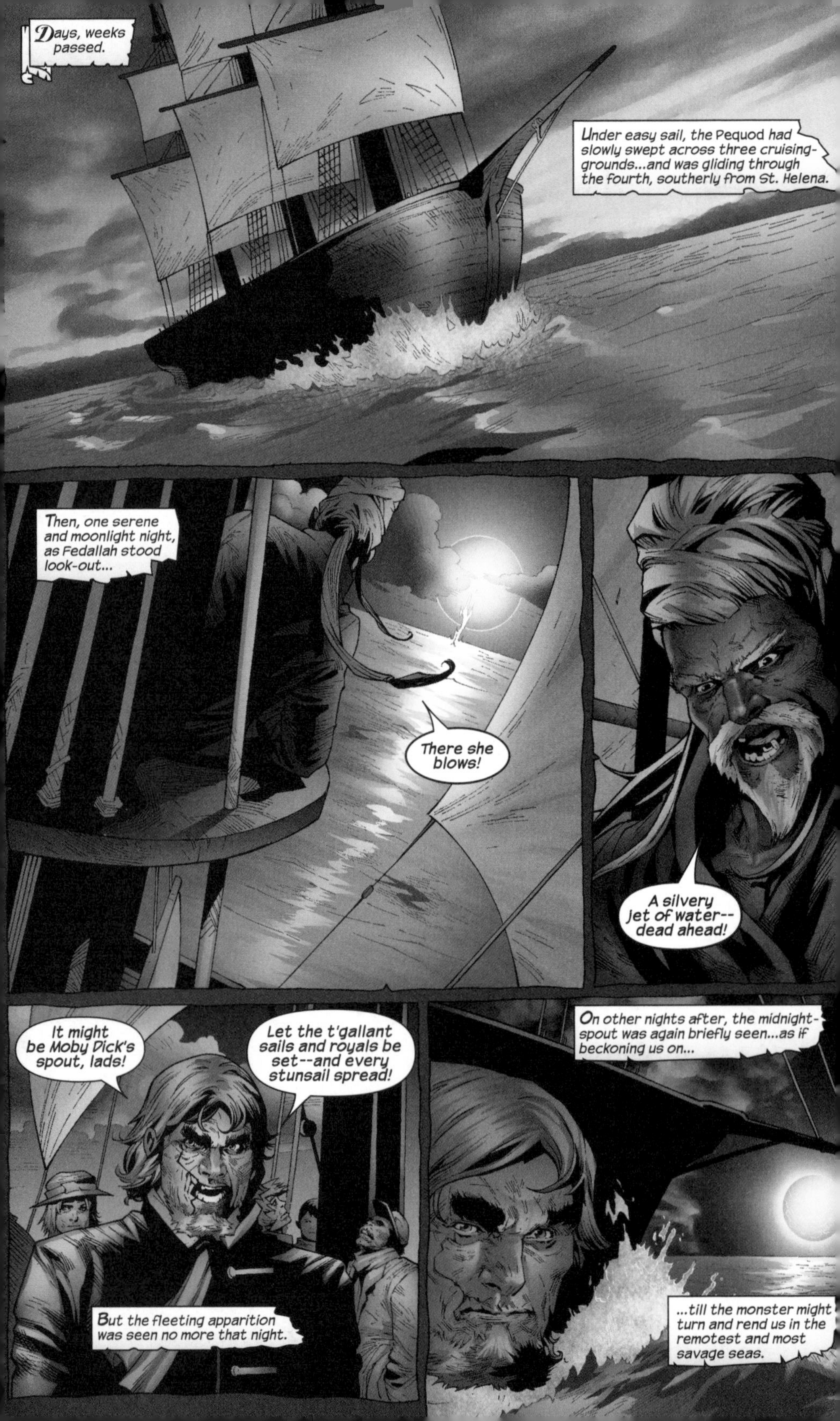
Days, weeks passed.
Under easy sail, the Pequod had slowly swept across three cruising-grounds...and was gliding through the fourth, southerly from St. Helena.
Then, one serene and moonlight night, as Fedallah stood look-out...
There she blows!
A silvery jet of water--dead ahead!
It might be Moby Dick's spout, lads!
Let the t'gallant sails and royals be set--and every stunsail spread!
But the fleeting apparition was seen no more that night.
On other nights after, the midnight-spout was again briefly seen...as if beckoning us on...
...till the monster might turn and rend us in the remotest and most savage seas.

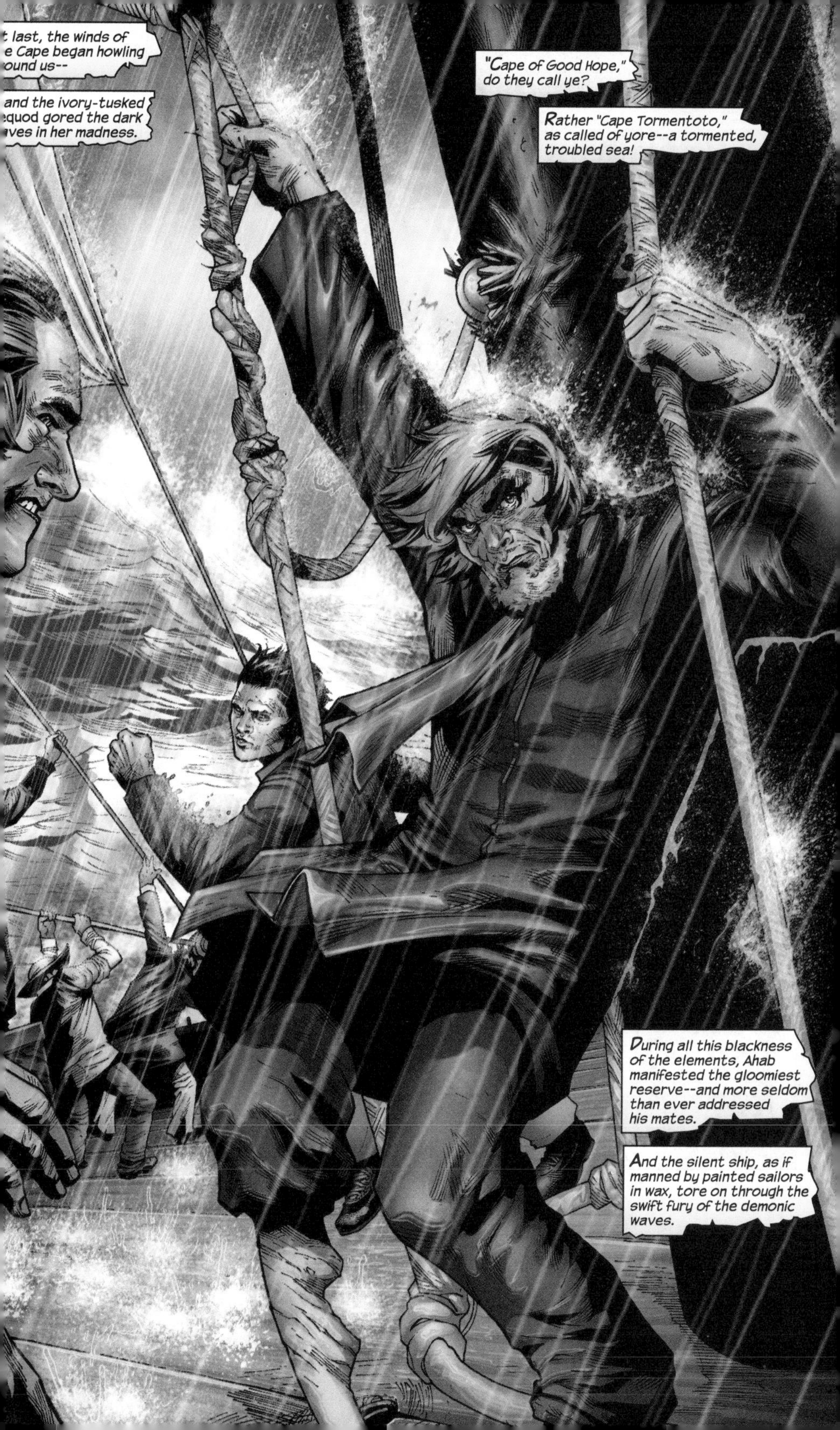
t last, the winds of e Cape began howling ound us--
and the ivory-tusked equod gored the dark ves in her madness.
"Cape of Good Hope," do they call ye?
Rather "Cape Tormentoto," as called of yore--a tormented, troubled sea!
During all this blackness of the elements, Ahab manifested the gloomiest reserve--and more seldom than ever addressed his mates.
And the silent ship, as if manned by painted sailors in wax, tore on through the swift fury of the demonic waves.

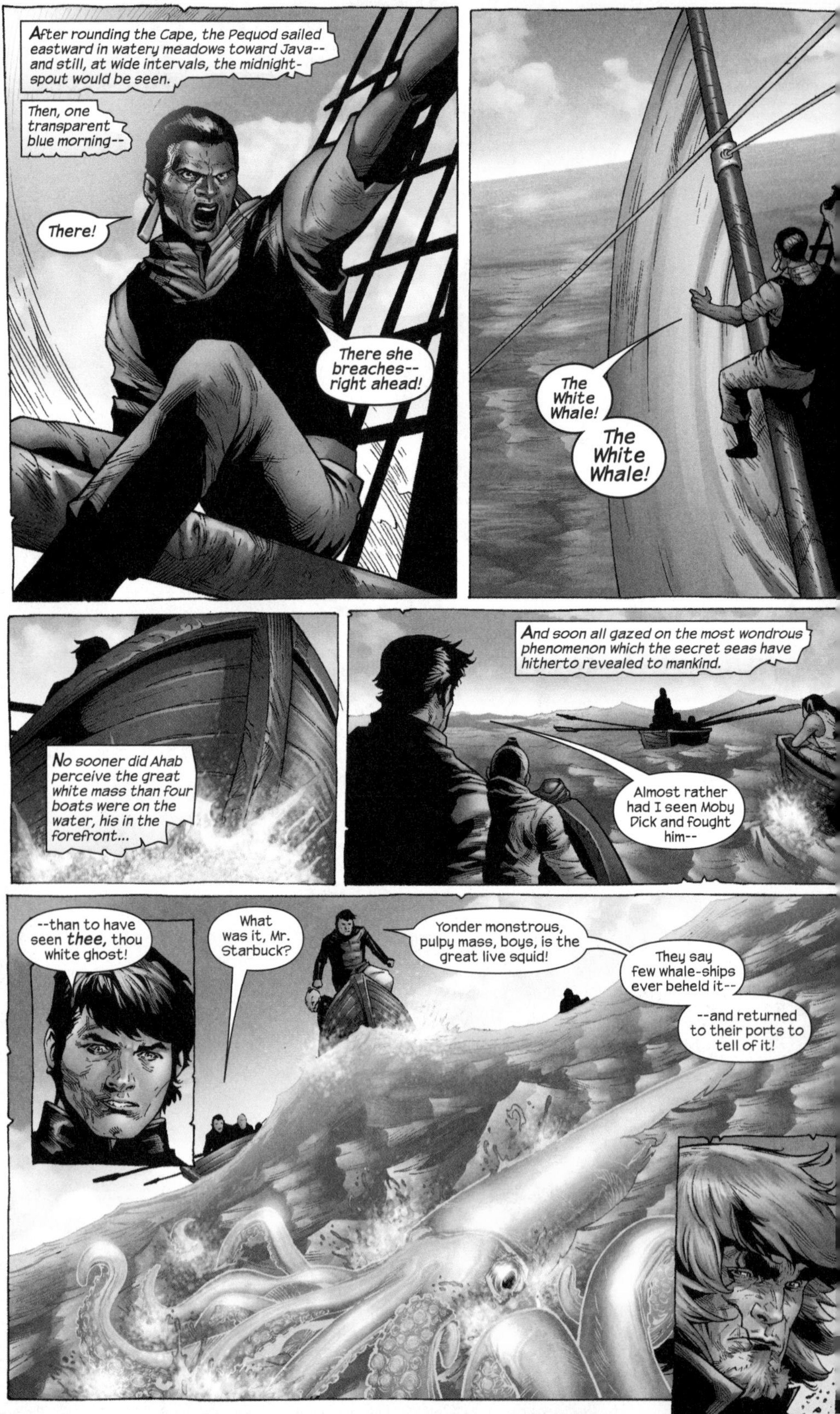
After rounding the Cape, the Pequod sailed eastward in watery meadows toward Java--and still, at wide intervals, the midnight-spout would be seen.
Then, one transparent blue morning--
There!
There she breaches--right ahead!
The White Whale!
The White Whale!
No sooner did Ahab perceive the great white mass than four boats were on the water, his in the forefront...
And soon all gazed on the most wondrous phenomenon which the secret seas have hitherto revealed to mankind.
Almost rather had I seen Moby Dick and fought him--
--than to have seen thee, thou white ghost!
What was it, Mr. Starbuck?
Yonder monstrous, pulpy mass, boys, is the great live squid!
They say few whale-ships ever beheld it--
--and returned to their ports to tell of it!

So said Queequeg, that night: "When you see him 'quid, then you quick see 'm 'parm whale!"

And indeed, the next day, I spotted from the foremast-head a Sperm whale...

...and Stubb and his harpooner made the first kill of the voyage.

He's dead, Mr. Stubb.

Yes, Tashtego...

Both pipes smoked out!

Stubb, be it known, was intemperately fond of the whale as a flavorish thing to his palate...

Fleece, you old cook--this steak is too tender! Don't I always say--

--a good whale-steak must be tough?

Nor was Stubb the only banqueter on the whale's flesh that night.

But the sharks would leave enough of the ship-lashed leviathan from which the crew could retrieve their precious whale oil...

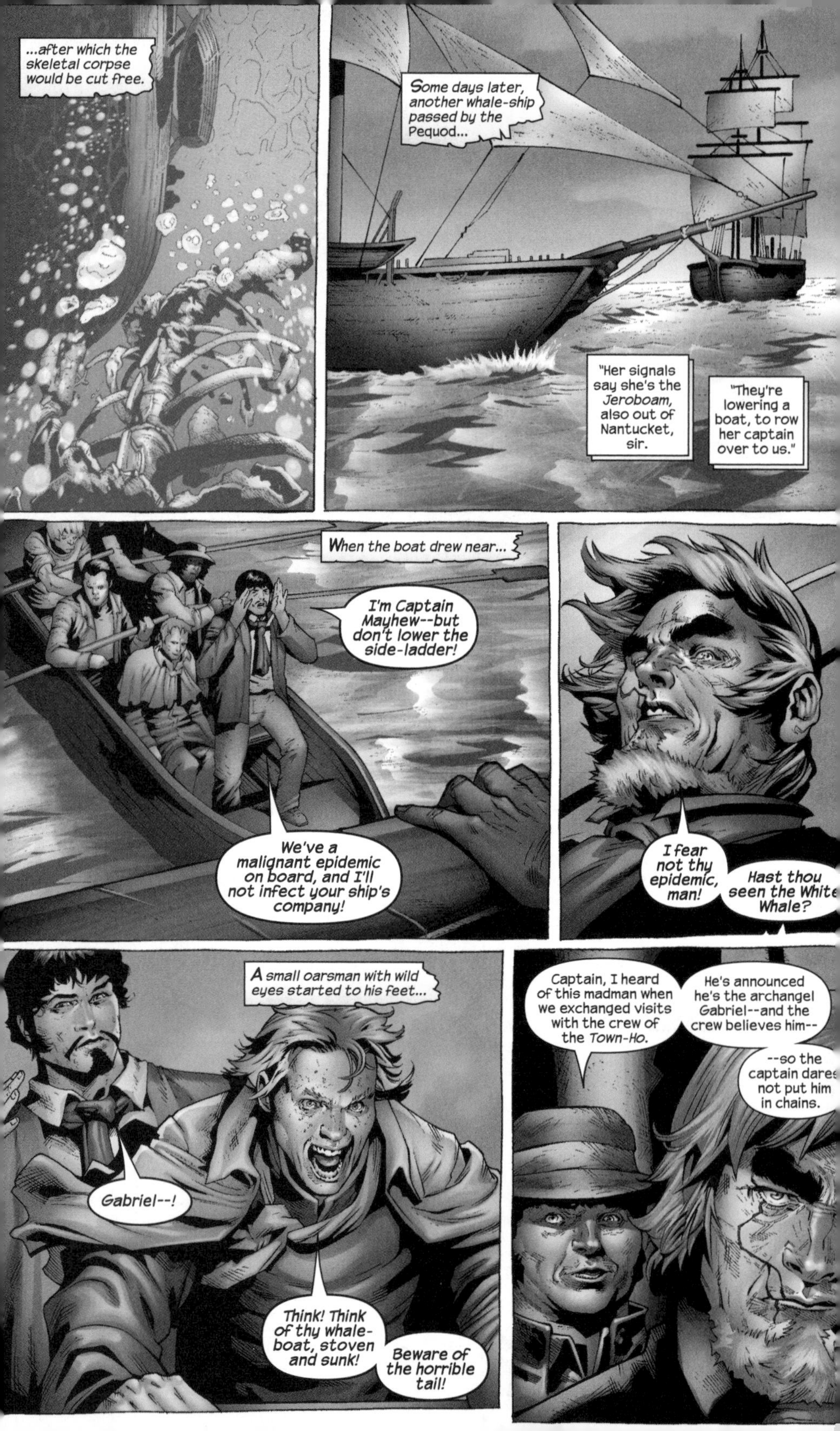
...after which the skeletal corpse would be cut free.
Some days later, another whale-ship passed by the Pequod...
"Her signals say she's the *Jeroboam*, also out of Nantucket, sir.
"They're lowering a boat, to row her captain over to us."
When the boat drew near...
I'm Captain Mayhew--but don't lower the side-ladder!
We've a malignant epidemic on board, and I'll not infect your ship's company!
I fear not thy epidemic, man!
Hast thou seen the White Whale?
A small oarsman with wild eyes started to his feet...
Gabriel--!
Think! Think of thy whale-boat, stoven and sunk!
Beware of the horrible tail!
Captain, I heard of this madman when we exchanged visits with the crew of the *Town-Ho*.
He's announced he's the archangel Gabriel--and the crew believes him--
--so the captain dares not put him in chains.

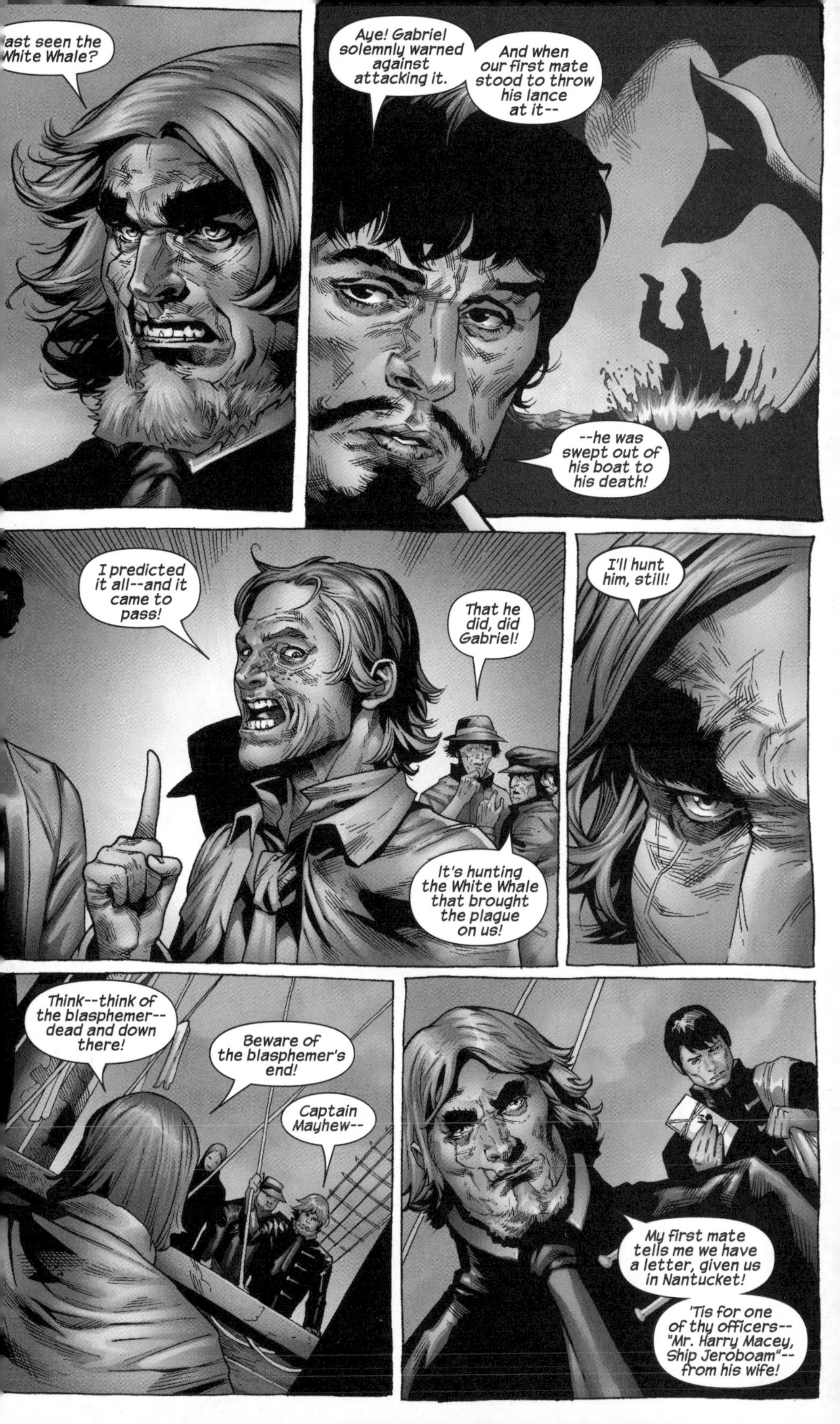
ast seen the White Whale?
Aye! Gabriel solemnly warned against attacking it.
And when our first mate stood to throw his lance at it--
--he was swept out of his boat to his death!
I predicted it all--and it came to pass!
That he did, did Gabriel!
It's hunting the White Whale that brought the plague on us!
I'll hunt him, still!
Think--think of the blasphemer--dead and down there!
Beware of the blasphemer's end!
Captain Mayhew--
My first mate tells me we have a letter, given us in Nantucket!
'Tis for one of thy officers--"Mr. Harry Macey, Ship Jeroboam"--from his wife!

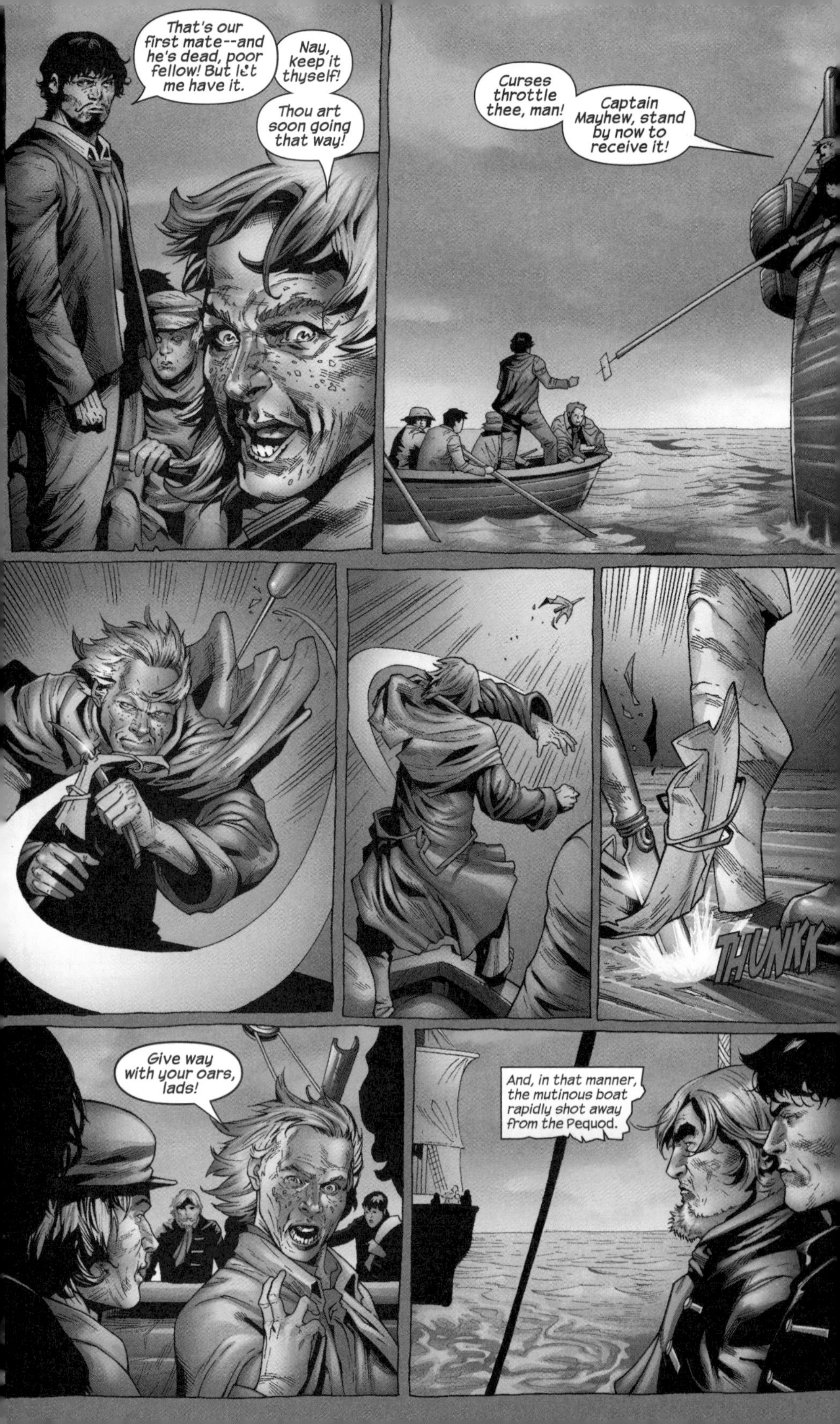
That's our first mate--and he's dead, poor fellow! But let me have it.
Nay, keep it thyself!
Thou art soon going that way!
Curses throttle thee, man!
Captain Mayhew, stand by now to receive it!
THUNKK
Give way with your oars, lads!
And, in that manner, the mutinous boat rapidly shot away from the Pequod.

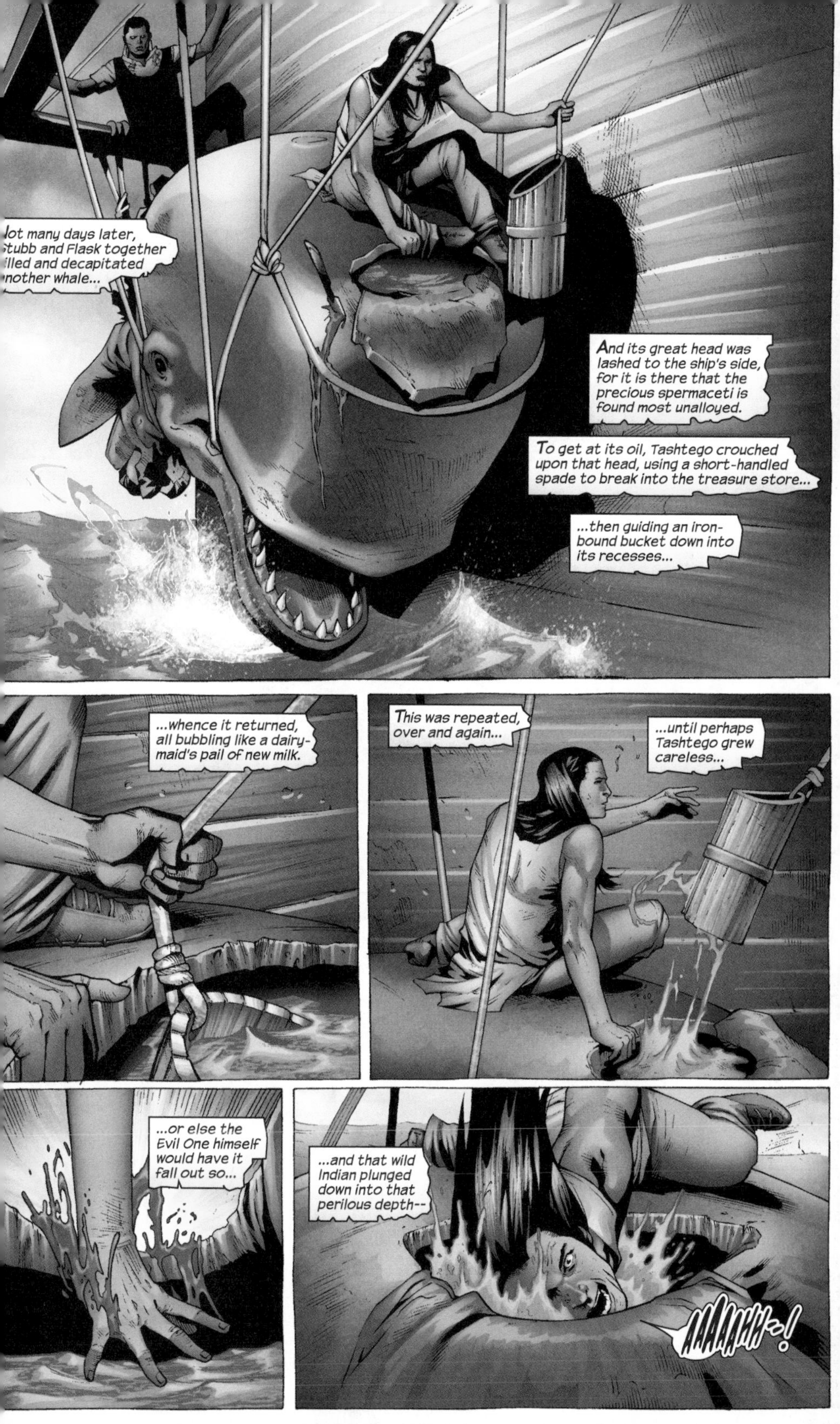

lot many days later, stubb and Flask together illed and decapitated nother whale...
And its great head was lashed to the ship's side, for it is there that the precious spermaceti is found most unalloyed.
To get at its oil, Tashtego crouched upon that head, using a short-handled spade to break into the treasure store...
...then guiding an iron-bound bucket down into its recesses...
...whence it returned, all bubbling like a dairy-maid's pail of new milk.
This was repeated, over and again...
...until perhaps Tashtego grew careless...
...or else the Evil One himself would have it fall out so...
...and that wild Indian plunged down into that perilous depth--
AAAAAHH--!

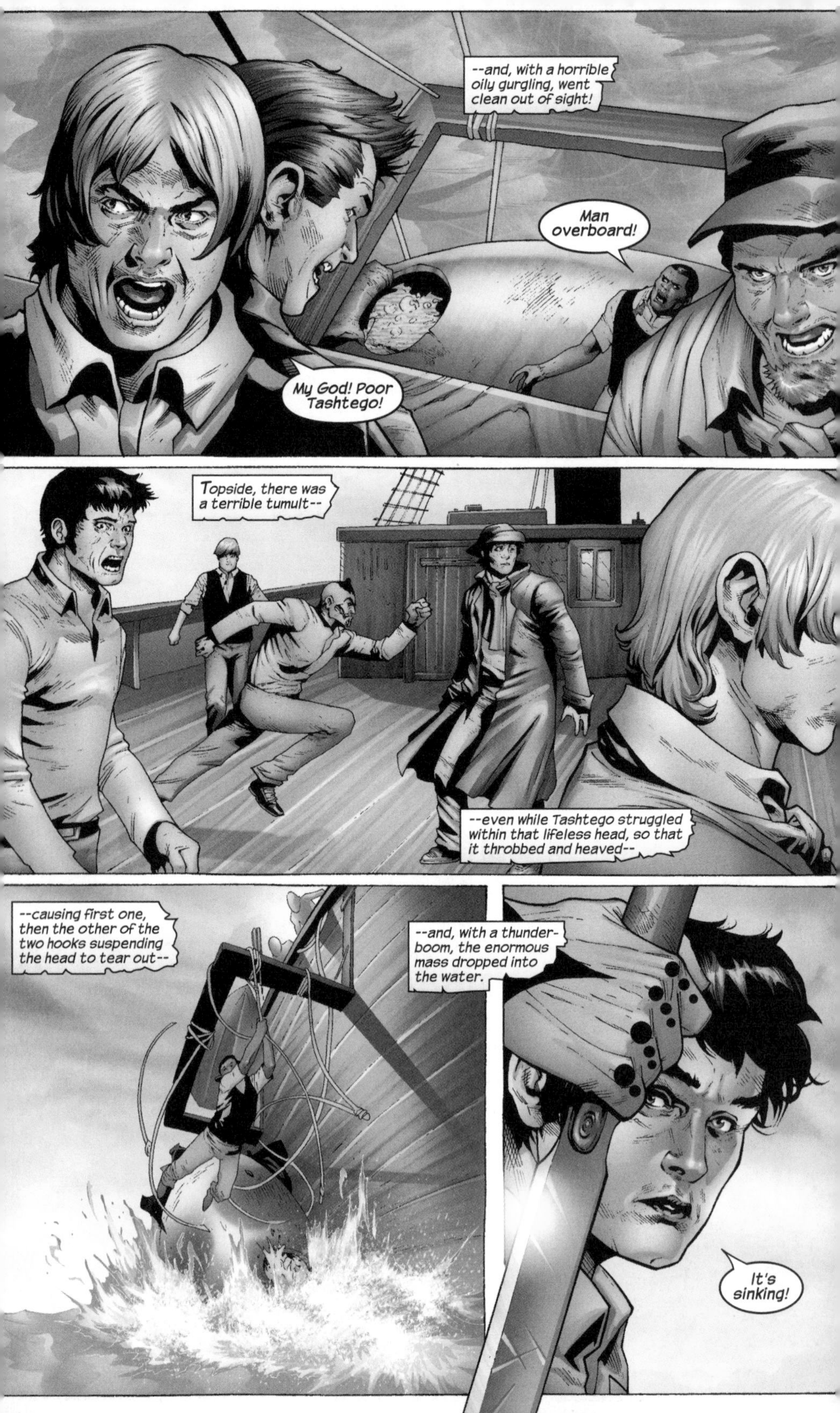
--and, with a horrible oily gurgling, went clean out of sight!
Man overboard!
My God! Poor Tashtego!
Topside, there was a terrible tumult--
--even while Tashtego struggled within that lifeless head, so that it throbbed and heaved--
--causing first one, then the other of the two hooks suspending the head to tear out--
--and, with a thunder-boom, the enormous mass dropped into the water.
It's sinking!

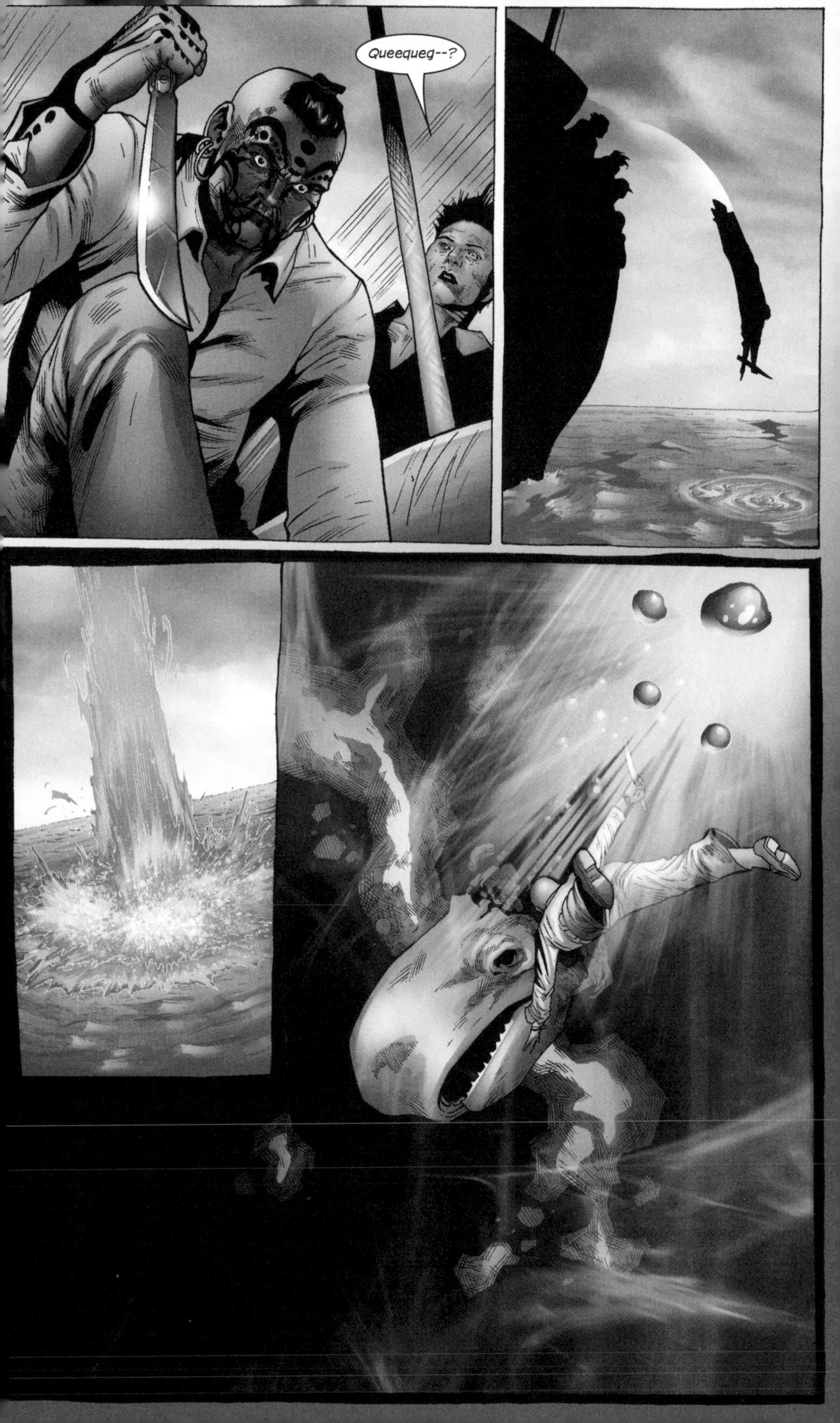
Queequeg--?

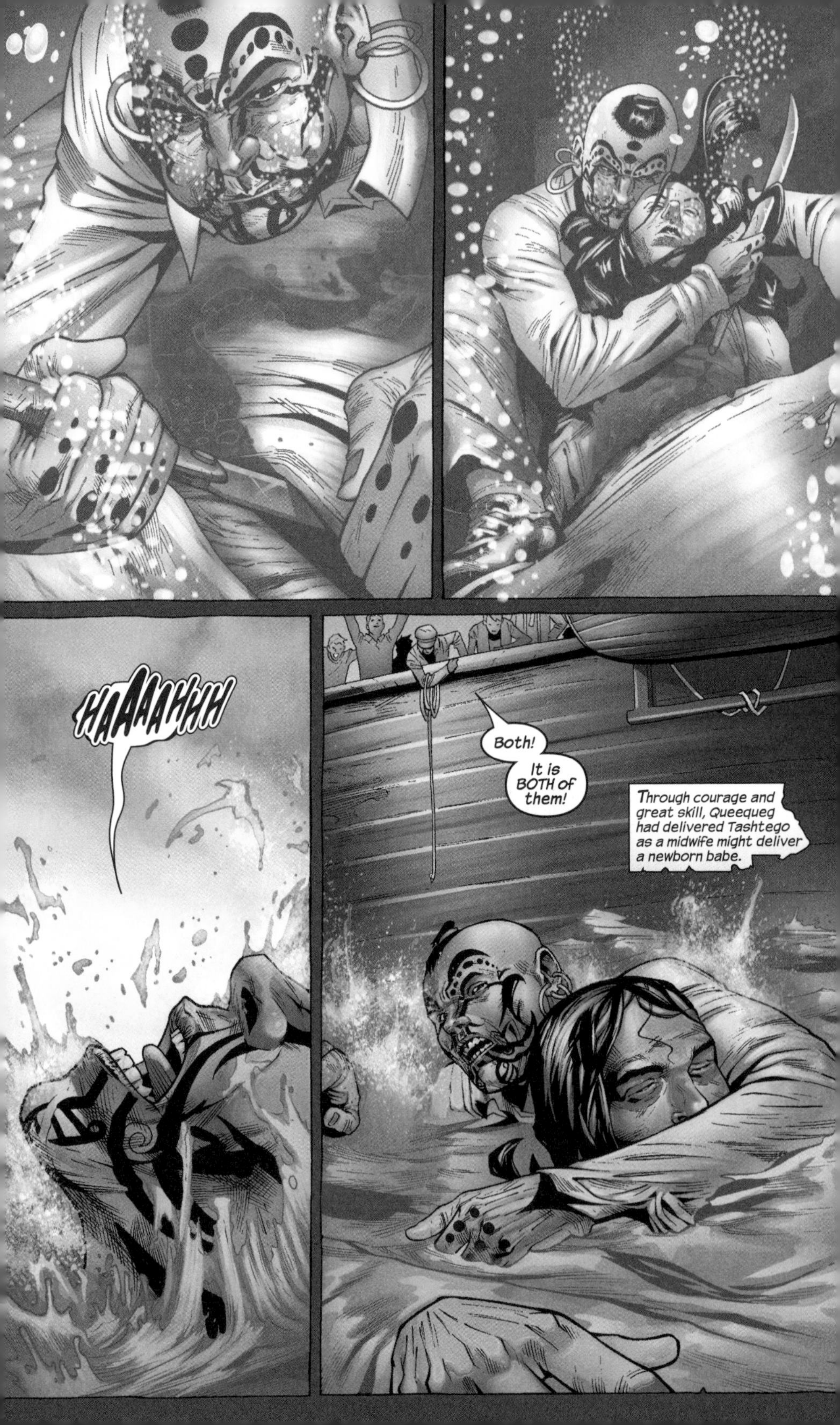
HAAAAHHH
Both!
It is BOTH of them!
Through courage and great skill, Queequeg had delivered Tashtego as a midwife might deliver a newborn babe.

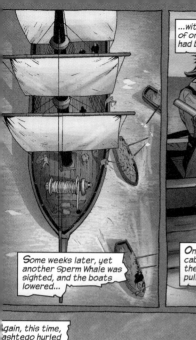

Some weeks later, yet another Sperm Whale was sighted, and the boats lowered...

...with little Pip rowing in place of one of Stubbs' oarsmen, who had badly maimed his hand.

On an earlier lowering, the cabin boy had leaped from the boat in fear, and been pulled from the brine.

...again, this time, ...ashtego hurled ...'s darted iron...

...and when this whale gave a hard rap right under the boat--

...Pip leaped ...ce more!

Jimmini!

Mr. Stubb! The whale's starting to run!

And we run with it!

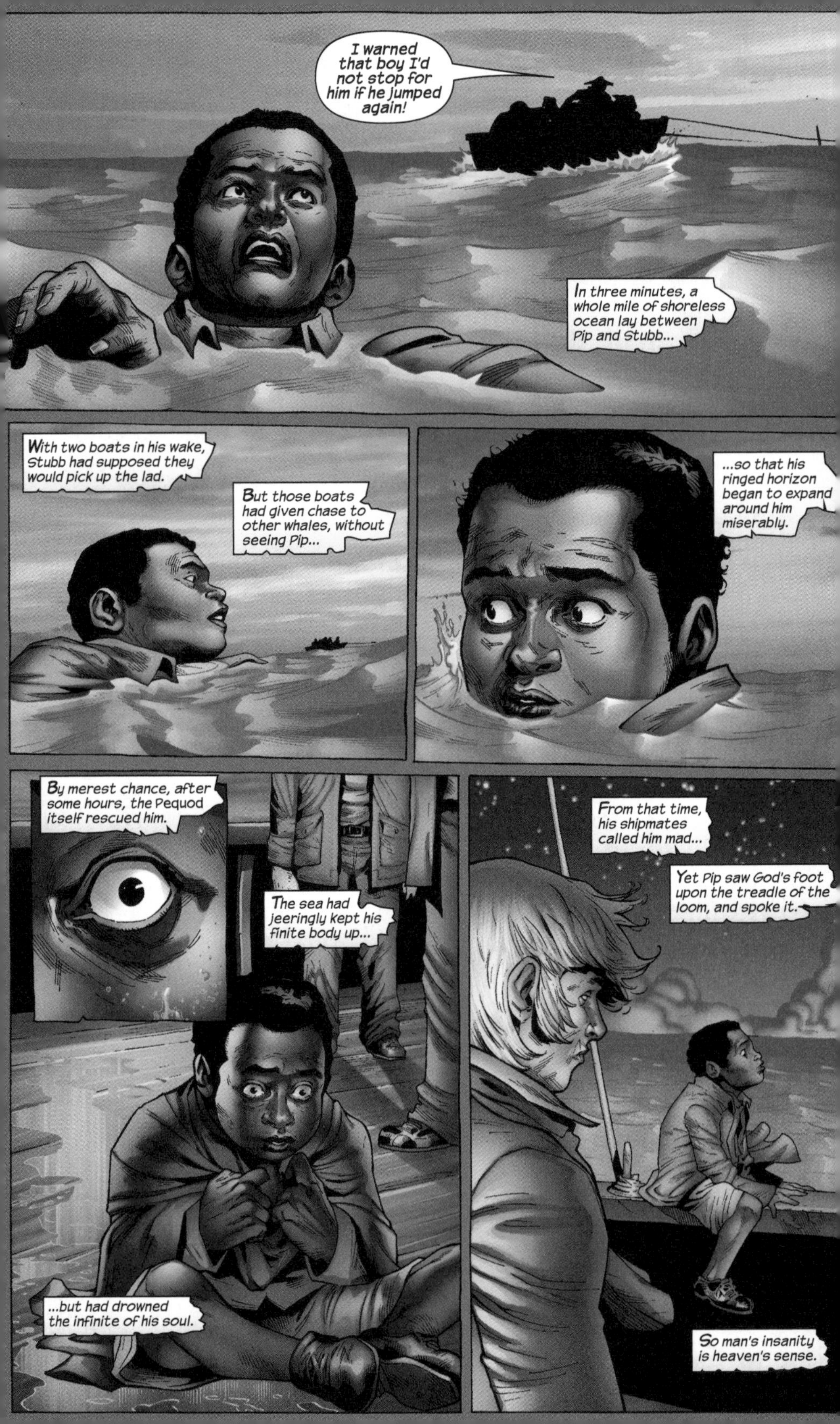

I warned that boy I'd not stop for him if he jumped again!
In three minutes, a whole mile of shoreless ocean lay between Pip and Stubb...
With two boats in his wake, Stubb had supposed they would pick up the lad.
But those boats had given chase to other whales, without seeing Pip...
...so that his ringed horizon began to expand around him miserably.
By merest chance, after some hours, the Pequod itself rescued him.
The sea had jeeringly kept his finite body up...
...but had drowned the infinite of his soul.
From that time, his shipmates called him mad...
Yet Pip saw God's foot upon the treadle of the loom, and spoke it.
So man's insanity is heaven's sense.

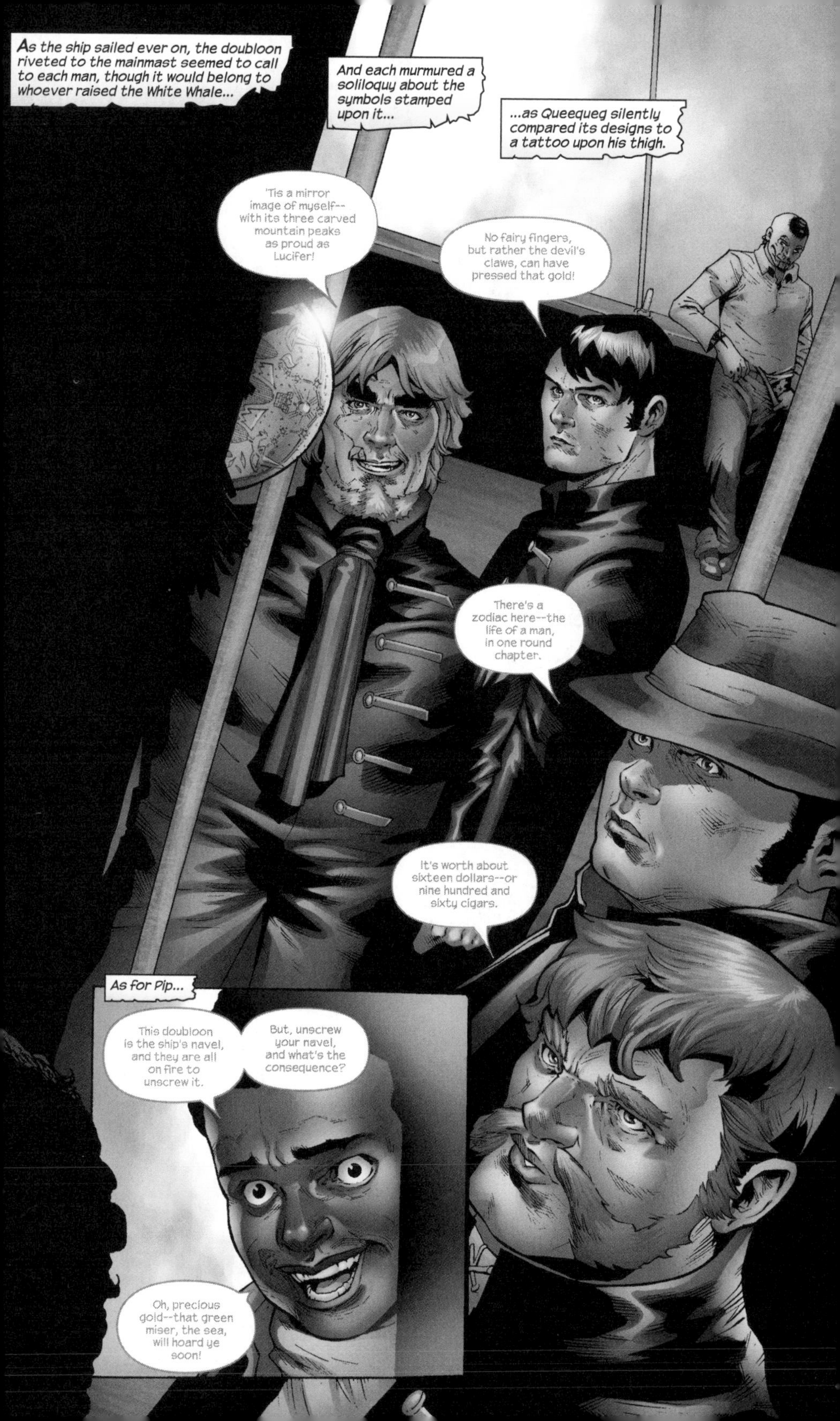
As the ship sailed ever on, the doubloon riveted to the mainmast seemed to call to each man, though it would belong to whoever raised the White Whale...
And each murmured a soliloquy about the symbols stamped upon it...
...as Queequeg silently compared its designs to a tattoo upon his thigh.
'Tis a mirror image of myself--with its three carved mountain peaks as proud as Lucifer!
No fairy fingers, but rather the devil's claws, can have pressed that gold!
There's a zodiac here--the life of a man, in one round chapter.
It's worth about sixteen dollars--or nine hundred and sixty cigars.
As for Pip...
This doubloon is the ship's navel, and they are all on fire to unscrew it.
But, unscrew your navel, and what's the consequence?
Oh, precious gold--that green miser, the sea, will hoard ye soon!

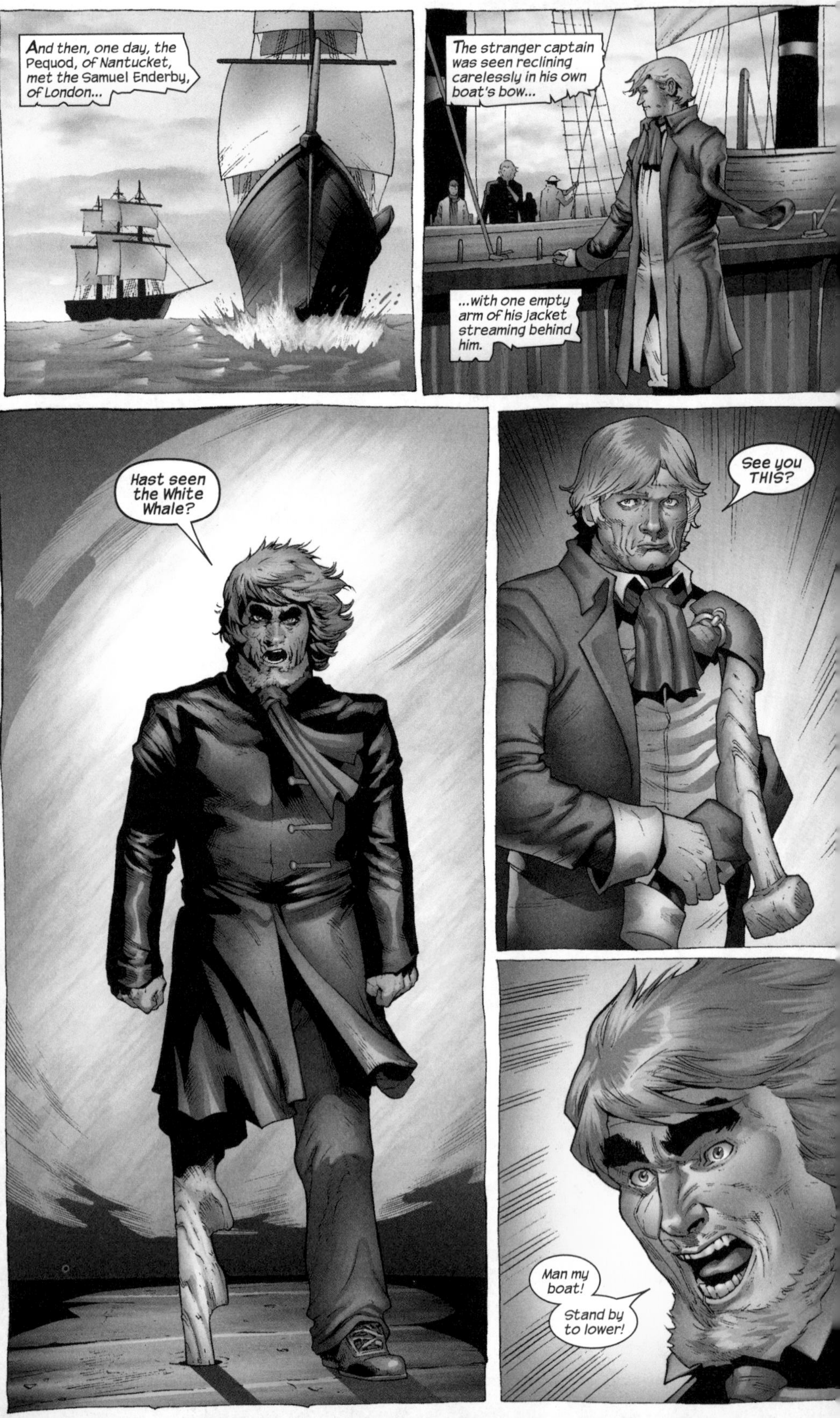
And then, one day, the Pequod, of Nantucket, met the Samuel Enderby, of London...
The stranger captain was seen reclining carelessly in his own boat's bow...
...with one empty arm of his jacket streaming behind him.
Hast seen the White Whale?
See you THIS?
Man my boat!
Stand by to lower!

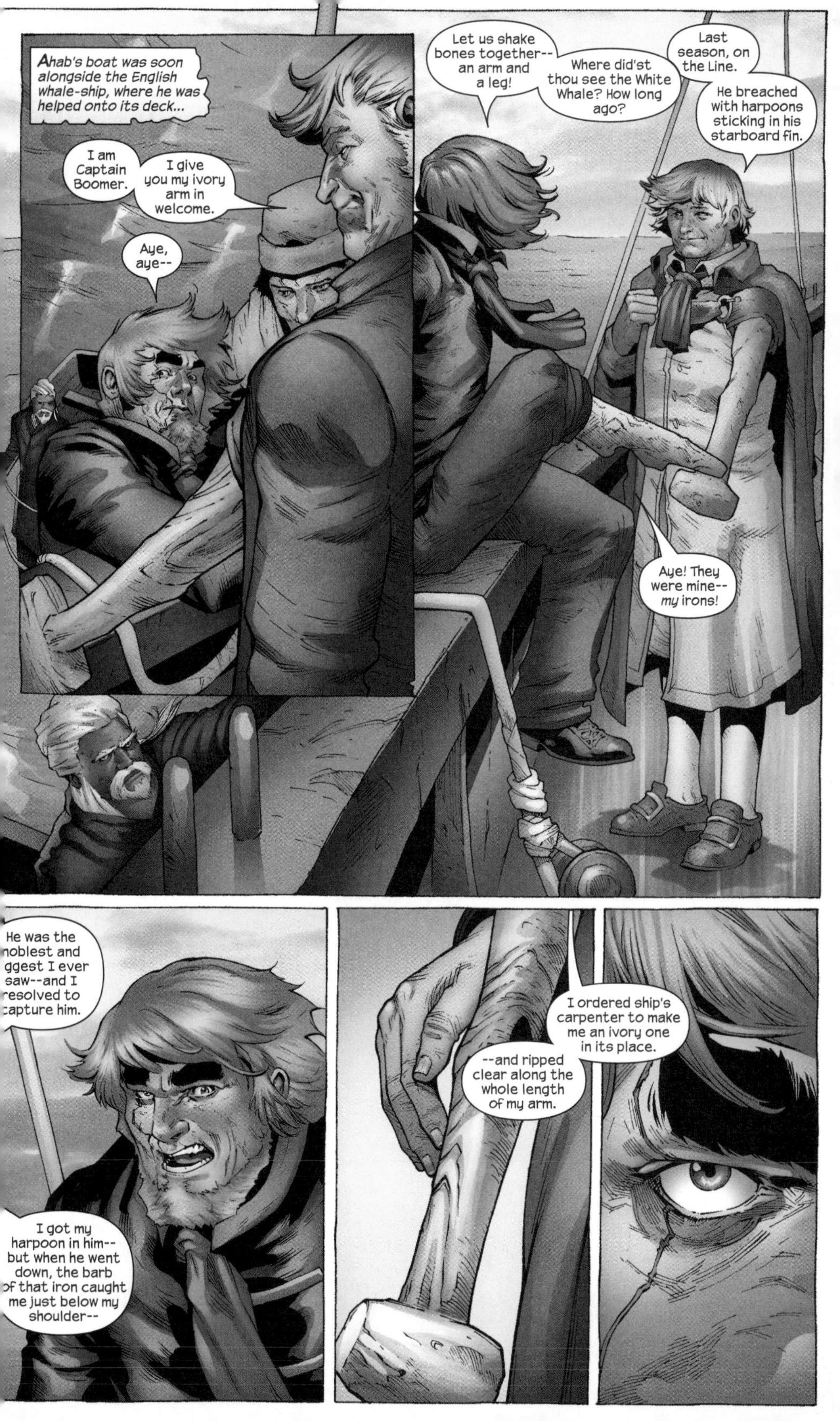

Ahab's boat was soon alongside the English whale-ship, where he was helped onto its deck...
I am Captain Boomer.
I give you my ivory arm in welcome.
Aye, aye--
Let us shake bones together-- an arm and a leg!
Where did'st thou see the White Whale? How long ago?
Last season, on the Line.
He breached with harpoons sticking in his starboard fin.
Aye! They were mine-- *my* irons!
He was the noblest and
ggest I ever saw--and I
esolved to
capture him.
I got my harpoon in him-- but when he went down, the barb
of that iron caught me just below my shoulder--
--and ripped clear along the whole length of my arm.
I ordered ship's carpenter to make me an ivory one in its place.

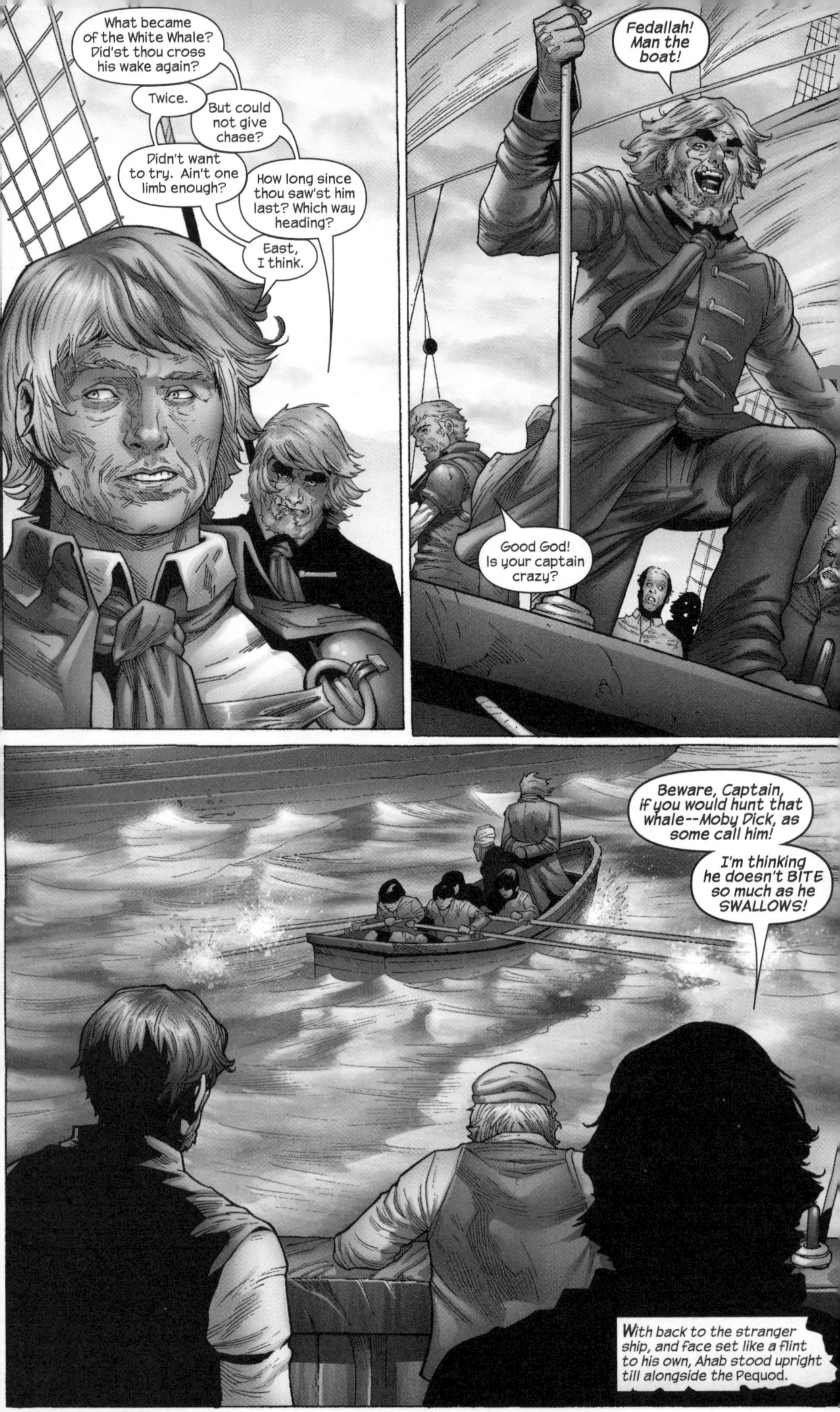
What became of the White Whale? Did'st thou cross his wake again?
Twice.
But could not give chase?
Didn't want to try. Ain't one limb enough?
How long since thou saw'st him last? Which way heading?
East, I think.
Fedallah! Man the boat!
Good God! Is your captain crazy?
Beware, Captain, if you would hunt that whale--Moby Dick, as some call him!
I'm thinking he doesn't BITE so much as he SWALLOWS!
With back to the stranger ship, and face set like a flint to his own, Ahab stood upright till alongside the Pequod.

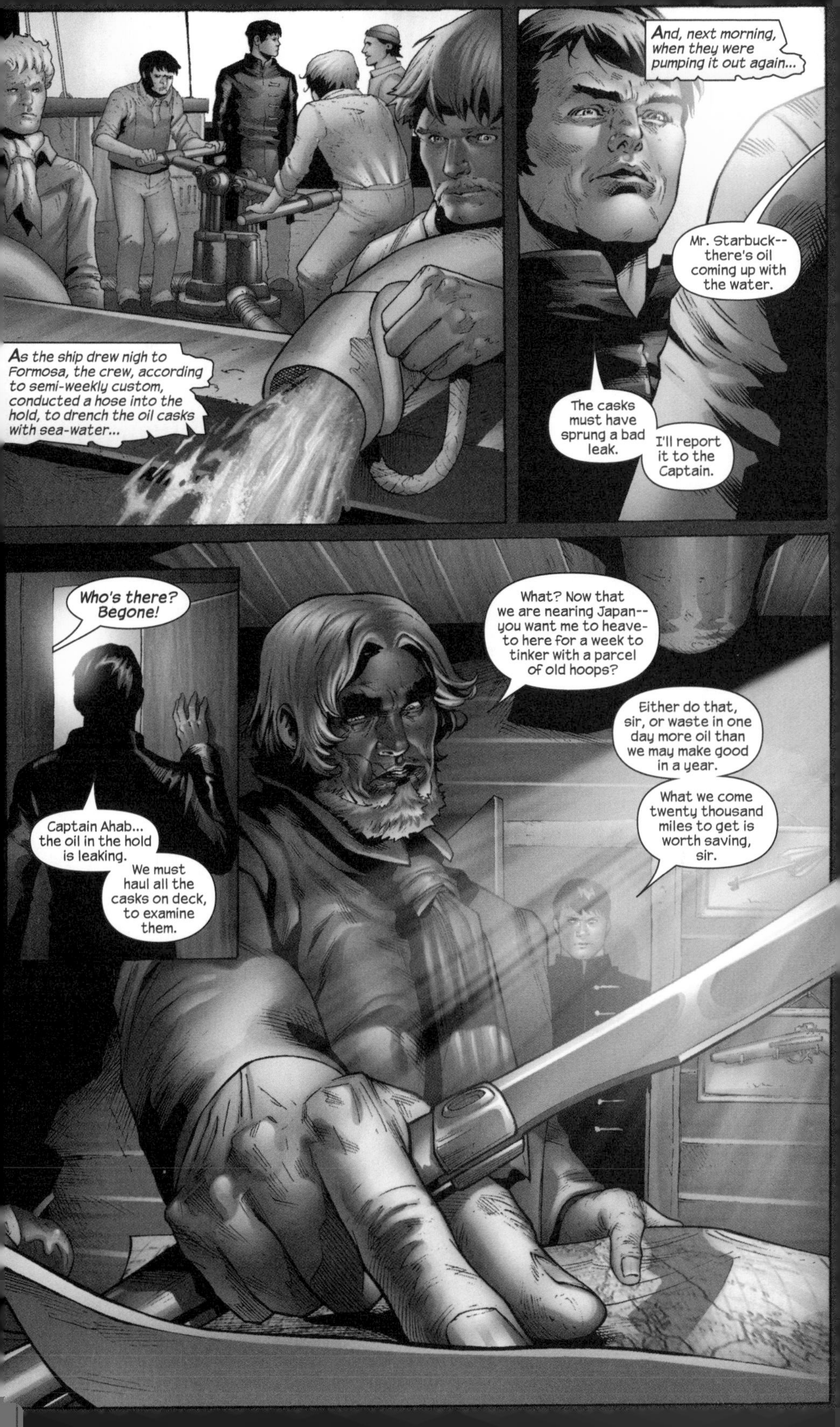
As the ship drew nigh to Formosa, the crew, according to semi-weekly custom, conducted a hose into the hold, to drench the oil casks with sea-water...
And, next morning, when they were pumping it out again...
Mr. Starbuck-- there's oil coming up with the water.
The casks must have sprung a bad leak.
I'll report it to the Captain.
Who's there? Begone!
Captain Ahab... the oil in the hold is leaking.
We must haul all the casks on deck, to examine them.
What? Now that we are nearing Japan-- you want me to heave-to here for a week to tinker with a parcel of old hoops?
Either do that, sir, or waste in one day more oil than we may make good in a year.
What we come twenty thousand miles to get is worth saving, sir.

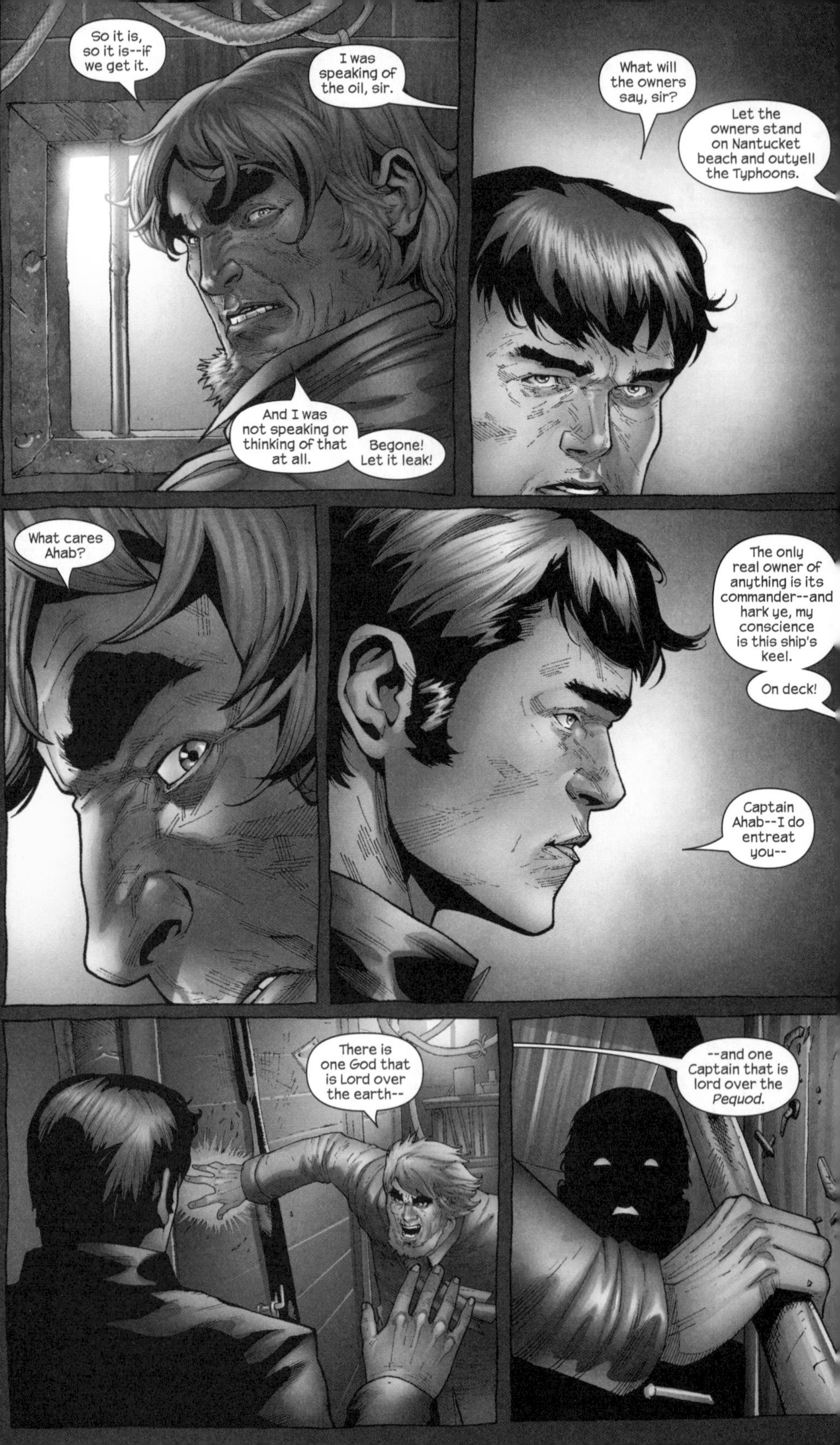

So it is, so it is--if we get it.
I was speaking of the oil, sir.
What will the owners say, sir?
Let the owners stand on Nantucket beach and outyell the Typhoons.
And I was not speaking or thinking of that at all.
Begone! Let it leak!
What cares Ahab?
The only real owner of anything is its commander--and hark ye, my conscience is this ship's keel.
On deck!
Captain Ahab--I do entreat you--
There is one God that is Lord over the earth--
--and one Captain that is lord over the *Pequod.*

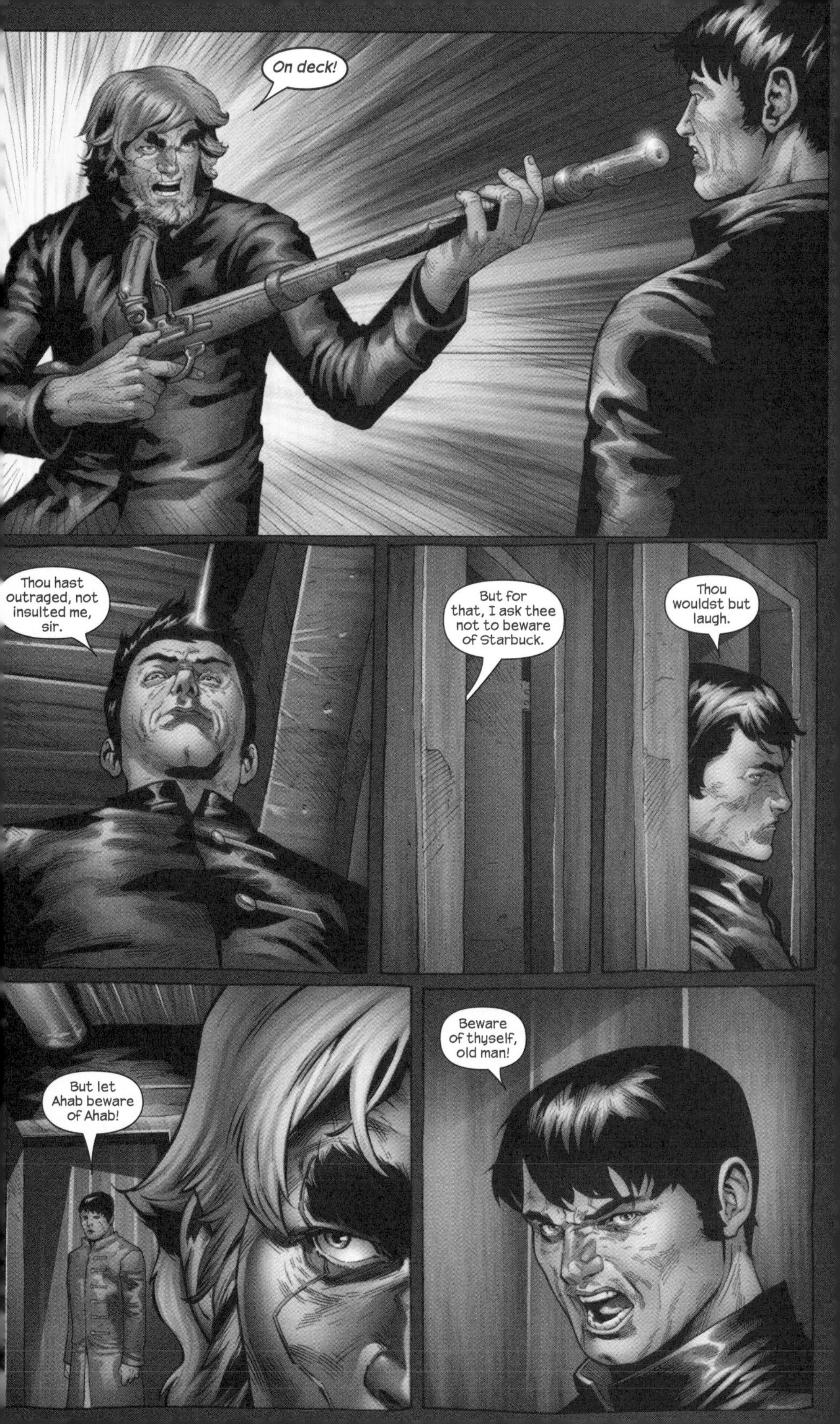
On deck!
Thou hast outraged, not insulted me, sir.
But for that, I ask thee not to beware of Starbuck.
Thou wouldst but laugh.
But let Ahab beware of Ahab!
Beware of thyself, old man!

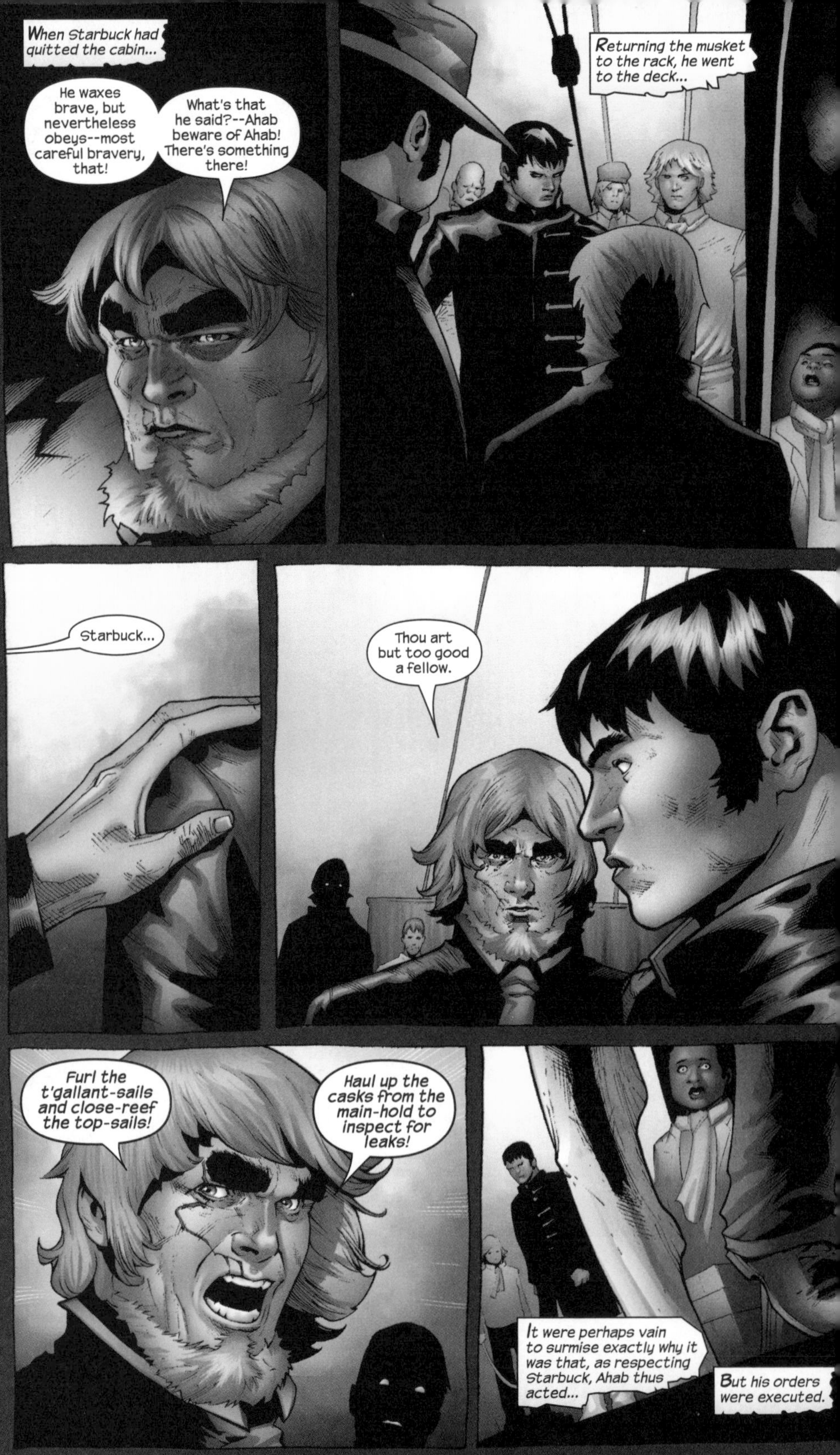
When Starbuck had quitted the cabin...
He waxes brave, but nevertheless obeys--most careful bravery, that!
What's that he said?--Ahab beware of Ahab! There's something there!
Returning the musket to the rack, he went to the deck...
Starbuck...
Thou art but too good a fellow.
Furl the t'gallant-sails and close-reef the top-sails!
Haul up the casks from the main-hold to inspect for leaks!
It were perhaps vain to surmise exactly why it was that, as respecting Starbuck, Ahab thus acted...
But his orders were executed.

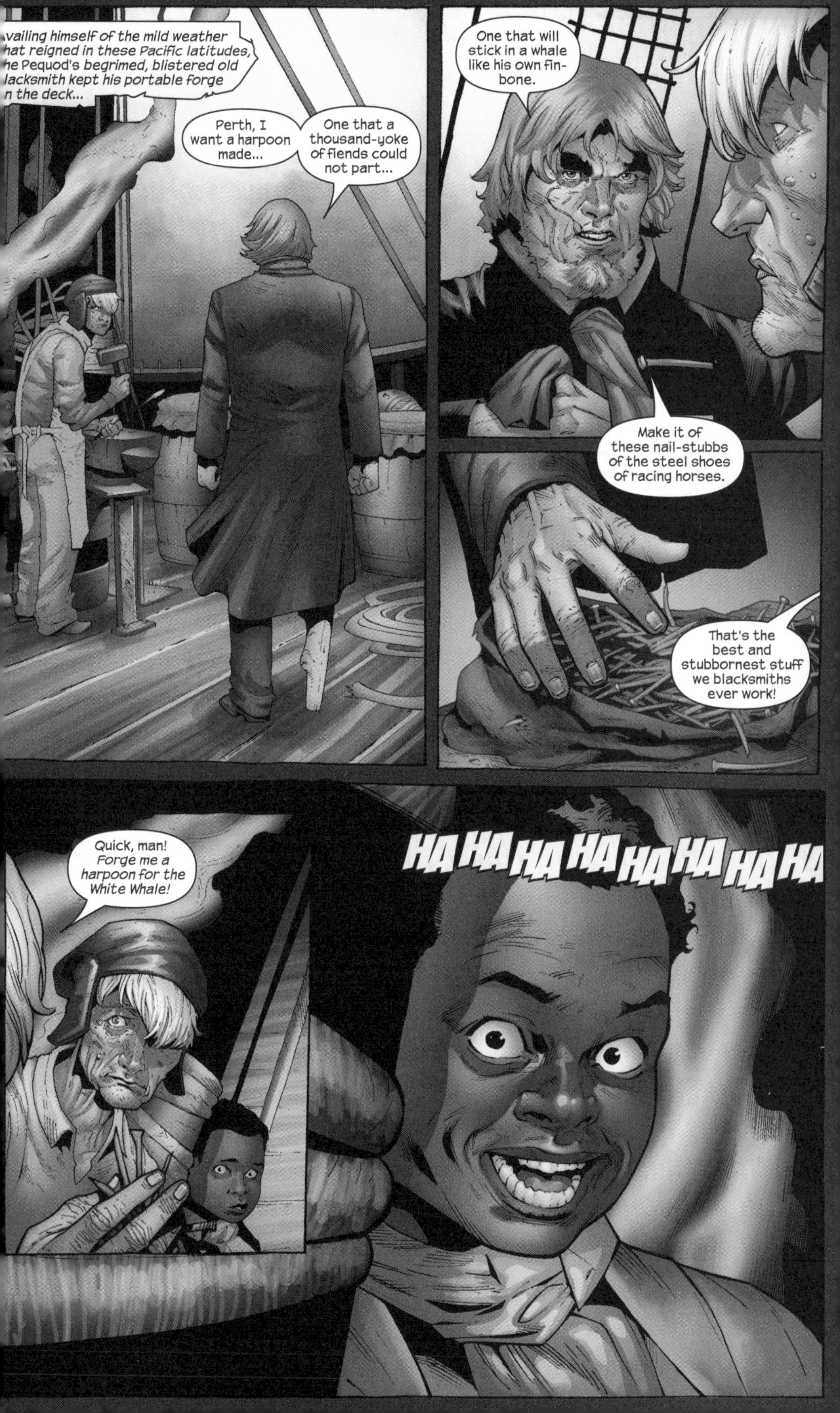
vailing himself of the mild weather hat reigned in these Pacific latitudes, he Pequod's begrimed, blistered old lacksmith kept his portable forge n the deck...
Perth, I want a harpoon made...
One that a thousand-yoke of fiends could not part...
One that will stick in a whale like his own fin-bone.
Make it of these nail-stubbs of the steel shoes of racing horses.
That's the best and stubbornest stuff we blacksmiths ever work!
Quick, man! Forge me a harpoon for the White Whale!
HA HA HA HA HA HA HA HA

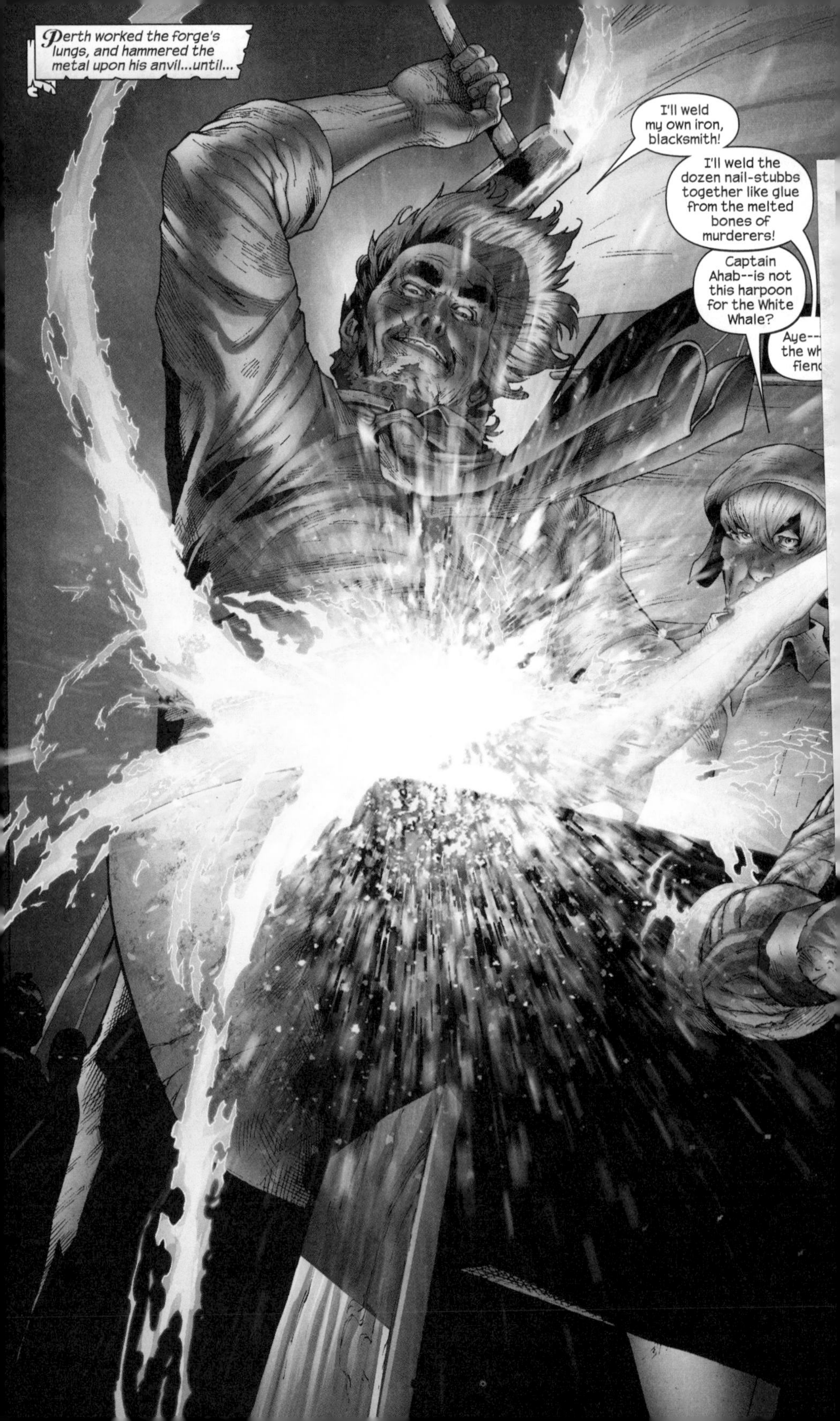
Perth worked the forge's lungs, and hammered the metal upon his anvil...until...
I'll weld my own iron, blacksmith!
I'll weld the dozen nail-stubbs together like glue from the melted bones of murderers!
Captain Ahab--is not this harpoon for the White Whale?
Aye--

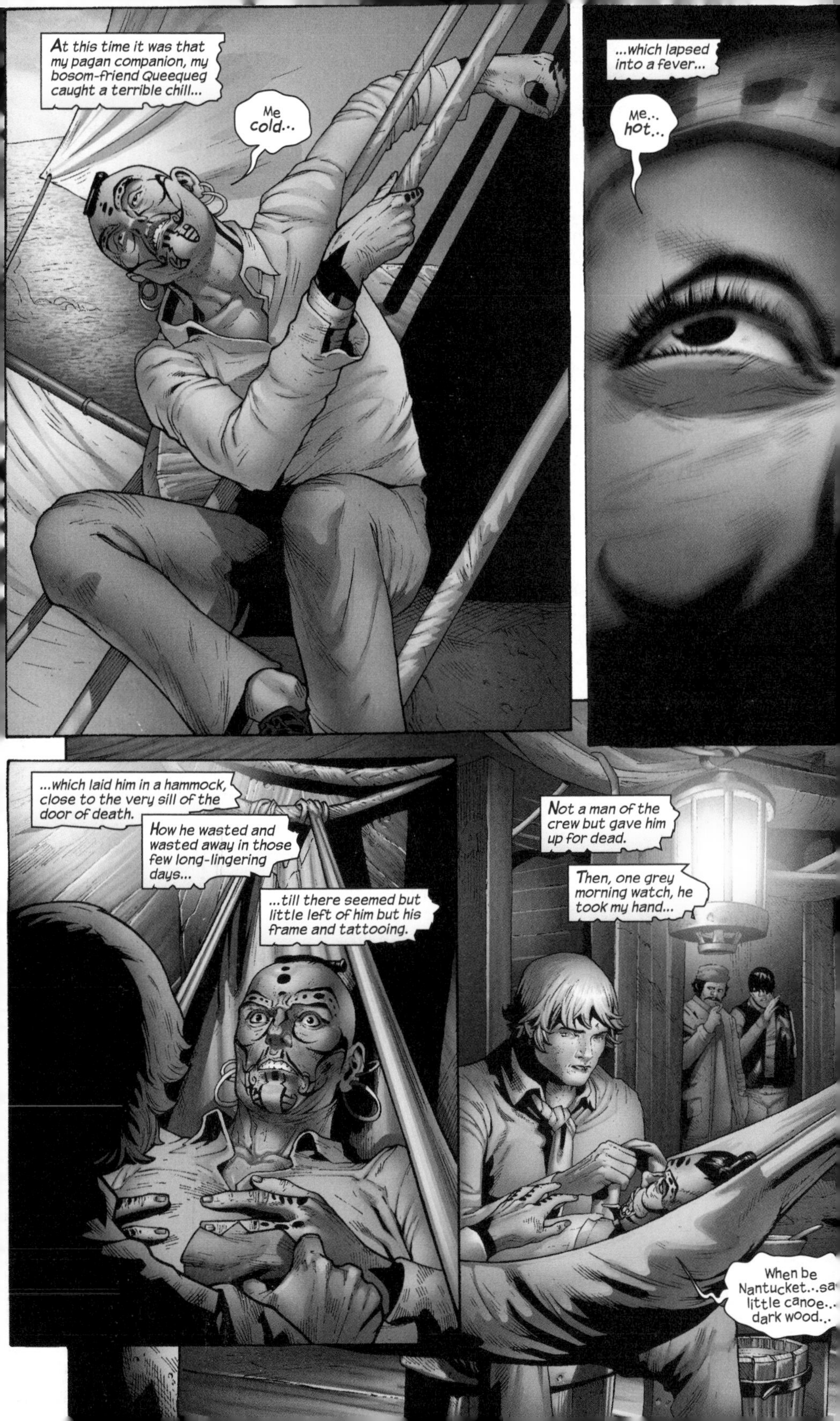
At this time it was that my pagan companion, my bosom-friend Queequeg caught a terrible chill...
Me cold...
...which lapsed into a fever...
Me... hot...
...which laid him in a hammock, close to the very sill of the door of death.
How he wasted and wasted away in those few long-lingering days...
...till there seemed but little left of him but his frame and tattooing.
Not a man of the crew but gave him up for dead.
Then, one grey morning watch, he took my hand...
When be Nantucket...sa little canoe... dark wood...

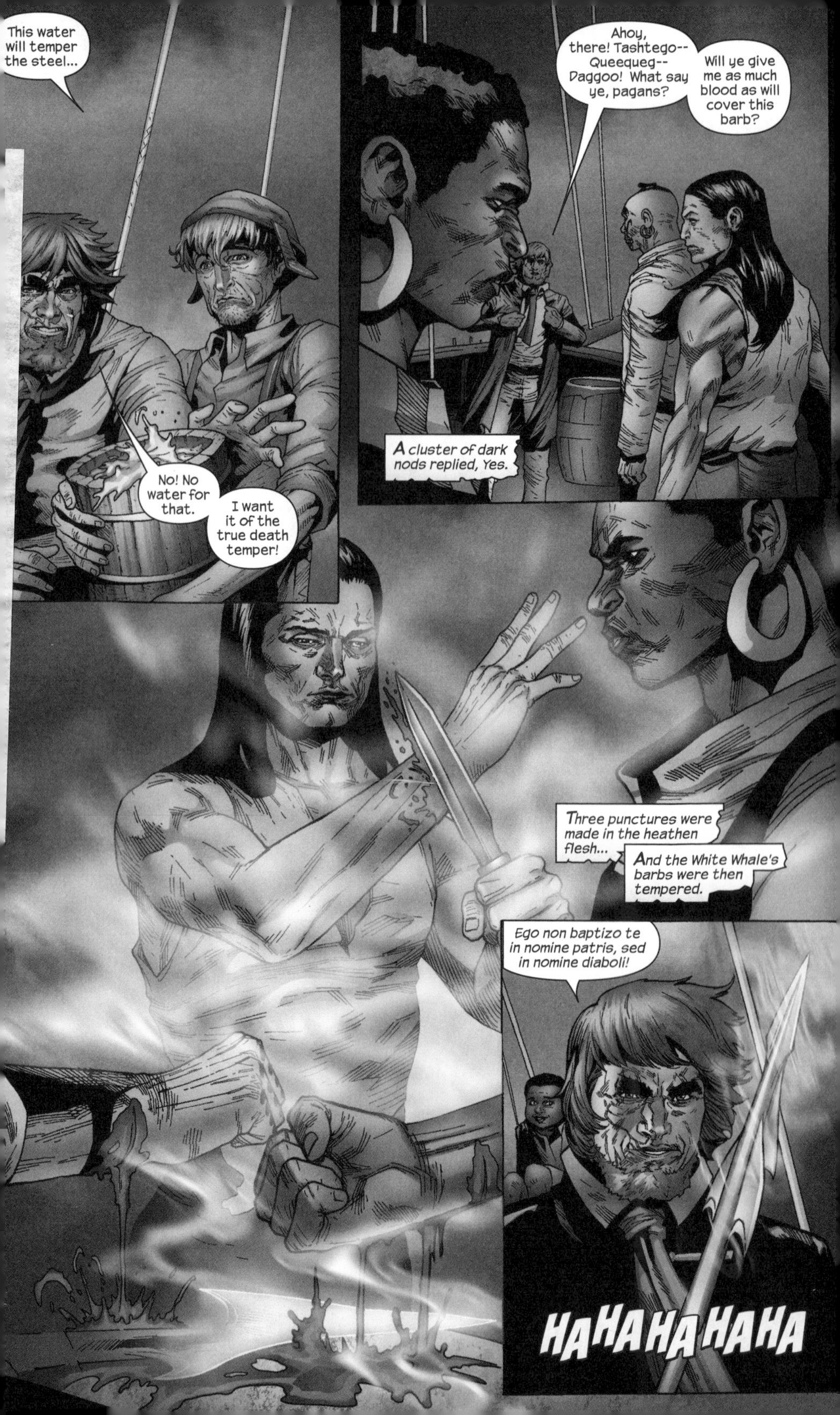

This water will temper the steel...
No! No water for that.
I want it of the true death temper!
Ahoy, there! Tashtego-- Queequeg-- Daggoo! What say ye, pagans?
Will ye give me as much blood as will cover this barb?
A cluster of dark nods replied, Yes.
Three punctures were made in the heathen flesh...
And the White Whale's barbs were then tempered.
Ego non baptizo te in nomine patris, sed in nomine diaboli!
HAHAHAHAHAHA

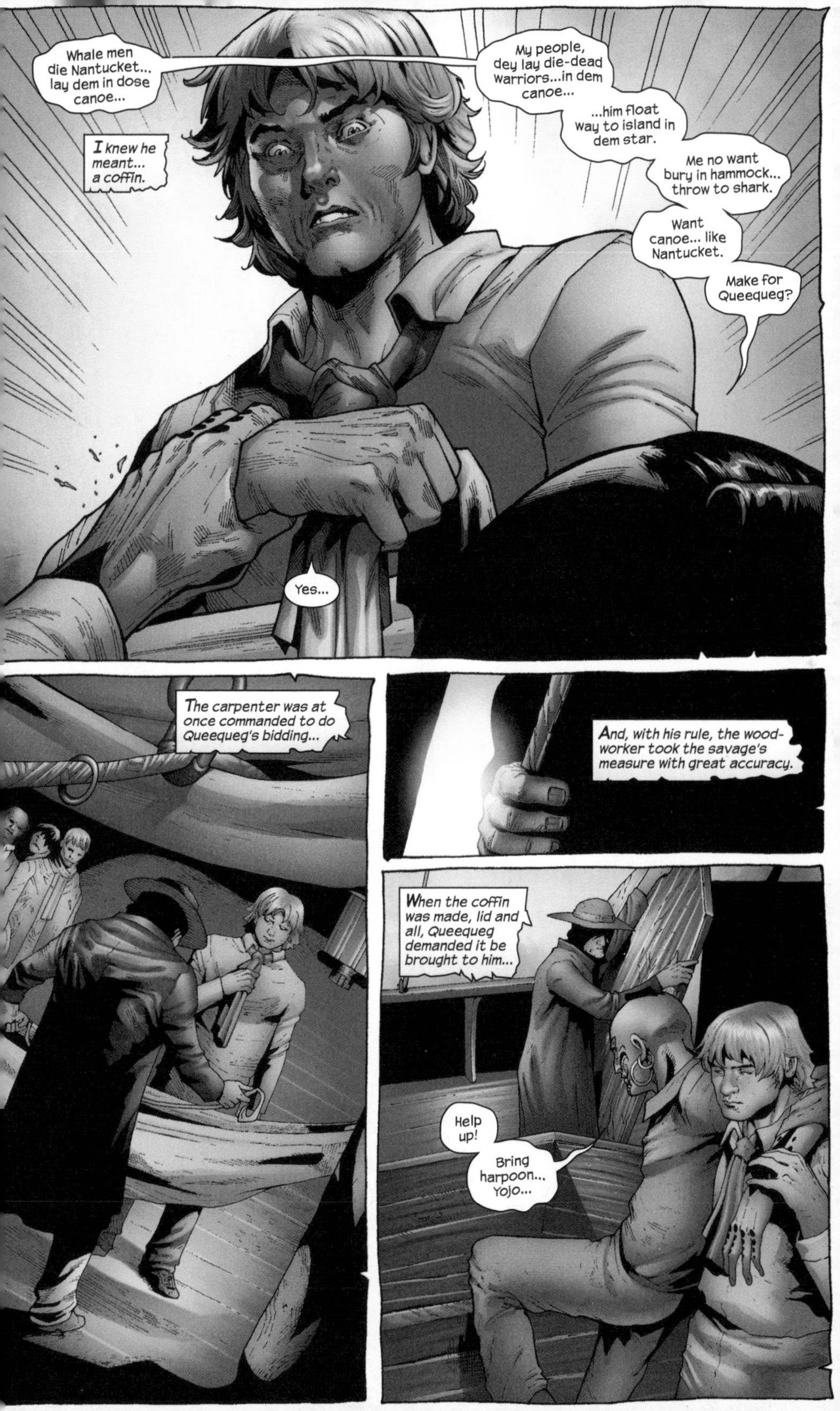
Whale men die Nantucket... lay dem in dose canoe...
My people, dey lay die-dead warriors...in dem canoe...
I knew he meant... a coffin.
...him float way to island in dem star.
Me no want bury in hammock... throw to shark.
Want canoe... like Nantucket.
Make for Queequeg?
Yes...
The carpenter was at once commanded to do Queequeg's bidding...
And, with his rule, the wood-worker took the savage's measure with great accuracy.
When the coffin was made, lid and all, Queequeg demanded it be brought to him...
Help up!
Bring harpoon... Yojo...

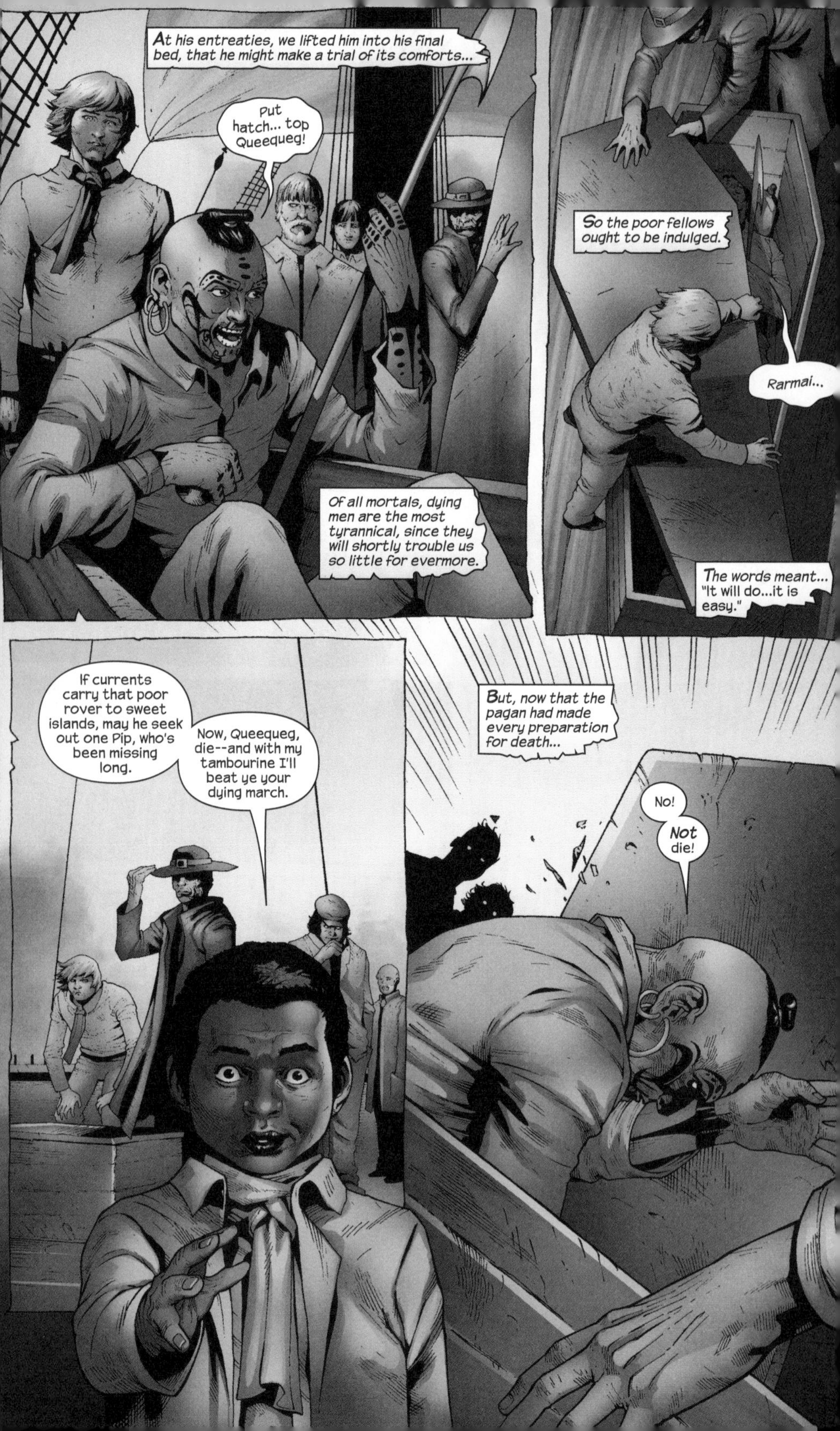
At his entreaties, we lifted him into his final bed, that he might make a trial of its comforts...
Put hatch... top Queequeg!
Of all mortals, dying men are the most tyrannical, since they will shortly trouble us so little for evermore.
So the poor fellows ought to be indulged.
Rarmai...
The words meant... "It will do...it is easy."
If currents carry that poor rover to sweet islands, may he seek out one Pip, who's been missing long.
Now, Queequeg, die--and with my tambourine I'll beat ye your dying march.
But, now that the pagan had made every preparation for death...
No!
Not die!

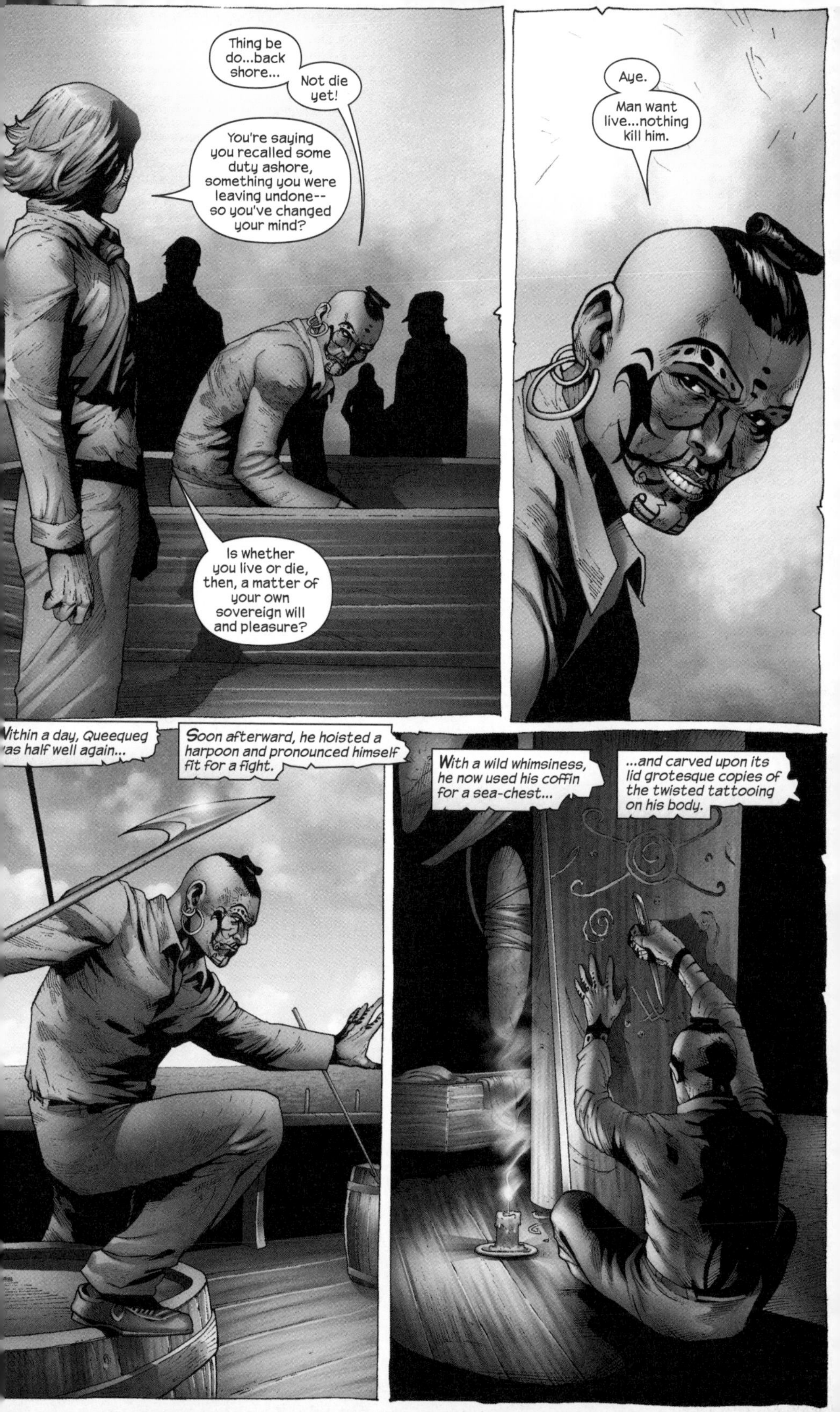
Thing be do...back shore...
Not die yet!
You're saying you recalled some duty ashore, something you were leaving undone--so you've changed your mind?
Is whether you live or die, then, a matter of your own sovereign will and pleasure?
Aye.
Man want live...nothing kill him.
Within a day, Queequeg was half well again...
Soon afterward, he hoisted a harpoon and pronounced himself fit for a fight.
With a wild whimsiness, he now used his coffin for a sea-chest...
...and carved upon its lid grotesque copies of the twisted tattooing on his body.

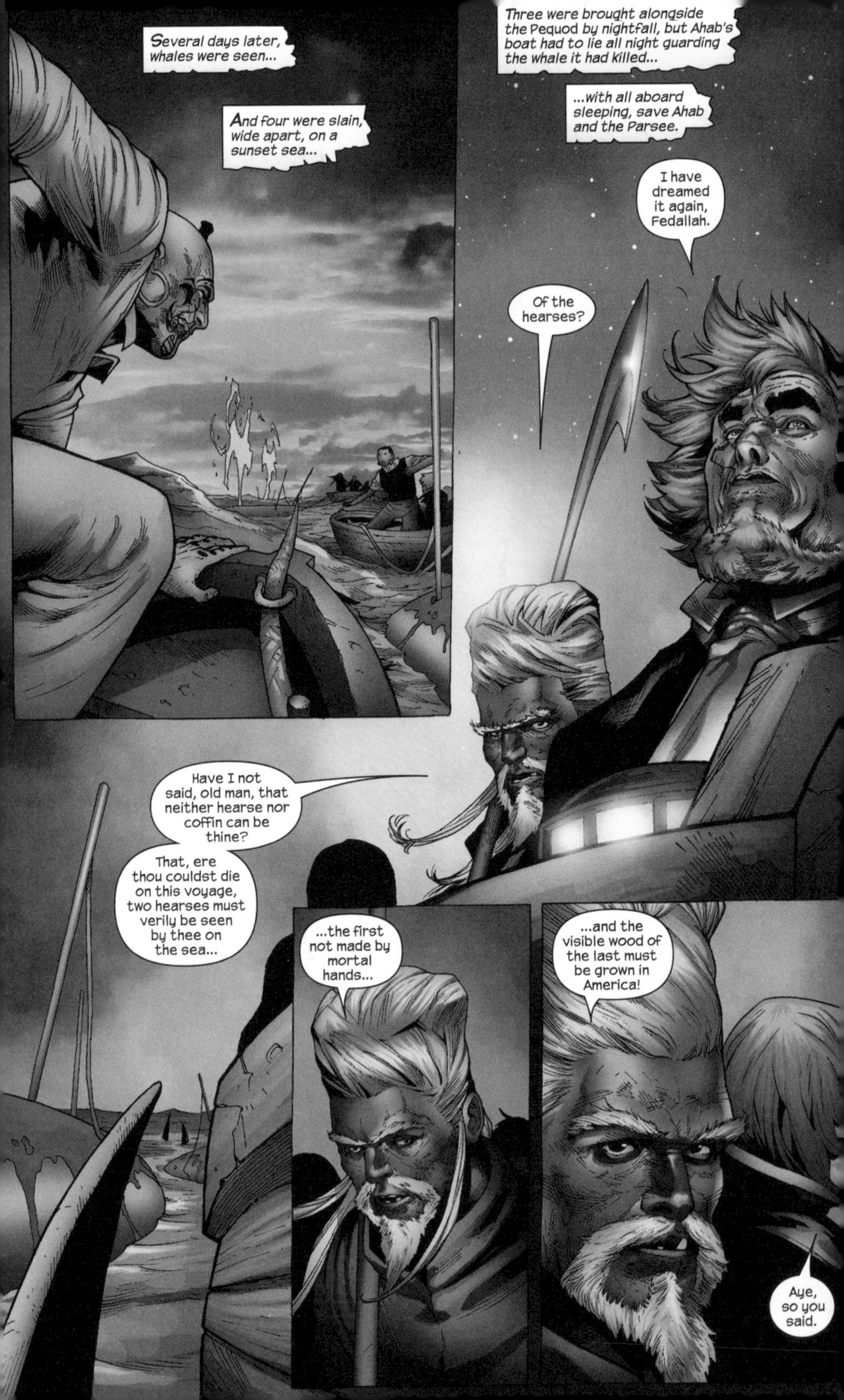

Several days later, whales were seen...
And four were slain, wide apart, on a sunset sea...
Three were brought alongside the Pequod by nightfall, but Ahab's boat had to lie all night guarding the whale it had killed...
...with all aboard sleeping, save Ahab and the Parsee.
I have dreamed it again, Fedallah.
Of the hearses?
Have I not said, old man, that neither hearse nor coffin can be thine?
That, ere thou couldst die on this voyage, two hearses must verily be seen by thee on the sea...
...the first not made by mortal hands...
...and the visible wood of the last must be grown in America!
Aye, so you said.

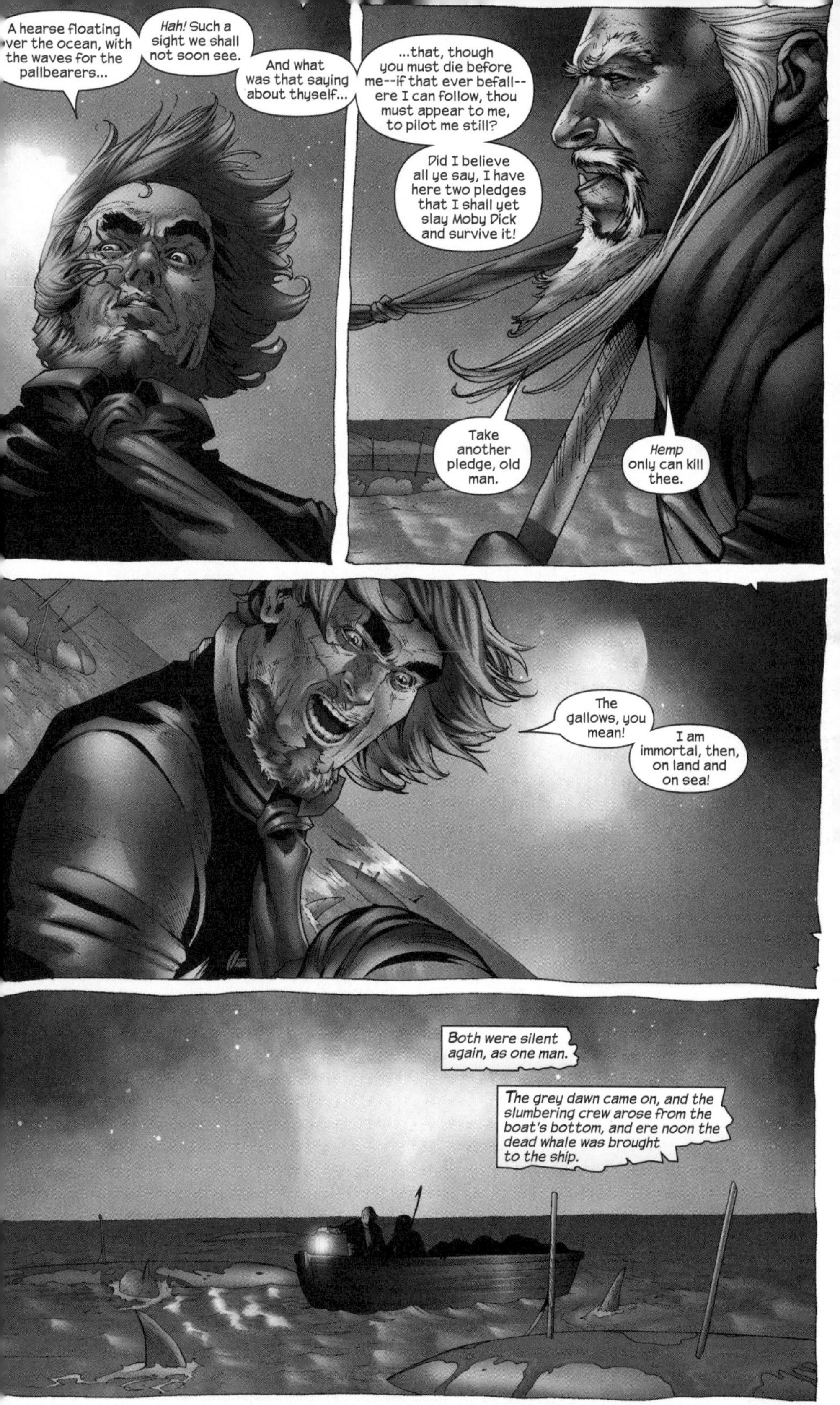
A hearse floating ver the ocean, with the waves for the pallbearers...
Hah! Such a sight we shall not soon see.
And what was that saying about thyself...
...that, though you must die before me--if that ever befall--ere I can follow, thou must appear to me, to pilot me still?
Did I believe all ye say, I have here two pledges that I shall yet slay Moby Dick and survive it!
Take another pledge, old man.
Hemp only can kill thee.
The gallows, you mean!
I am immortal, then, on land and on sea!
Both were silent again, as one man.
The grey dawn came on, and the slumbering crew arose from the boat's bottom, and ere noon the dead whale was brought to the ship.

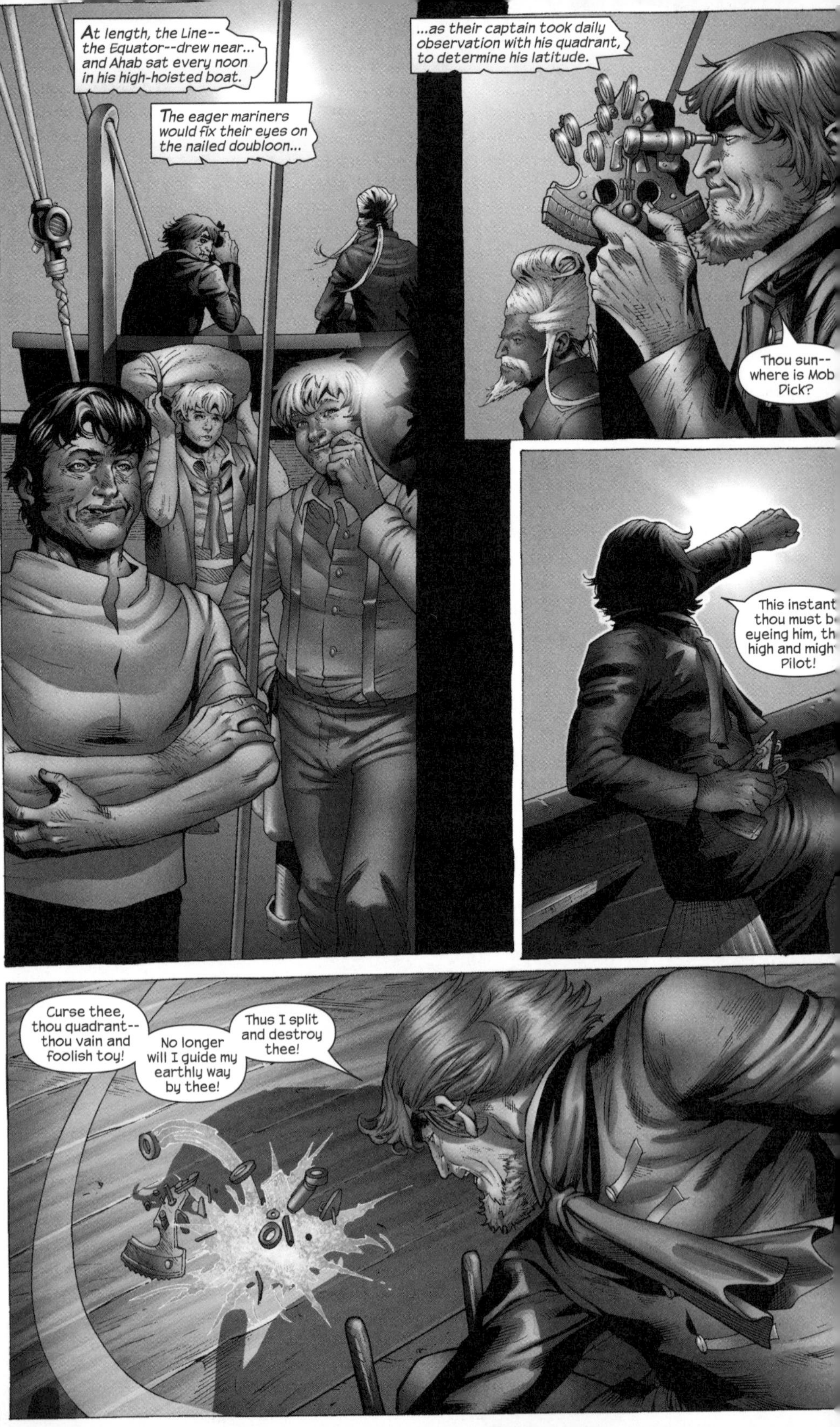
At length, the Line--the Equator--drew near... and Ahab sat every noon in his high-hoisted boat.
The eager mariners would fix their eyes on the nailed doubloon...
...as their captain took daily observation with his quadrant, to determine his latitude.
Thou sun--where is Mob Dick?
This instant thou must b eyeing him, th high and migh Pilot!
Curse thee, thou quadrant--thou vain and foolish toy!
No longer will I guide my earthly way by thee!
Thus I split and destroy thee!

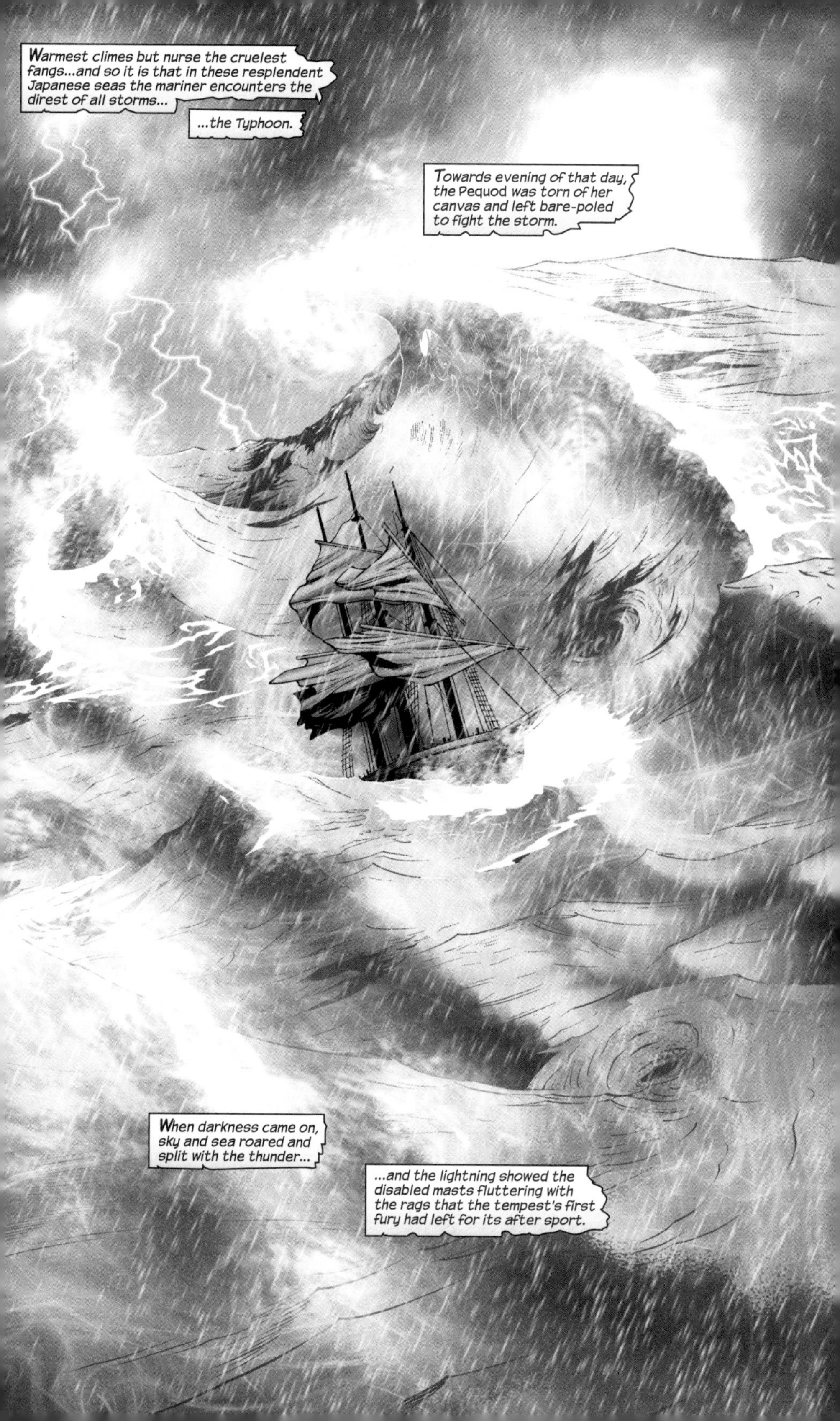
Warmest climes but nurse the cruelest fangs...and so it is that in these resplendent Japanese seas the mariner encounters the direst of all storms...
...the Typhoon.
Towards evening of that day, the Pequod was torn of her canvas and left bare-poled to fight the storm.
When darkness came on, sky and sea roared and split with the thunder...
...and the lightning showed the disabled masts fluttering with the rags that the tempest's first fury had left for its after sport.

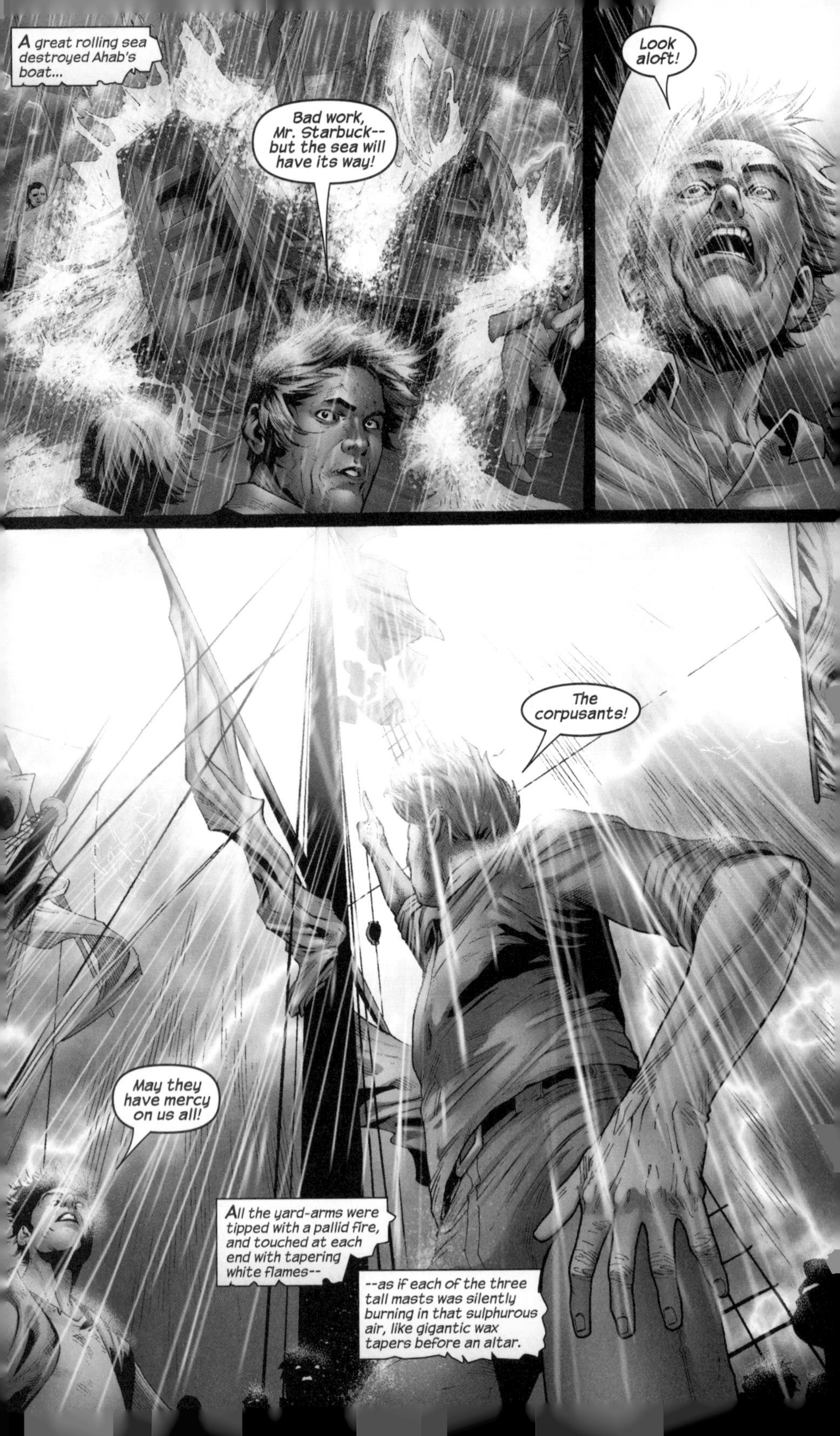
A great rolling sea destroyed Ahab's boat...
Bad work, Mr. Starbuck--but the sea will have its way!
Look aloft!
The corpusants!
May they have mercy on us all!
All the yard-arms were tipped with a pallid fire, and touched at each end with tapering white flames--
--as if each of the three tall masts was silently burning in that sulphurous air, like gigantic wax tapers before an altar.

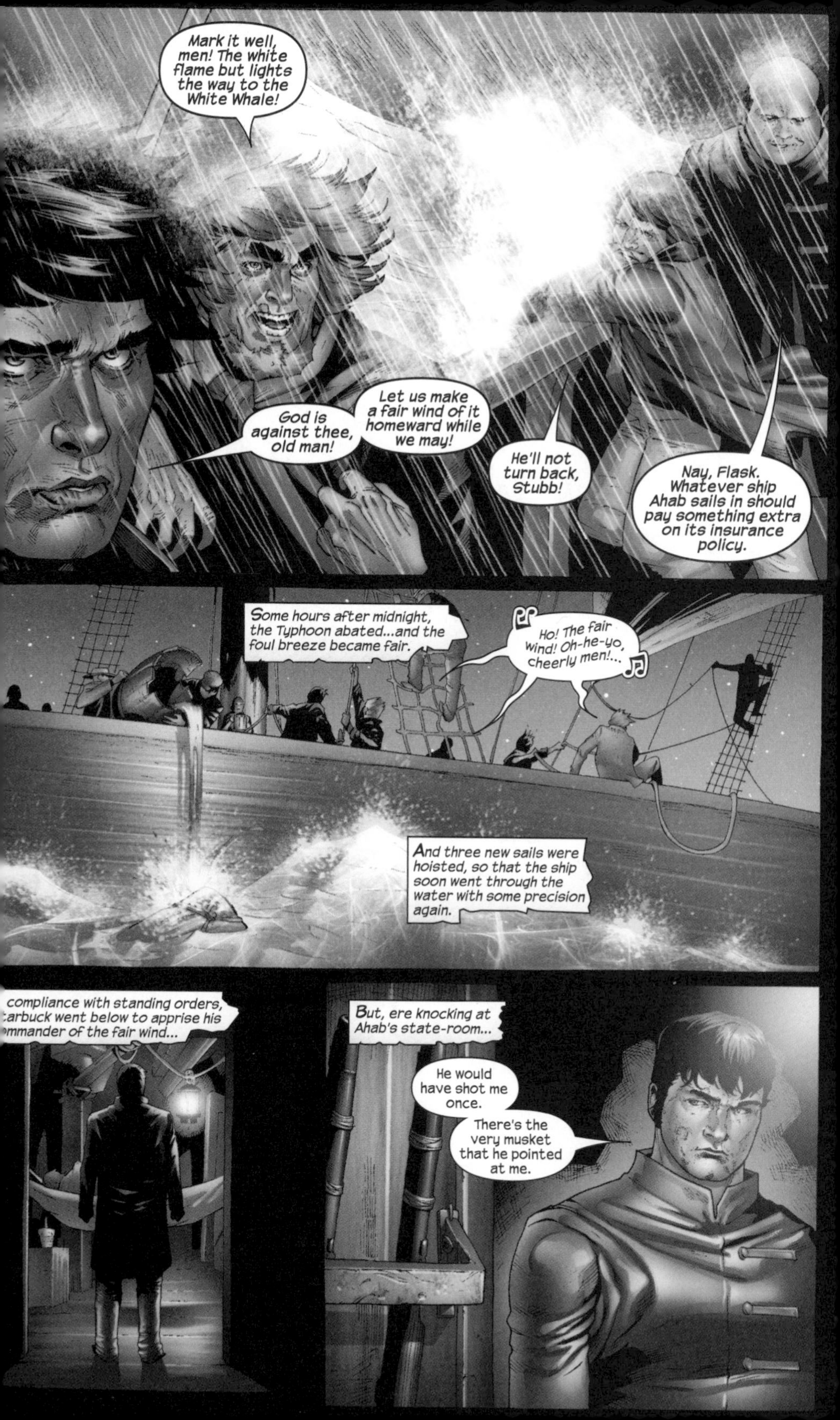
Mark it well, men! The white flame but lights the way to the White Whale!
God is against thee, old man!
Let us make a fair wind of it homeward while we may!
He'll not turn back, Stubb!
Nay, Flask. Whatever ship Ahab sails in should pay something extra on its insurance policy.
Some hours after midnight, the Typhoon abated...and the foul breeze became fair.
Ho! The fair wind! Oh-he-yo, cheerly men!...
And three new sails were hoisted, so that the ship soon went through the water with some precision again.
compliance with standing orders, tarbuck went below to apprise his mmander of the fair wind...
But, ere knocking at Ahab's state-room...
He would have shot me once.
There's the very musket that he pointed at me.

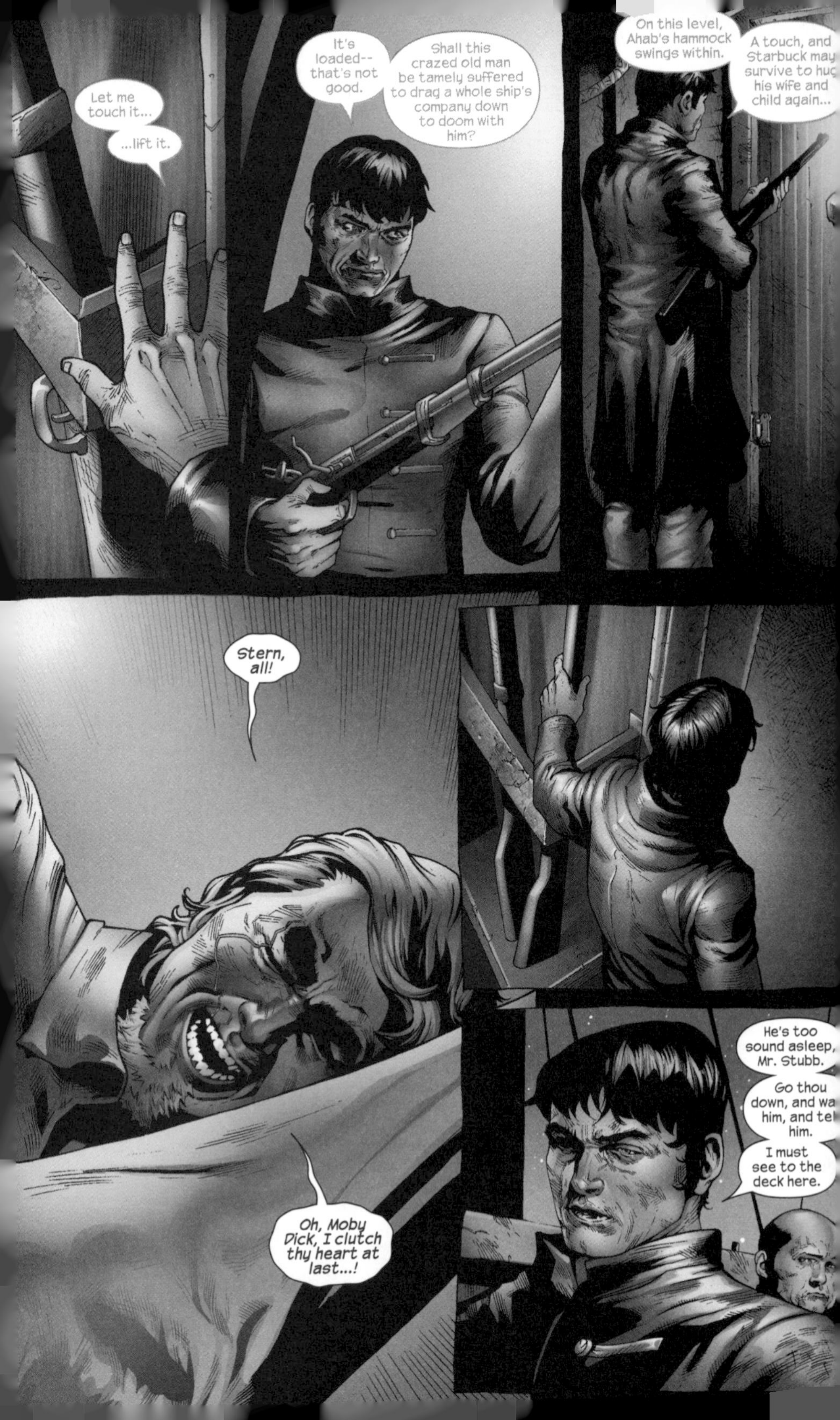
Let me touch it...
...lift it.
It's loaded--that's not good.
Shall this crazed old man be tamely suffered to drag a whole ship's company down to doom with him?
On this level, Ahab's hammock swings within.
A touch, and Starbuck may survive to hug his wife and child again...
Stern, all!
Oh, Moby Dick, I clutch thy heart at last...!
He's too sound asleep, Mr. Stubb.
Go thou down, and wake him, and tell him.
I must see to the deck here.

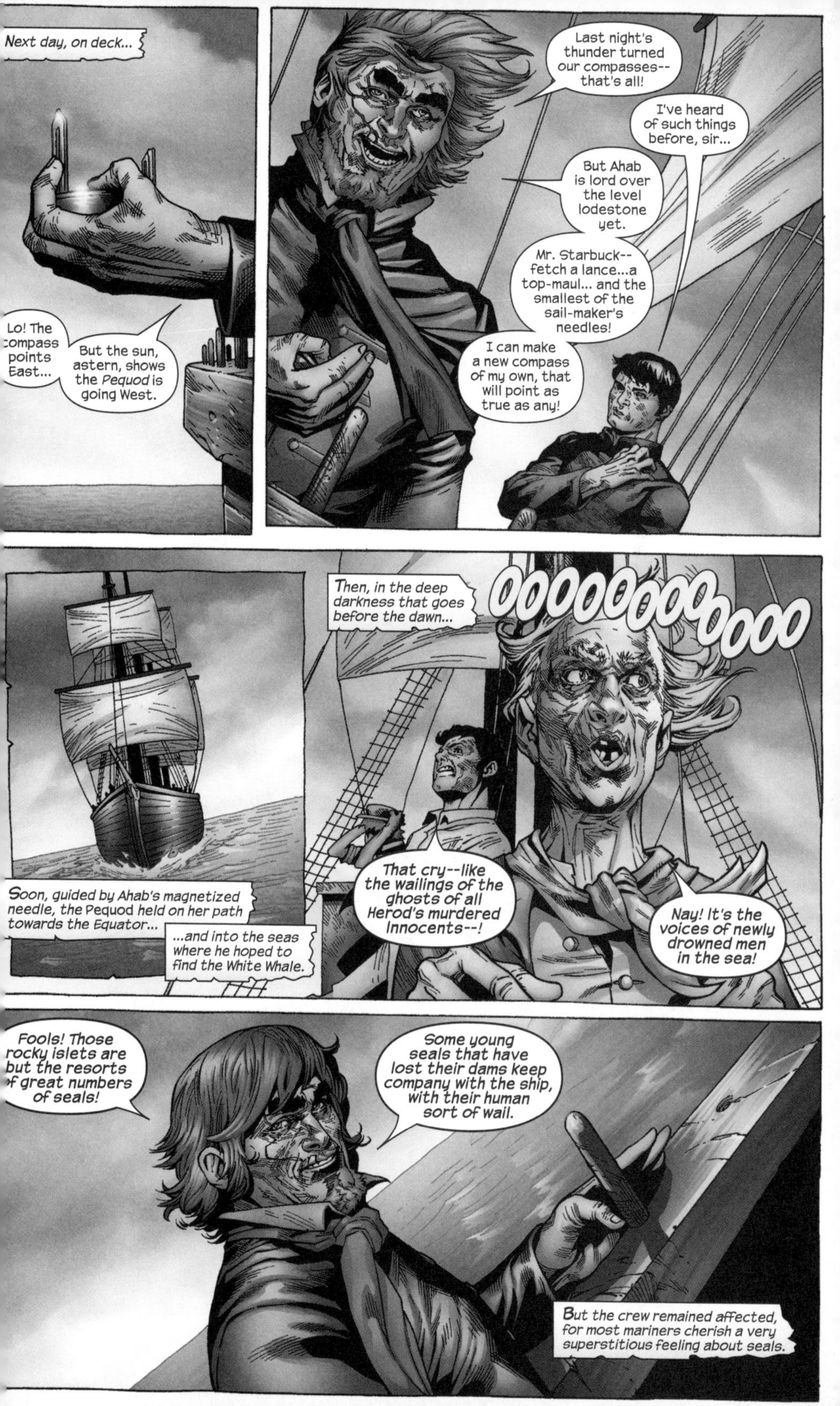
Next day, on deck...
Lo! The compass points East...
But the sun, astern, shows the *Pequod* is going West.
Last night's thunder turned our compasses--that's all!
I've heard of such things before, sir...
But Ahab is lord over the level lodestone yet.
Mr. Starbuck--fetch a lance...a top-maul... and the smallest of the sail-maker's needles!
I can make a new compass of my own, that will point as true as any!
Soon, guided by Ahab's magnetized needle, the Pequod held on her path towards the Equator...
...and into the seas where he hoped to find the White Whale.
Then, in the deep darkness that goes before the dawn...
OOOOOOOOOOOO
That cry--like the wailings of the ghosts of all Herod's murdered Innocents--!
Nay! It's the voices of newly drowned men in the sea!
Fools! Those rocky islets are but the resorts of great numbers of seals!
Some young seals that have lost their dams keep company with the ship, with their human sort of wail.
But the crew remained affected, for most mariners cherish a very superstitious feeling about seals.

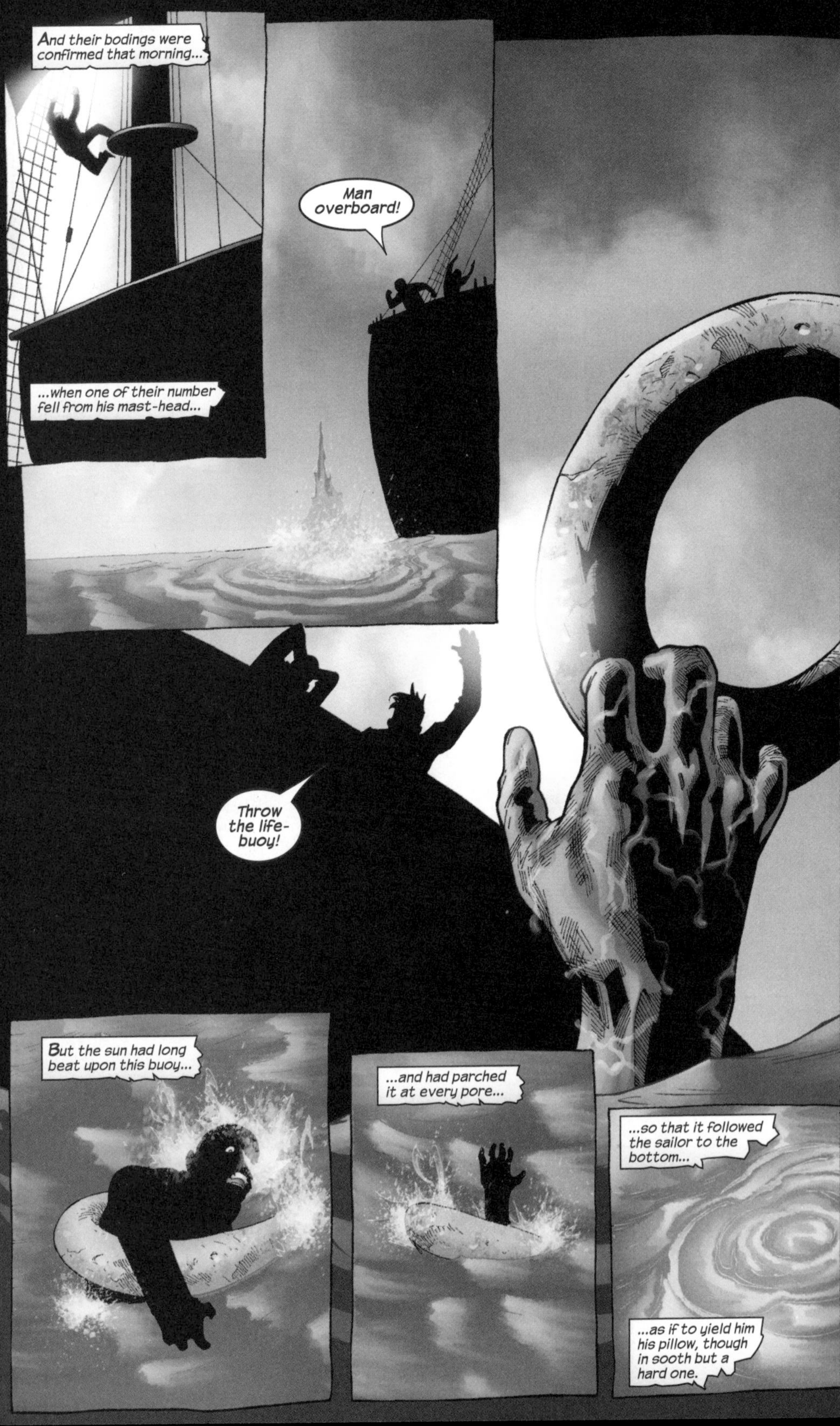
And their bodings were confirmed that morning...
...when one of their number fell from his mast-head...
Man overboard!
Throw the life-buoy!
But the sun had long beat upon this buoy...
...and had parched it at every pore...
...so that it followed the sailor to the bottom...
...as if to yield him his pillow, though in sooth but a hard one.

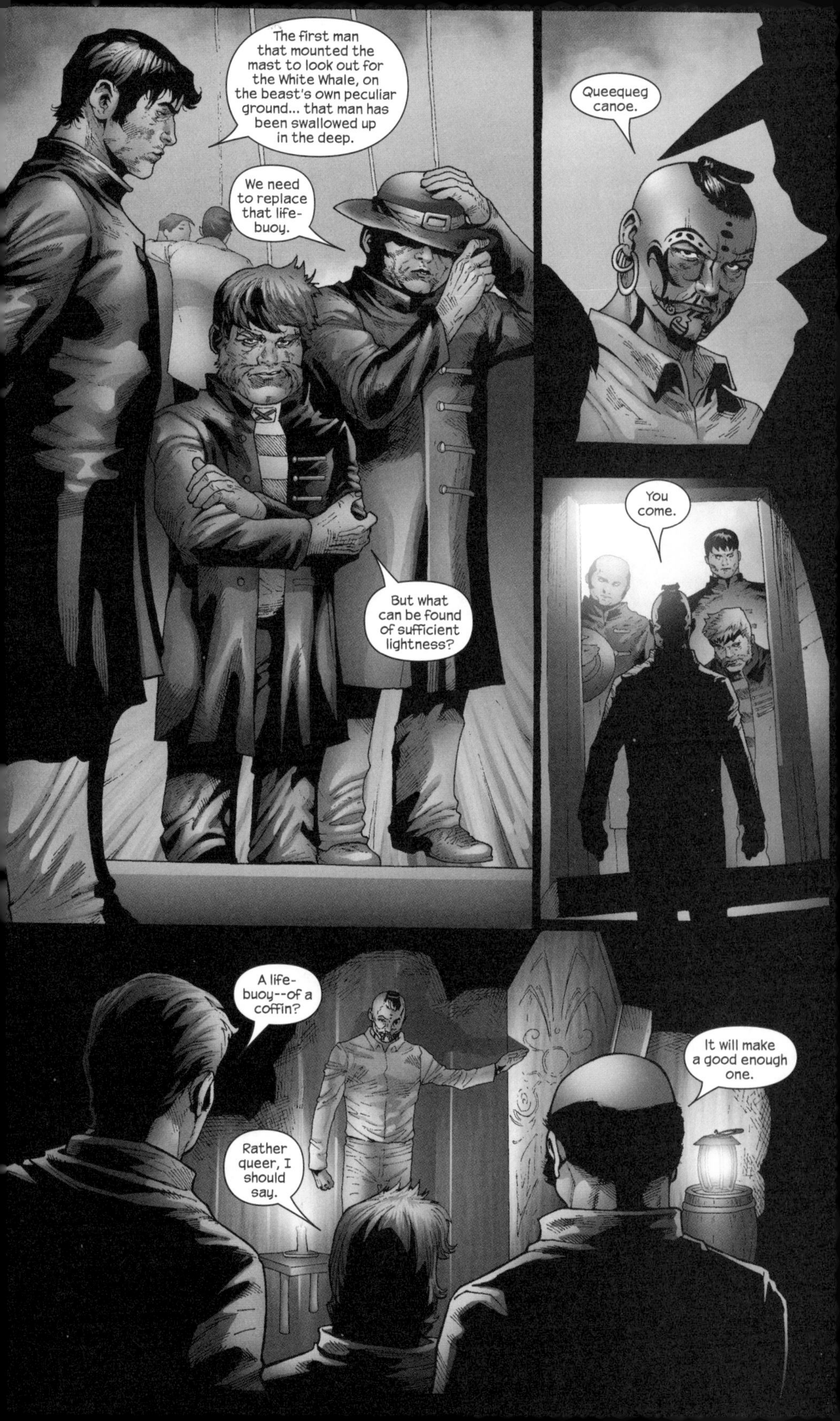
The first man that mounted the mast to look out for the White Whale, on the beast's own peculiar ground... that man has been swallowed up in the deep.
We need to replace that life-buoy.
But what can be found of sufficient lightness?
Queequeg canoe.
You come.
A life-buoy--of a coffin?
Rather queer, I should say.
It will make a good enough one.

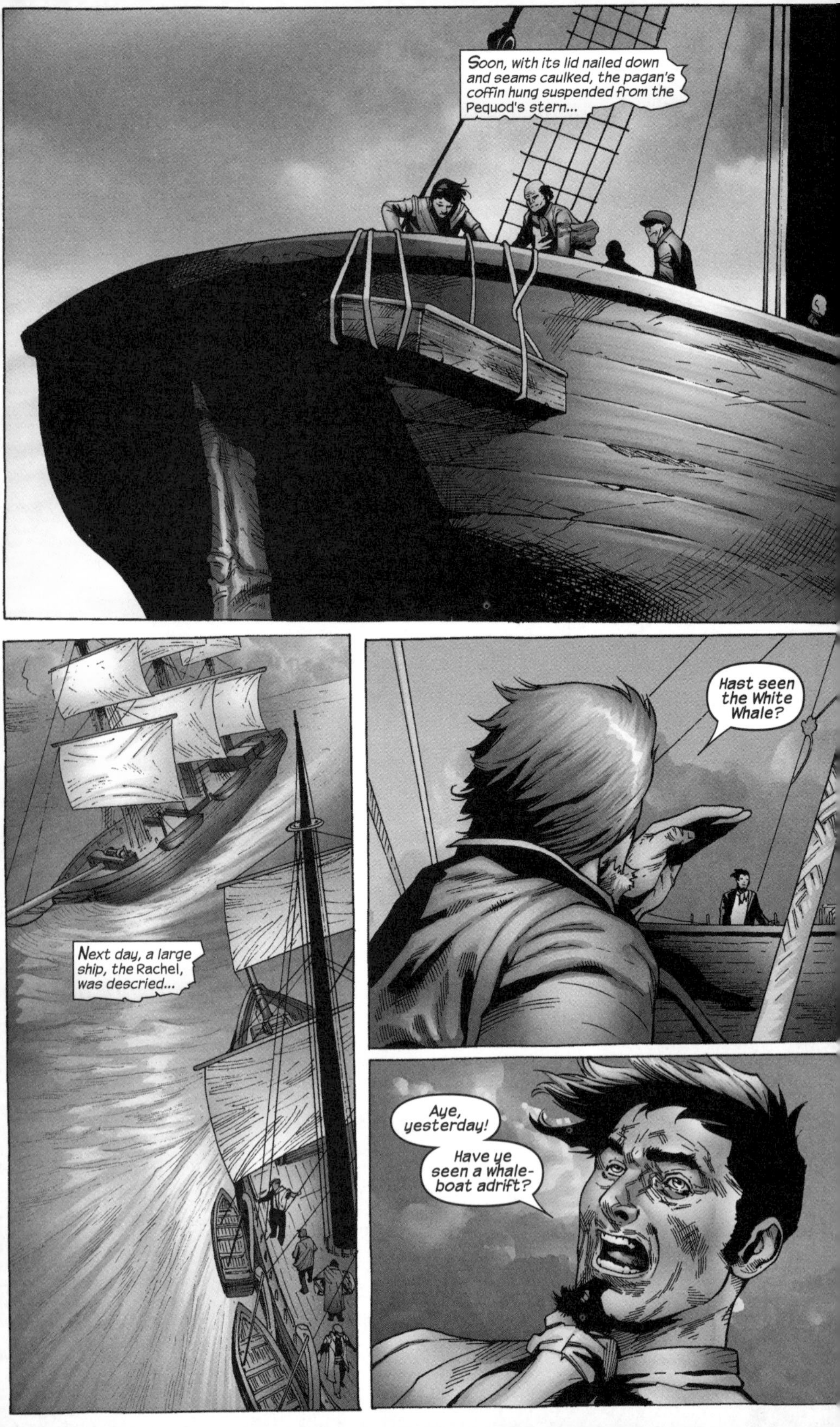
Soon, with its lid nailed down and seams caulked, the pagan's coffin hung suspended from the Pequod's stern...
Next day, a large ship, the Rachel, was descried...
Hast seen the White Whale?
Aye, yesterday!
Have ye seen a whale-boat adrift?

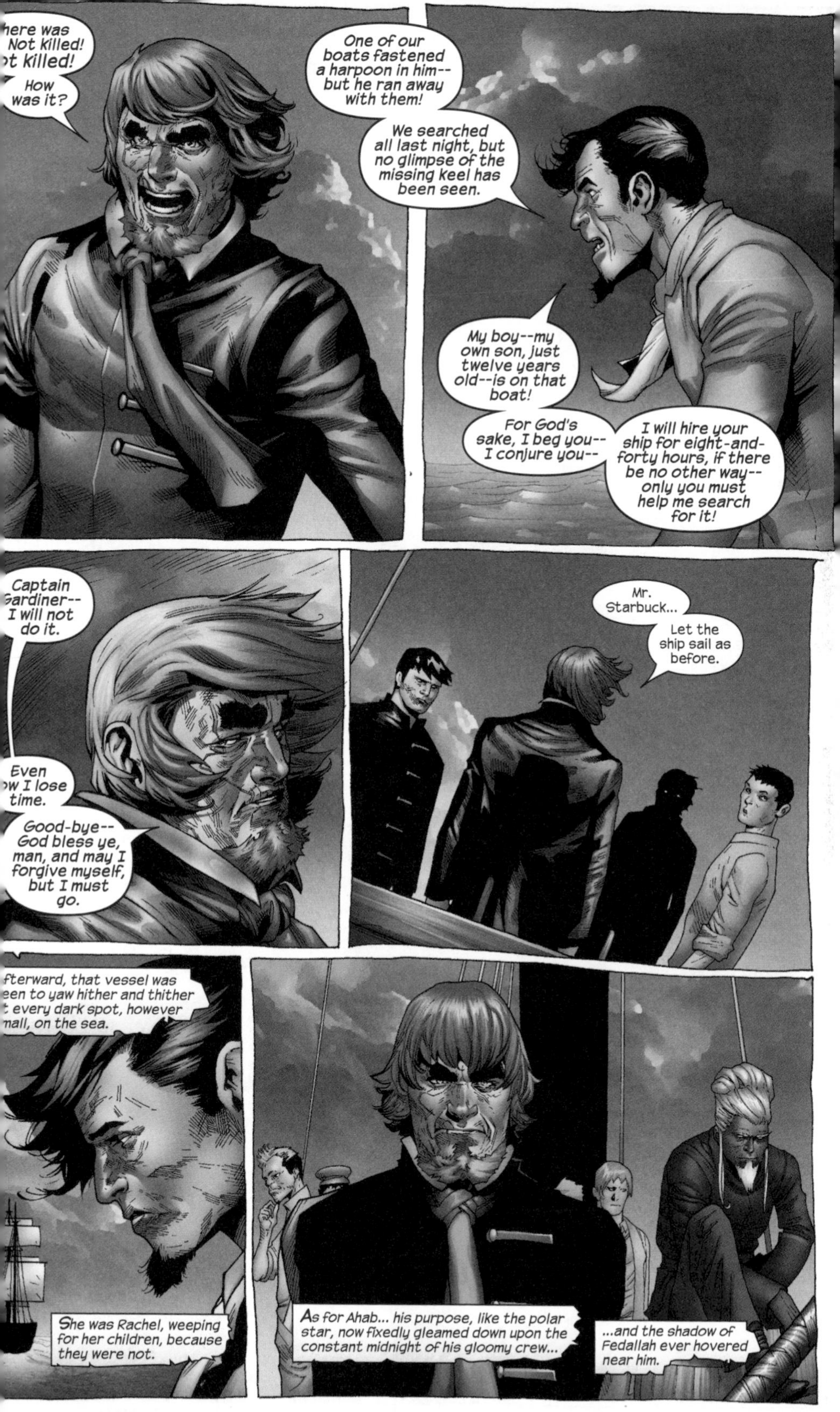
here was Not killed! ot killed!
How was it?
One of our boats fastened a harpoon in him--but he ran away with them!
We searched all last night, but no glimpse of the missing keel has been seen.
My boy--my own son, just twelve years old--is on that boat!
For God's sake, I beg you--I conjure you--
I will hire your ship for eight-and-forty hours, if there be no other way--only you must help me search for it!
Captain Gardiner--I will not do it.
Even w I lose time.
Good-bye--God bless ye, man, and may I forgive myself, but I must go.
Mr. Starbuck...
Let the ship sail as before.
fterward, that vessel was een to yaw hither and thither every dark spot, however mall, on the sea.
She was Rachel, weeping for her children, because they were not.
As for Ahab... his purpose, like the polar star, now fixedly gleamed down upon the constant midnight of his gloomy crew...
...and the shadow of Fedallah ever hovered near him.

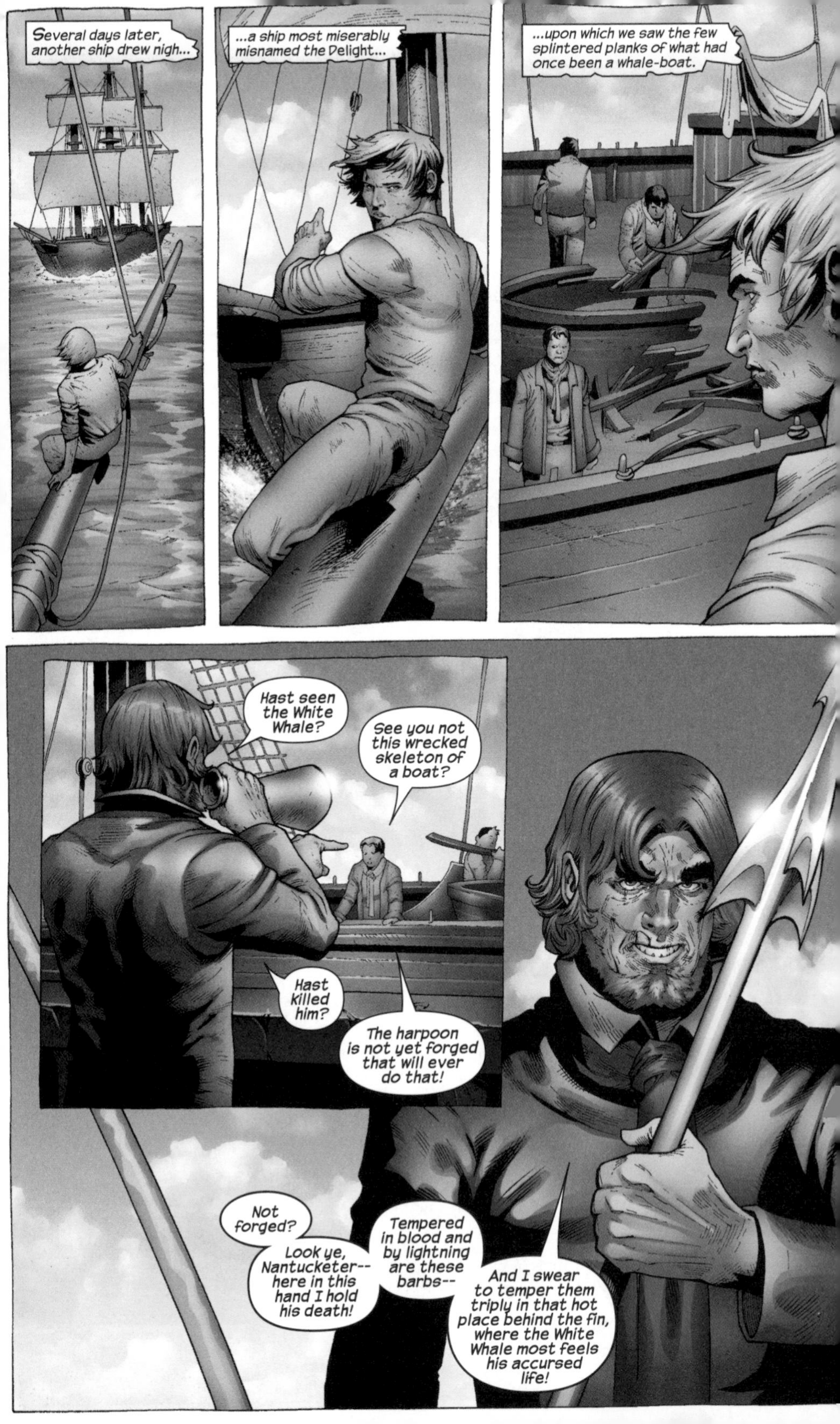
Several days later, another ship drew nigh...
...a ship most miserably misnamed the Delight...
...upon which we saw the few splintered planks of what had once been a whale-boat.
Hast seen the White Whale?
See you not this wrecked skeleton of a boat?
Hast killed him?
The harpoon is not yet forged that will ever do that!
Not forged?
Look ye, Nantucketer-- here in this hand I hold his death!
Tempered in blood and by lightning are these barbs--
And I swear to temper them triply in that hot place behind the fin, where the White Whale most feels his accursed life!

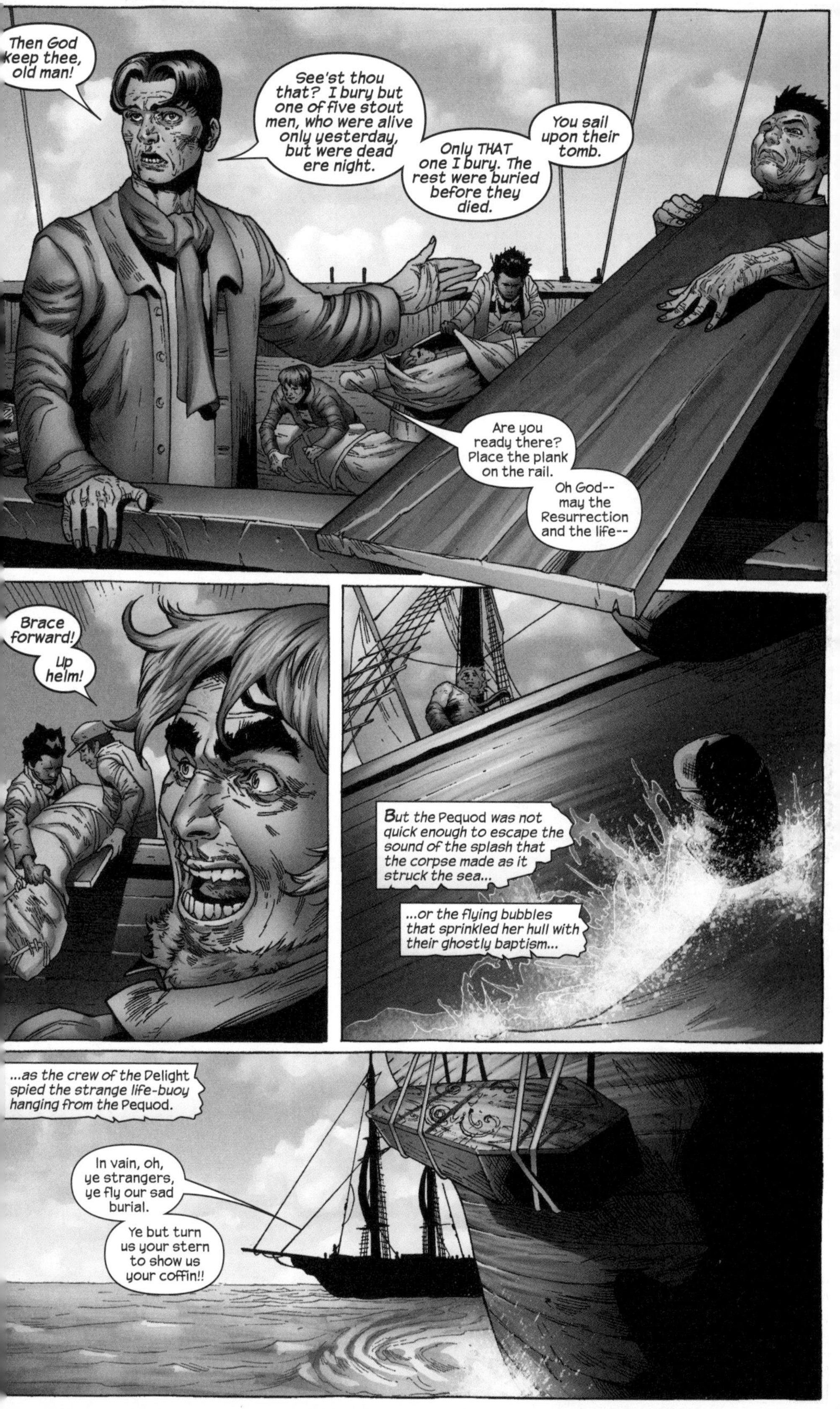

Then God keep thee, old man!
See'st thou that? I bury but one of five stout men, who were alive only yesterday, but were dead ere night.
Only THAT one I bury. The rest were buried before they died.
You sail upon their tomb.
Are you ready there? Place the plank on the rail.
Oh God-- may the Resurrection and the life--
Brace forward!
Up helm!
But the Pequod was not quick enough to escape the sound of the splash that the corpse made as it struck the sea...
...or the flying bubbles that sprinkled her hull with their ghostly baptism...
...as the crew of the Delight spied the strange life-buoy hanging from the Pequod.
In vain, oh, ye strangers, ye fly our sad burial.
Ye but turn us your stern to show us your coffin!!

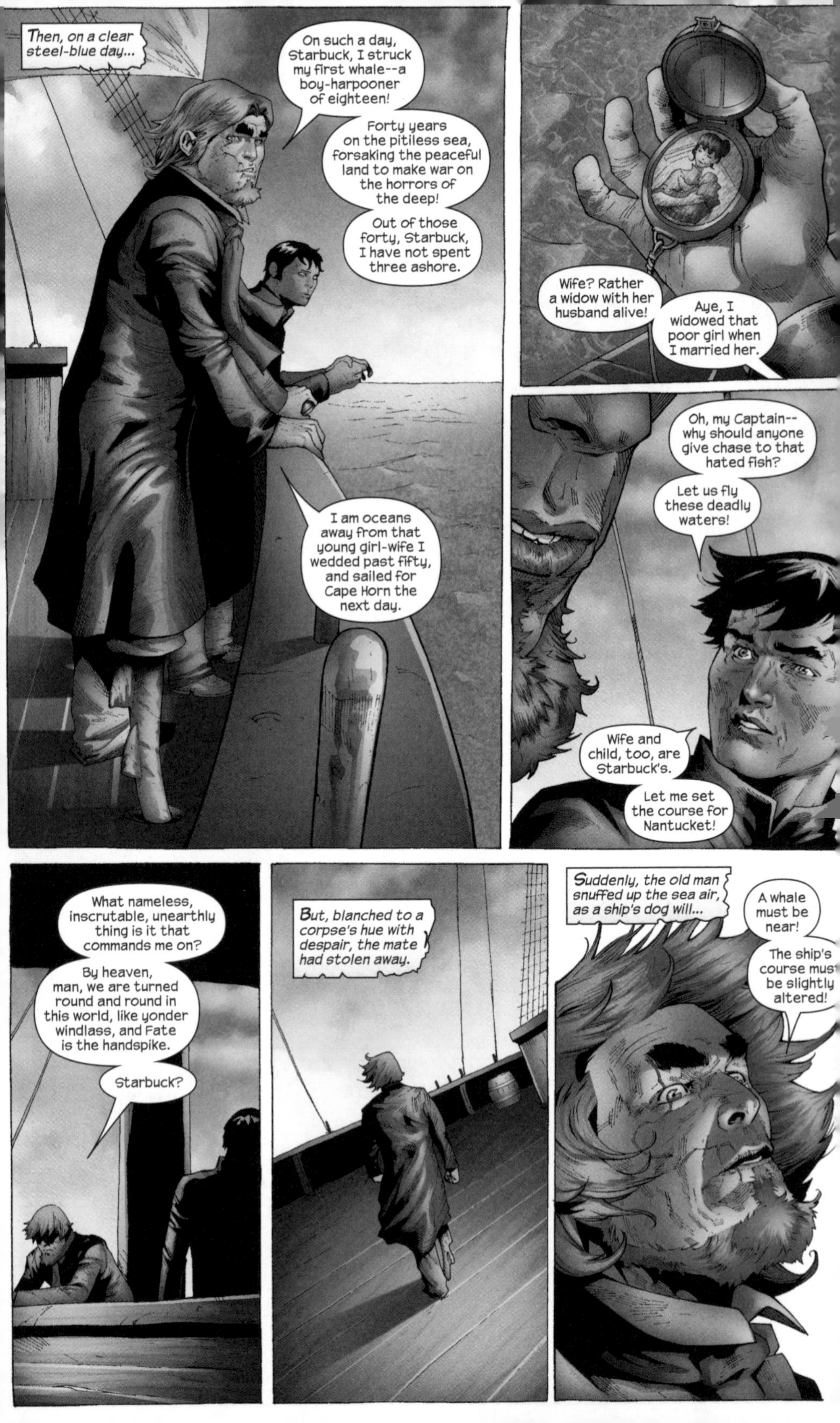
Then, on a clear steel-blue day...
On such a day, Starbuck, I struck my first whale--a boy-harpooner of eighteen!
Forty years on the pitiless sea, forsaking the peaceful land to make war on the horrors of the deep!
Out of those forty, Starbuck, I have not spent three ashore.
I am oceans away from that young girl-wife I wedded past fifty, and sailed for Cape Horn the next day.
Wife? Rather a widow with her husband alive!
Aye, I widowed that poor girl when I married her.
Oh, my Captain--why should anyone give chase to that hated fish?
Let us fly these deadly waters!
Wife and child, too, are Starbuck's.
Let me set the course for Nantucket!
What nameless, inscrutable, unearthly thing is it that commands me on?
By heaven, man, we are turned round and round in this world, like yonder windlass, and Fate is the handspike.
Starbuck?
But, blanched to a corpse's hue with despair, the mate had stolen away.
Suddenly, the old man snuffed up the sea air, as a ship's dog will...
A whale must be near!
The ship's course mus be slightly altered!

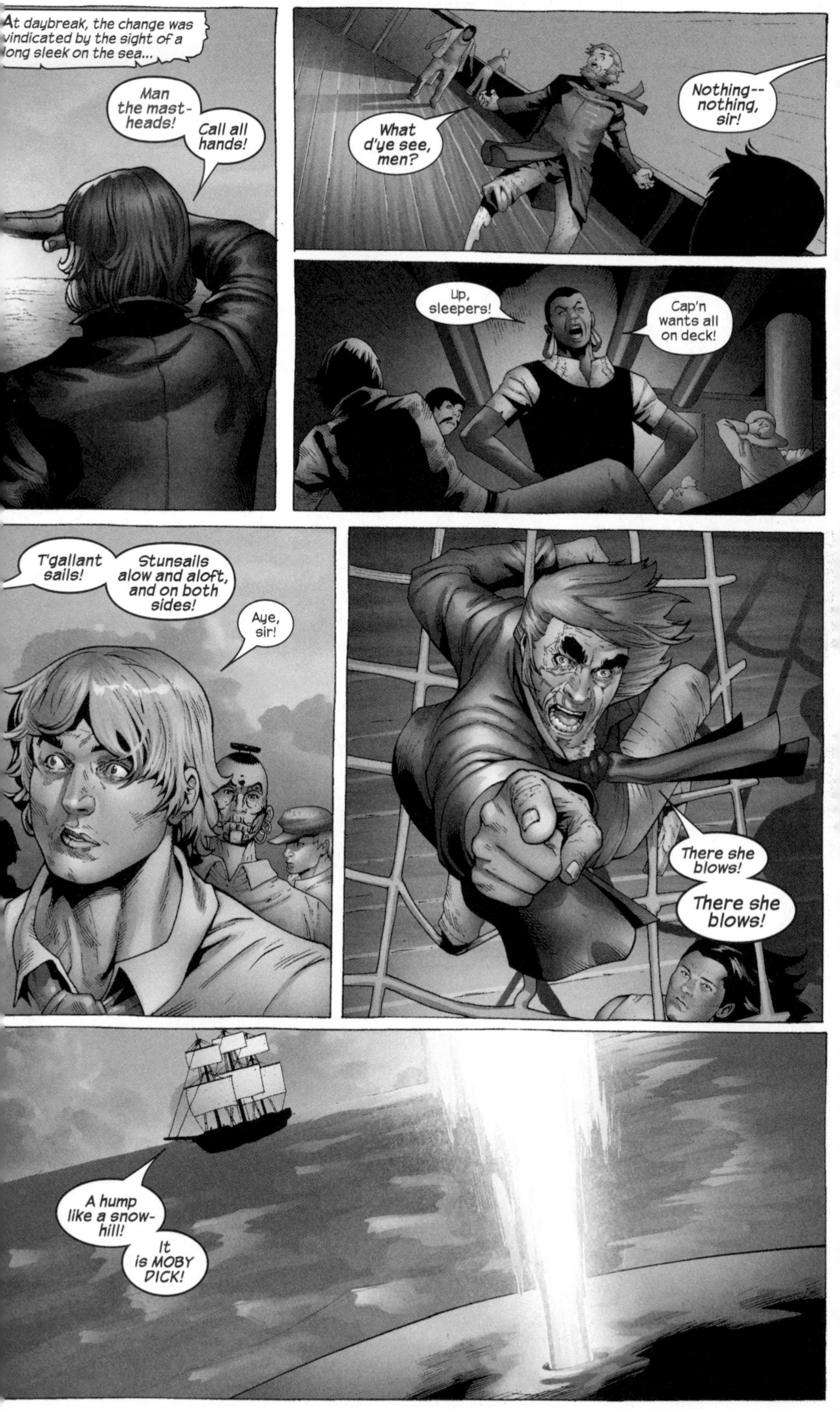

At daybreak, the change was vindicated by the sight of a long sleek on the sea...
Man the mast-heads!
Call all hands!
What d'ye see, men?
Nothing-- nothing, sir!
Up, sleepers!
Cap'n wants all on deck!
T'gallant sails!
Stunsails alow and aloft, and on both sides!
Aye, sir!
There she blows!
There she blows!
A hump like a snow-hill!
It is MOBY DICK!

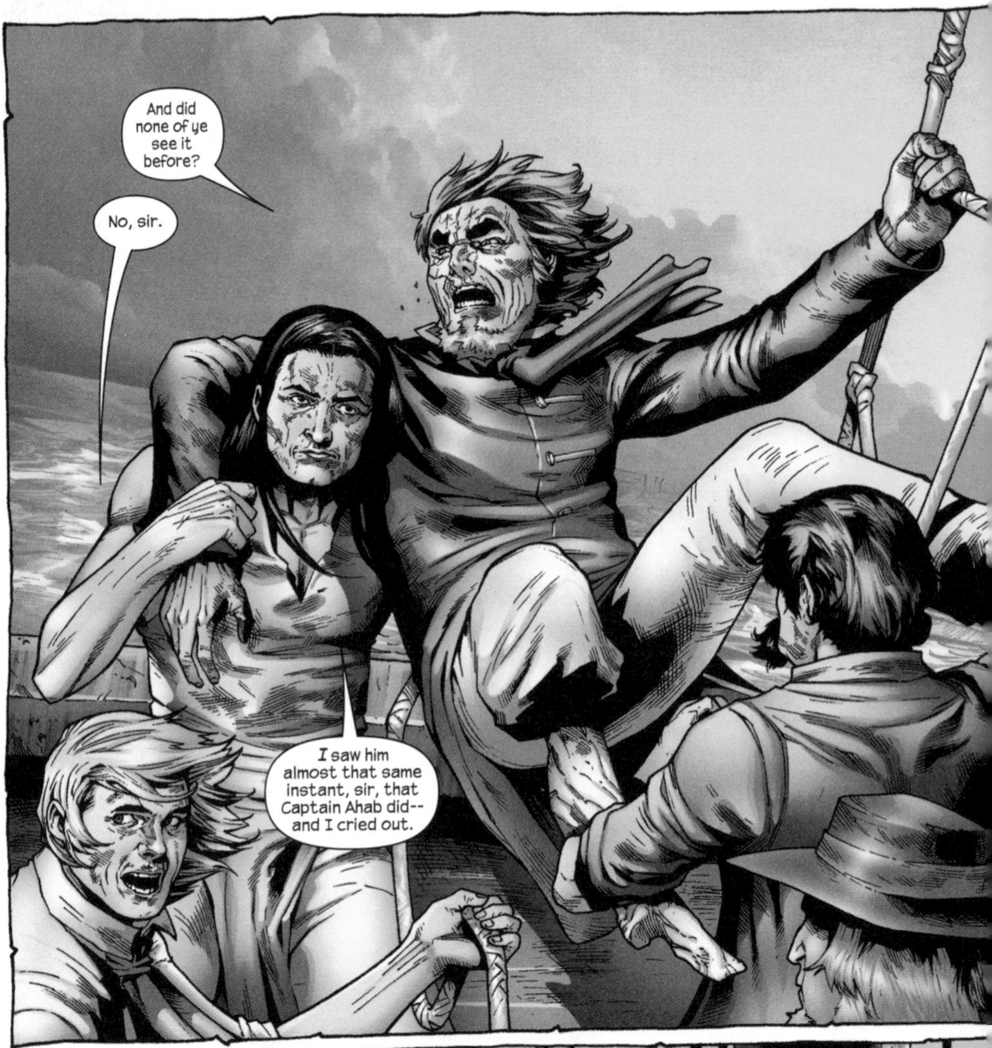
And did none of ye see it before?
No, sir.
I saw him almost that same instant, sir, that Captain Ahab did--and I cried out.

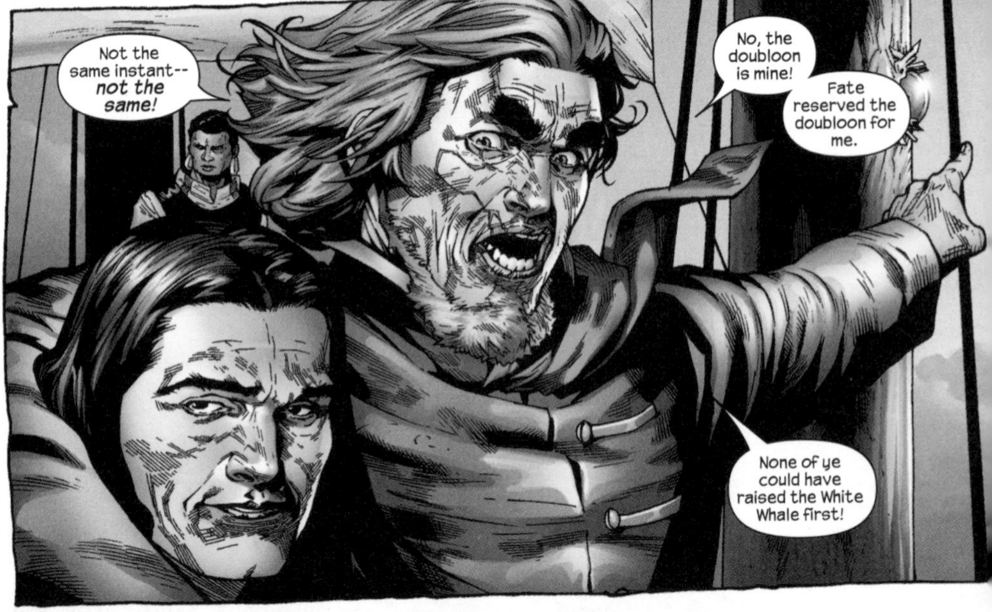
Not the same instant--not the same!
No, the doubloon is mine!
Fate reserved the doubloon for me.
None of ye could have raised the White Whale first!

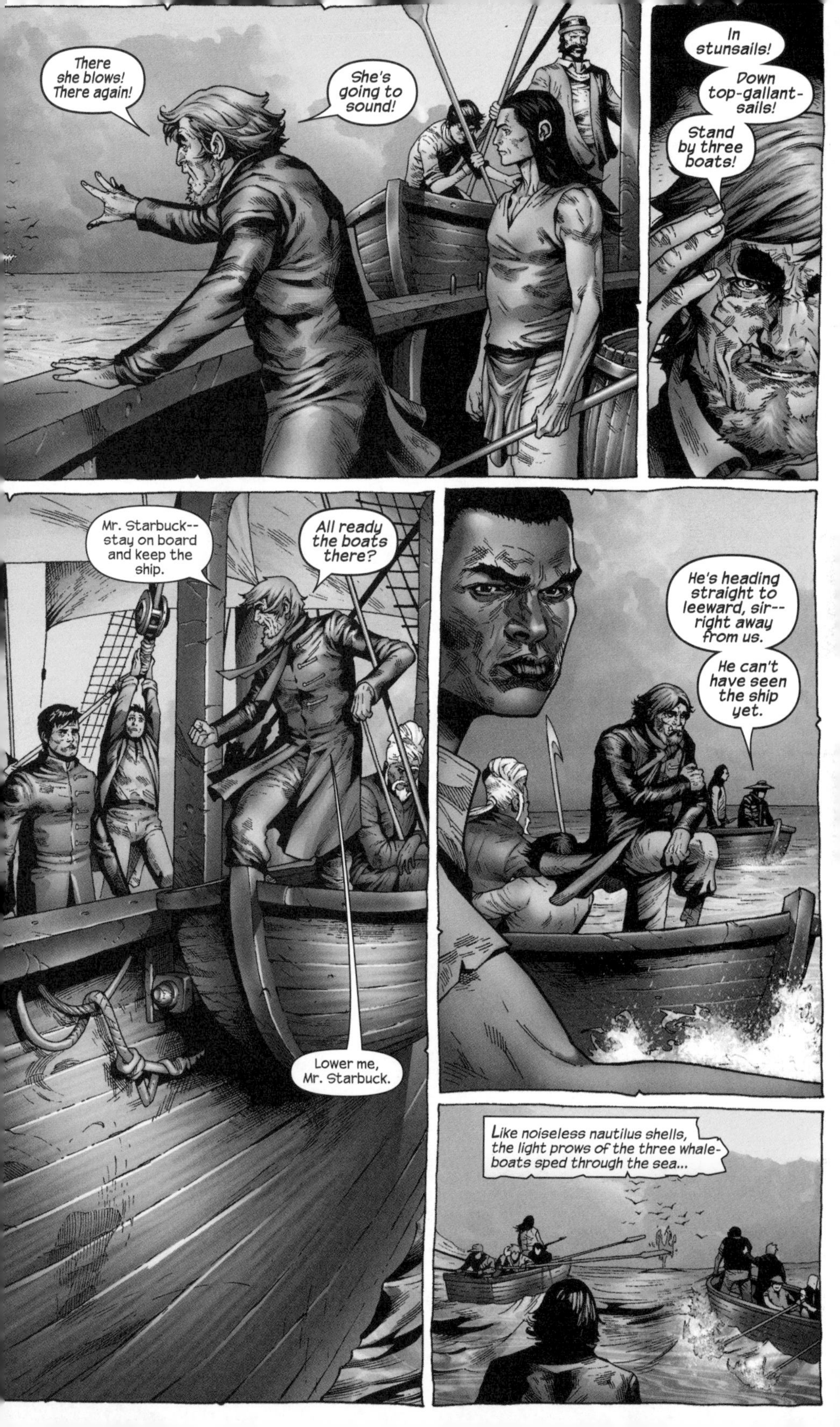
There she blows! There again!
She's going to sound!
In stunsails!
Down top-gallant-sails!
Stand by three boats!
Mr. Starbuck-- stay on board and keep the ship.
All ready the boats there?
Lower me, Mr. Starbuck.
He's heading straight to leeward, sir-- right away from us.
He can't have seen the ship yet.
Like noiseless nautilus shells, the light prows of the three whale-boats sped through the sea...

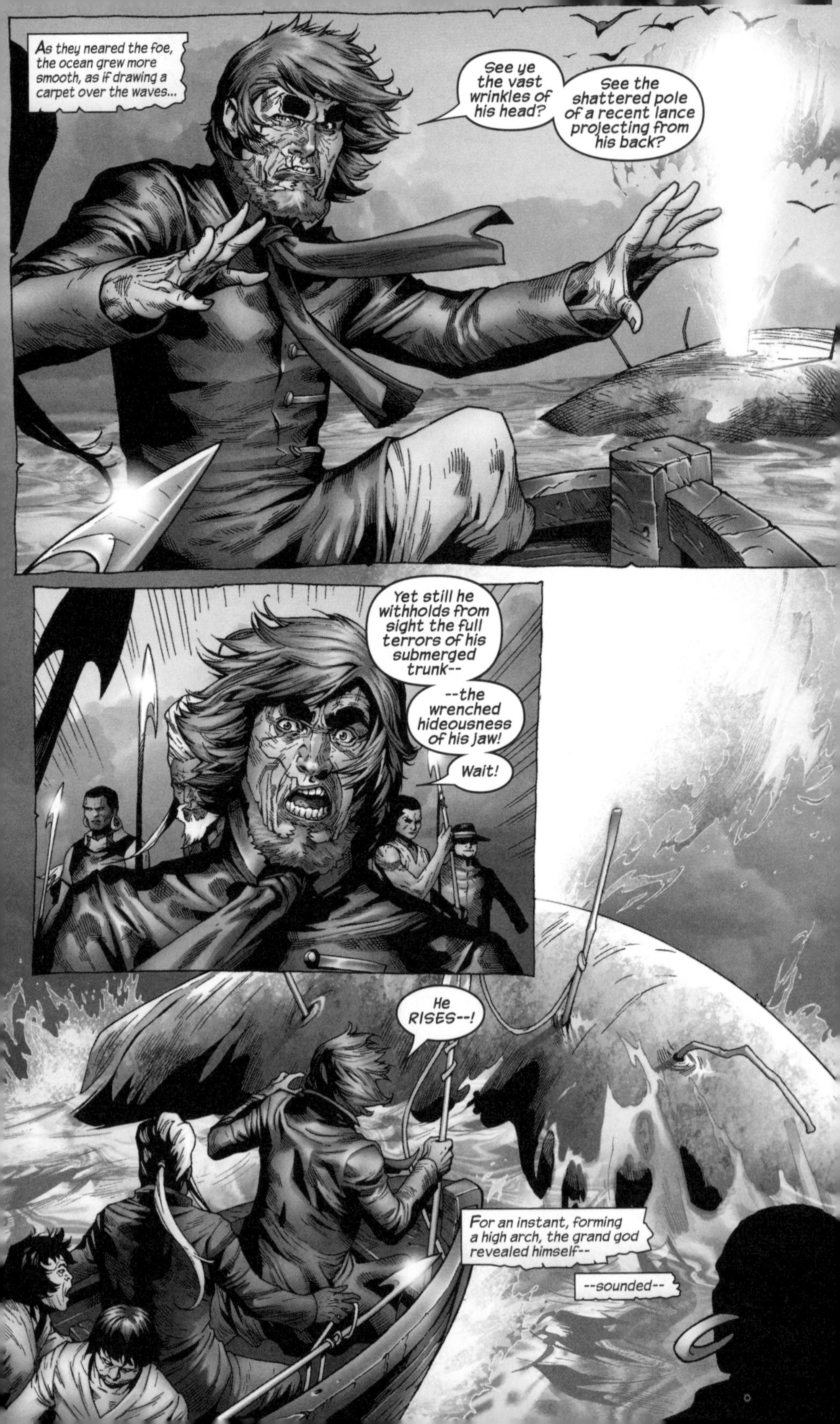
As they neared the foe, the ocean grew more smooth, as if drawing a carpet over the waves...
See ye the vast wrinkles of his head?
See the shattered pole of a recent lance projecting from his back?
Yet still he withholds from sight the full terrors of his submerged trunk--
--the wrenched hideousness of his jaw!
Wait!
He RISES--!
For an instant, forming a high arch, the grand god revealed himself--
--sounded--

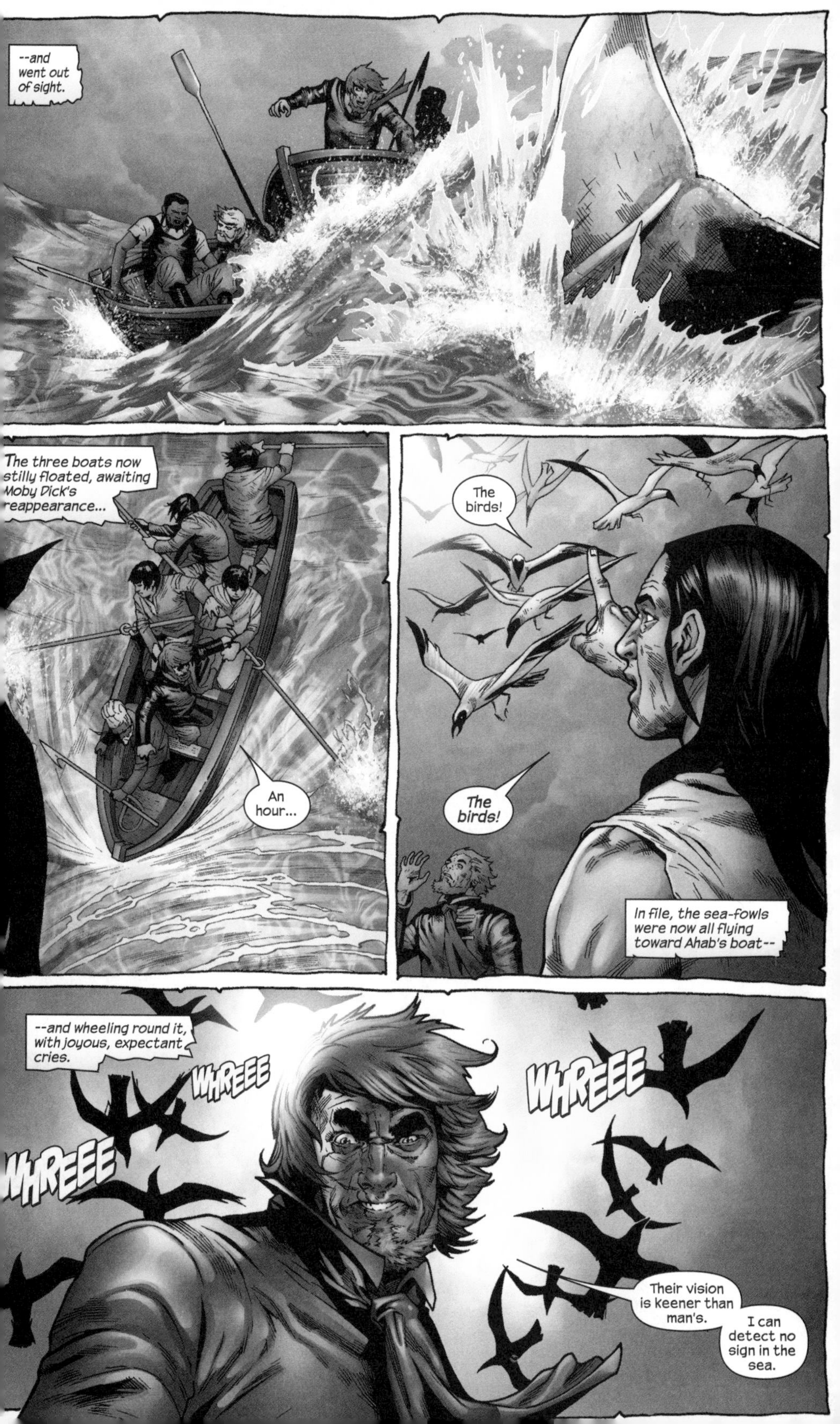
--and went out of sight.
The three boats now stilly floated, awaiting Moby Dick's reappearance...
An hour...
The birds!
The birds!
In file, the sea-fowls were now all flying toward Ahab's boat--
--and wheeling round it, with joyous, expectant cries.
WHREEE
WHREEE
WHREEE
Their vision is keener than man's.
I can detect no sign in the sea.

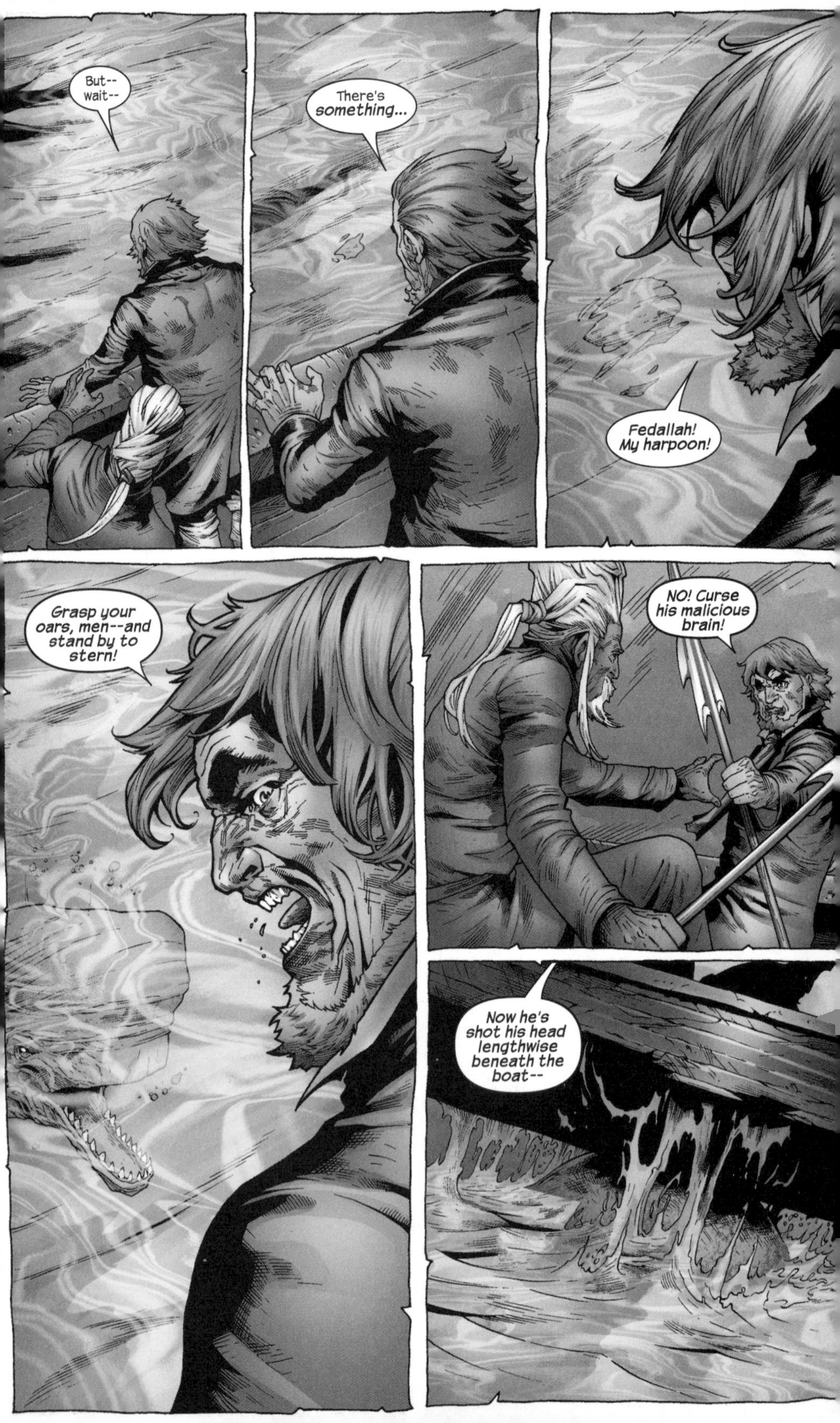
But-- wait--
There's something...
Fedallah! My harpoon!
Grasp your oars, men--and stand by to stern!
NO! Curse his malicious brain!
Now he's shot his head lengthwise beneath the boat--

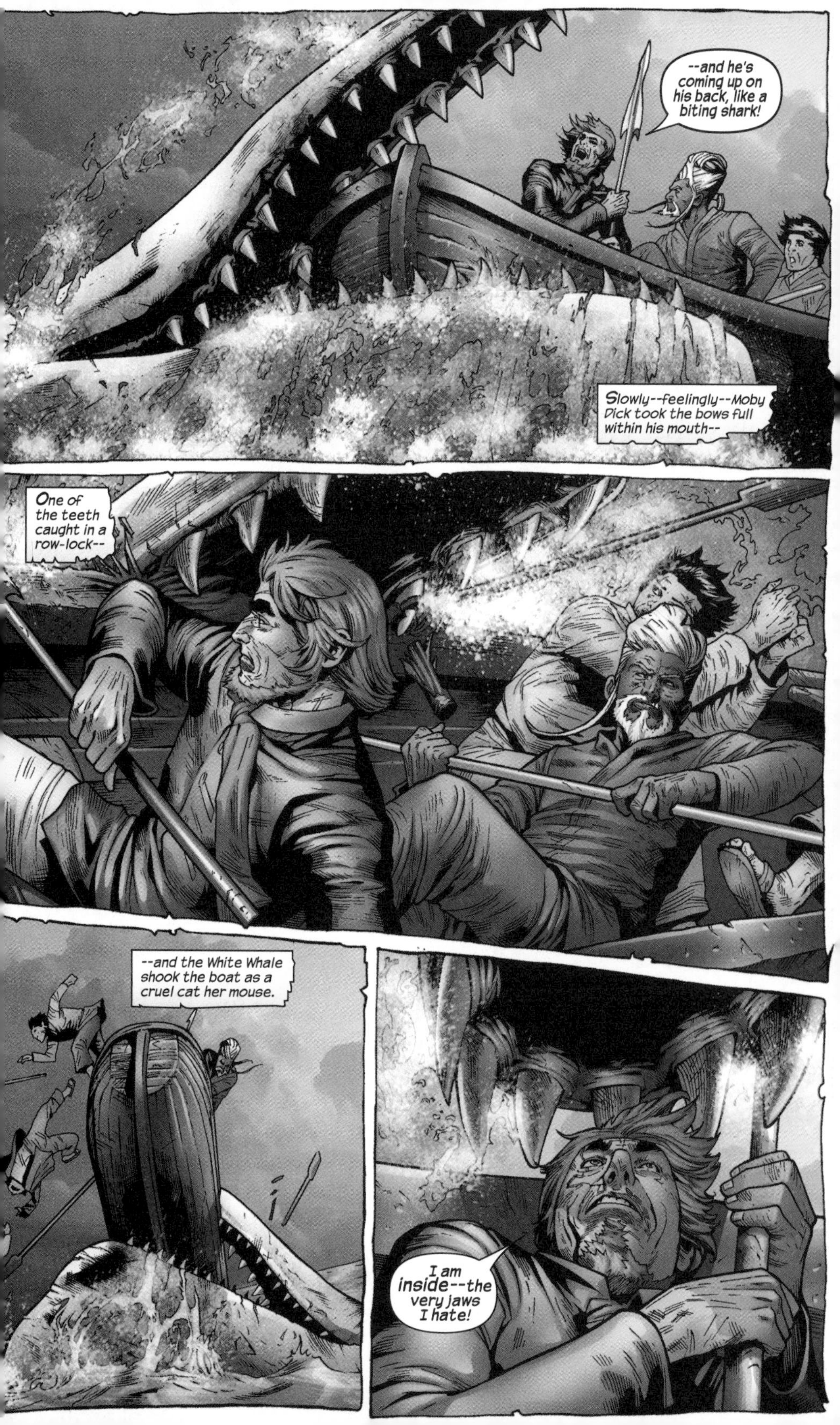
--and he's coming up on his back, like a biting shark!
Slowly--feelingly--Moby Dick took the bows full within his mouth--
One of the teeth caught in a row-lock--
--and the White Whale shook the boat as a cruel cat her mouse.
I am inside--the very jaws I hate!

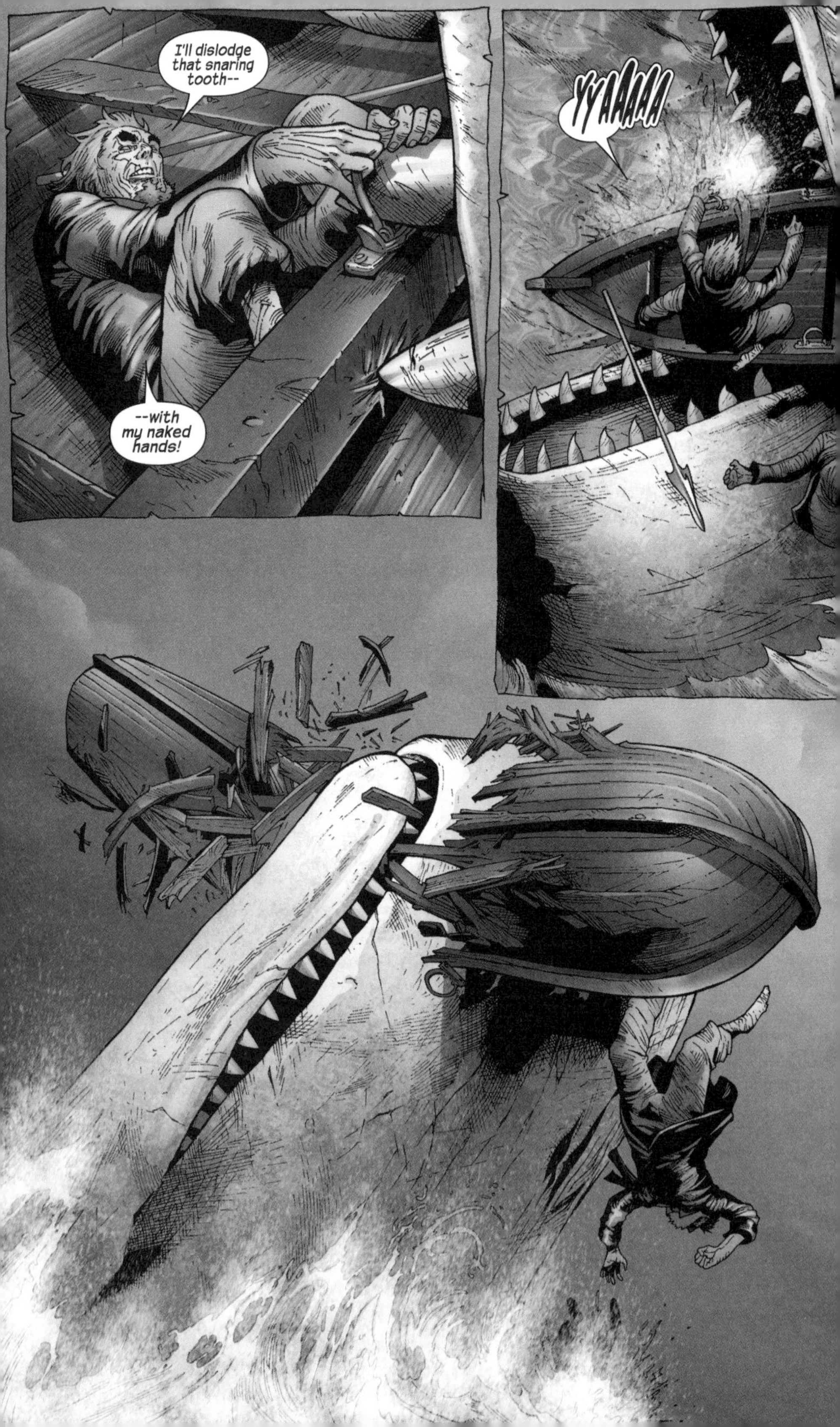
I'll dislodge that snaring tooth--
--with my naked hands!
YYAAAAA

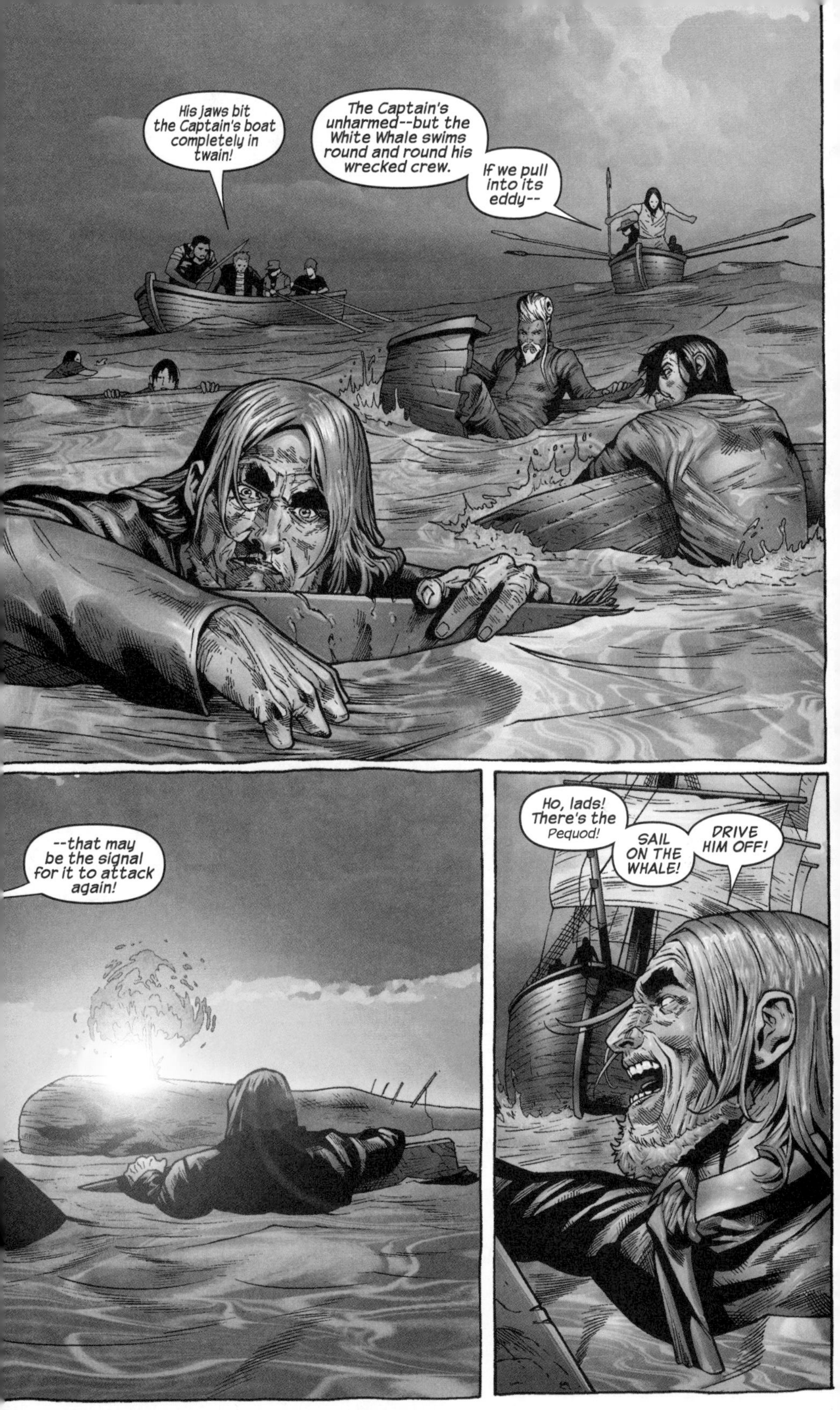
His jaws bit the Captain's boat completely in twain!
The Captain's unharmed--but the White Whale swims round and round his wrecked crew.
If we pull into its eddy--
--that may be the signal for it to attack again!
Ho, lads! There's the Pequod!
SAIL ON THE WHALE!
DRIVE HIM OFF!

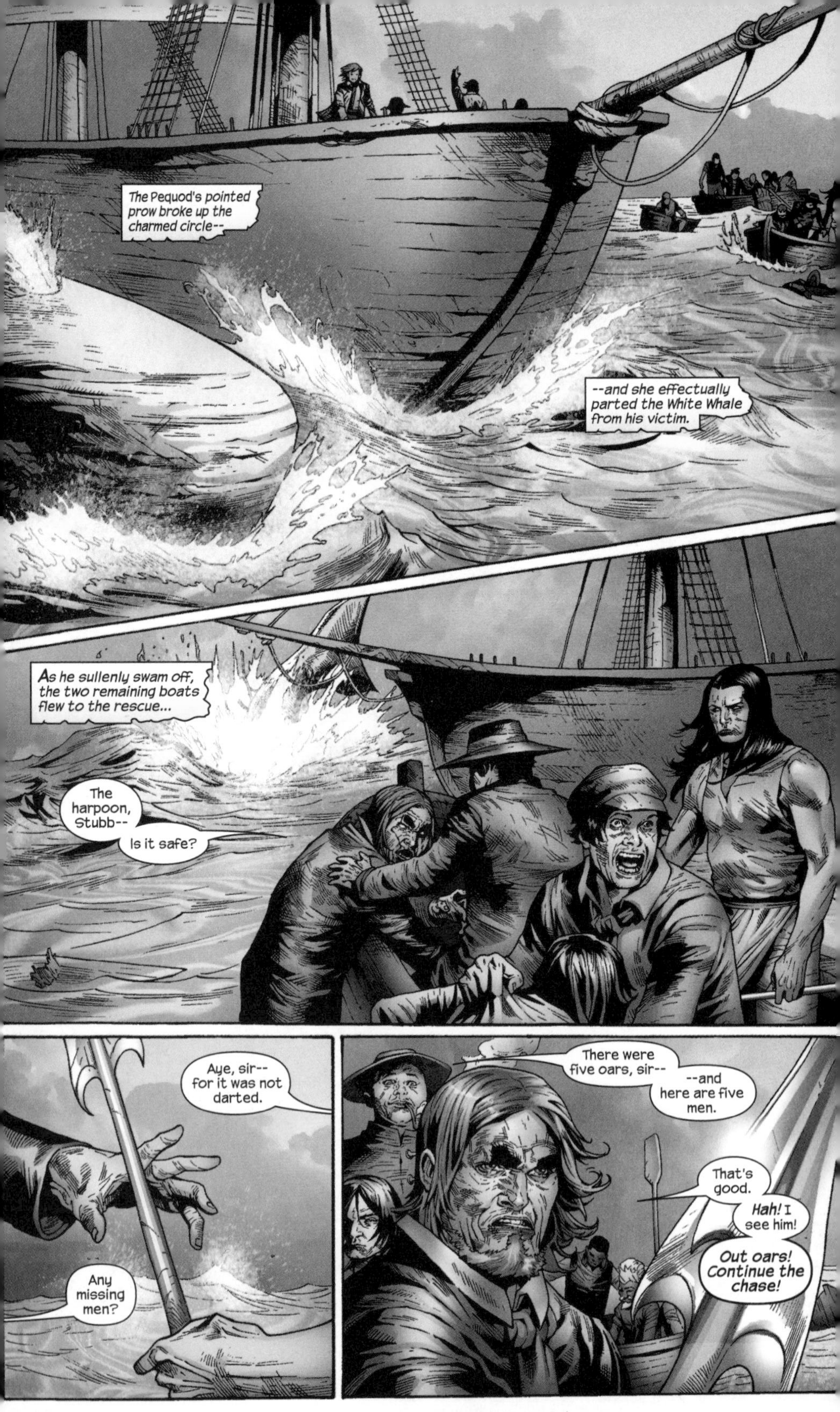
The Pequod's pointed prow broke up the charmed circle--
--and she effectually parted the White Whale from his victim.
As he sullenly swam off, the two remaining boats flew to the rescue...
The harpoon, Stubb--
Is it safe?
Aye, sir-- for it was not darted.
Any missing men?
There were five oars, sir--
--and here are five men.
That's good.
Hah! I see him!
Out oars! Continue the chase!

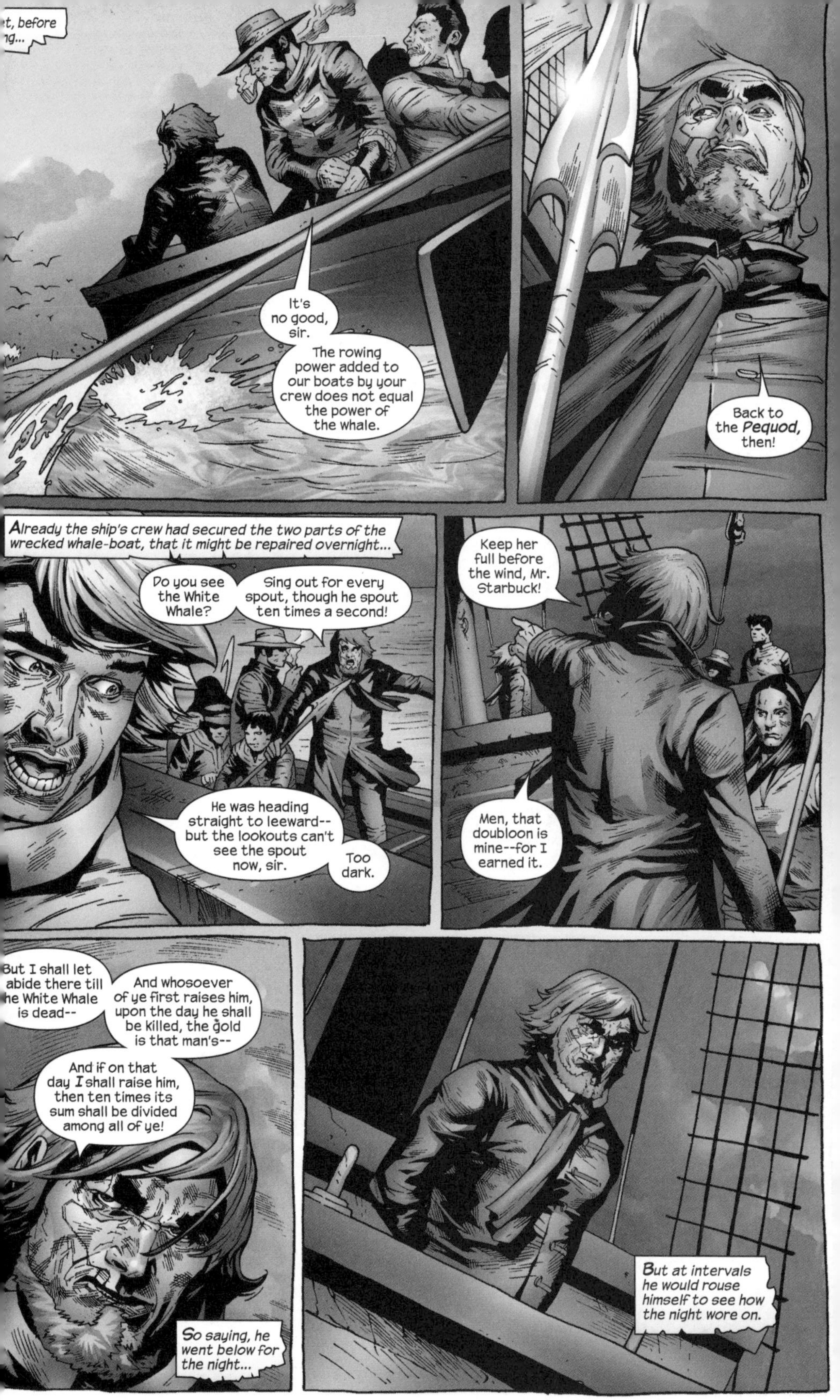

...t, before
...ng...
It's no good, sir.
The rowing power added to our boats by your crew does not equal the power of the whale.
Back to the *Pequod,* then!
Already the ship's crew had secured the two parts of the wrecked whale-boat, that it might be repaired overnight...
Do you see the White Whale?
Sing out for every spout, though he spout ten times a second!
He was heading straight to leeward--but the lookouts can't see the spout now, sir.
Too dark.
Keep her full before the wind, Mr. Starbuck!
Men, that doubloon is mine--for I earned it.
But I shall let abide there till the White Whale is dead--
And whosoever of ye first raises him, upon the day he shall be killed, the gold is that man's--
And if on that day *I* shall raise him, then ten times its sum shall be divided among all of ye!
So saying, he went below for the night...
But at intervals he would rouse himself to see how the night wore on.

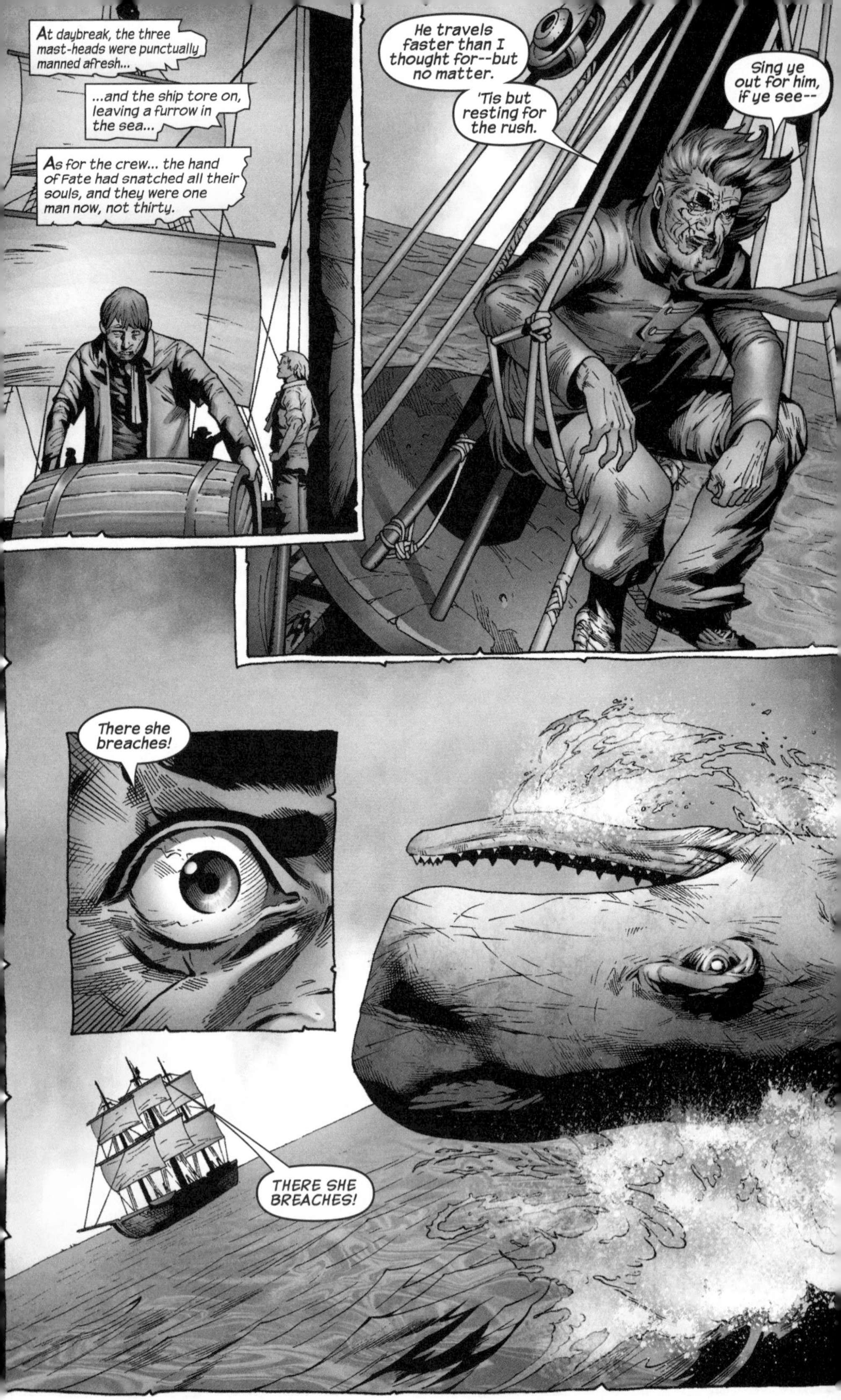

At daybreak, the three mast-heads were punctually manned afresh...
...and the ship tore on, leaving a furrow in the sea...
As for the crew... the hand of Fate had snatched all their souls, and they were one man now, not thirty.
He travels faster than I thought for--but no matter.
'Tis but resting for the rush.
Sing ye out for him, if ye see--
There she breaches!
THERE SHE BREACHES!

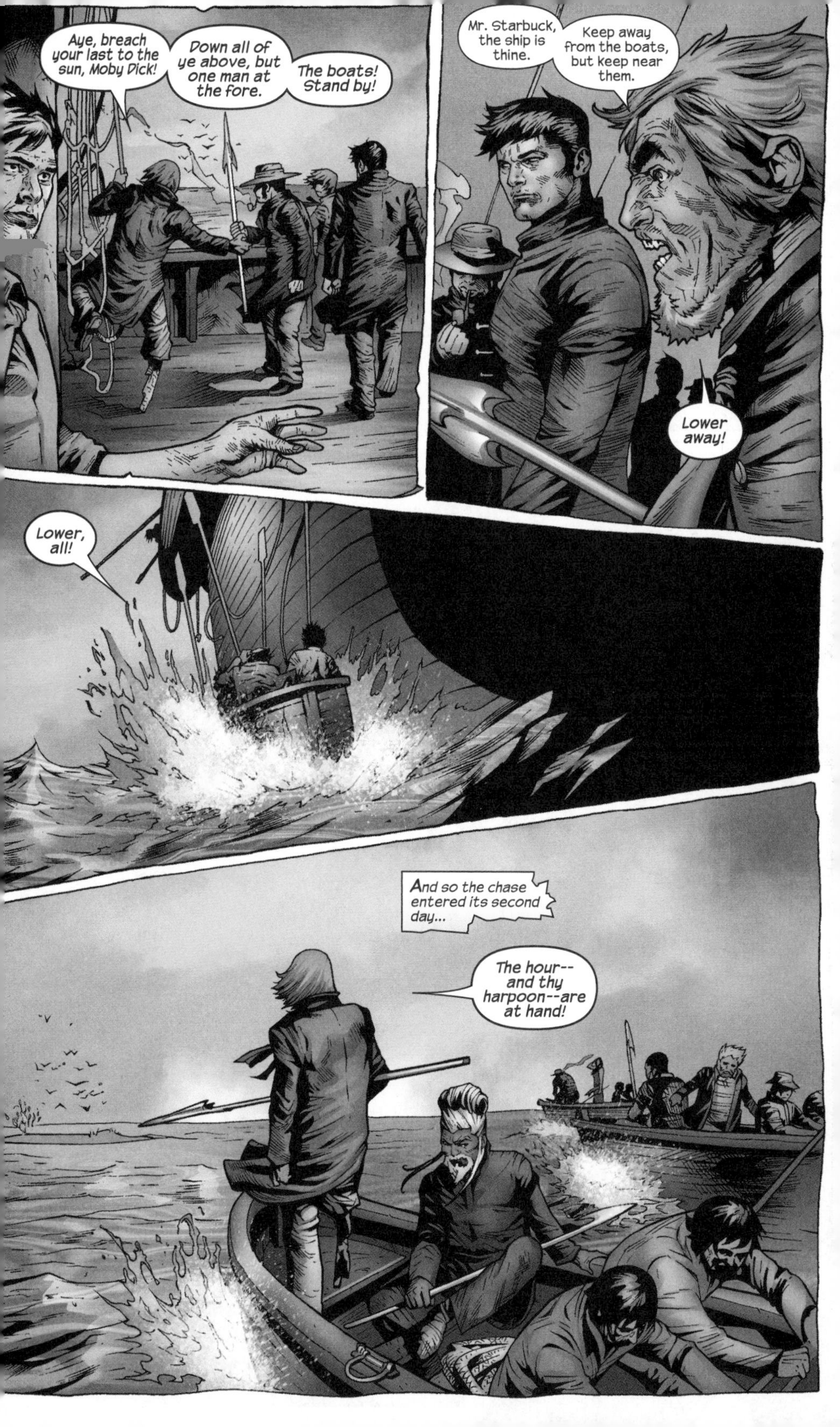
Aye, breach your last to the sun, Moby Dick!
Down all of ye above, but one man at the fore.
The boats! Stand by!
Mr. Starbuck, the ship is thine.
Keep away from the boats, but keep near them.
Lower away!
Lower, all!
And so the chase entered its second day...
The hour--and thy harpoon--are at hand!

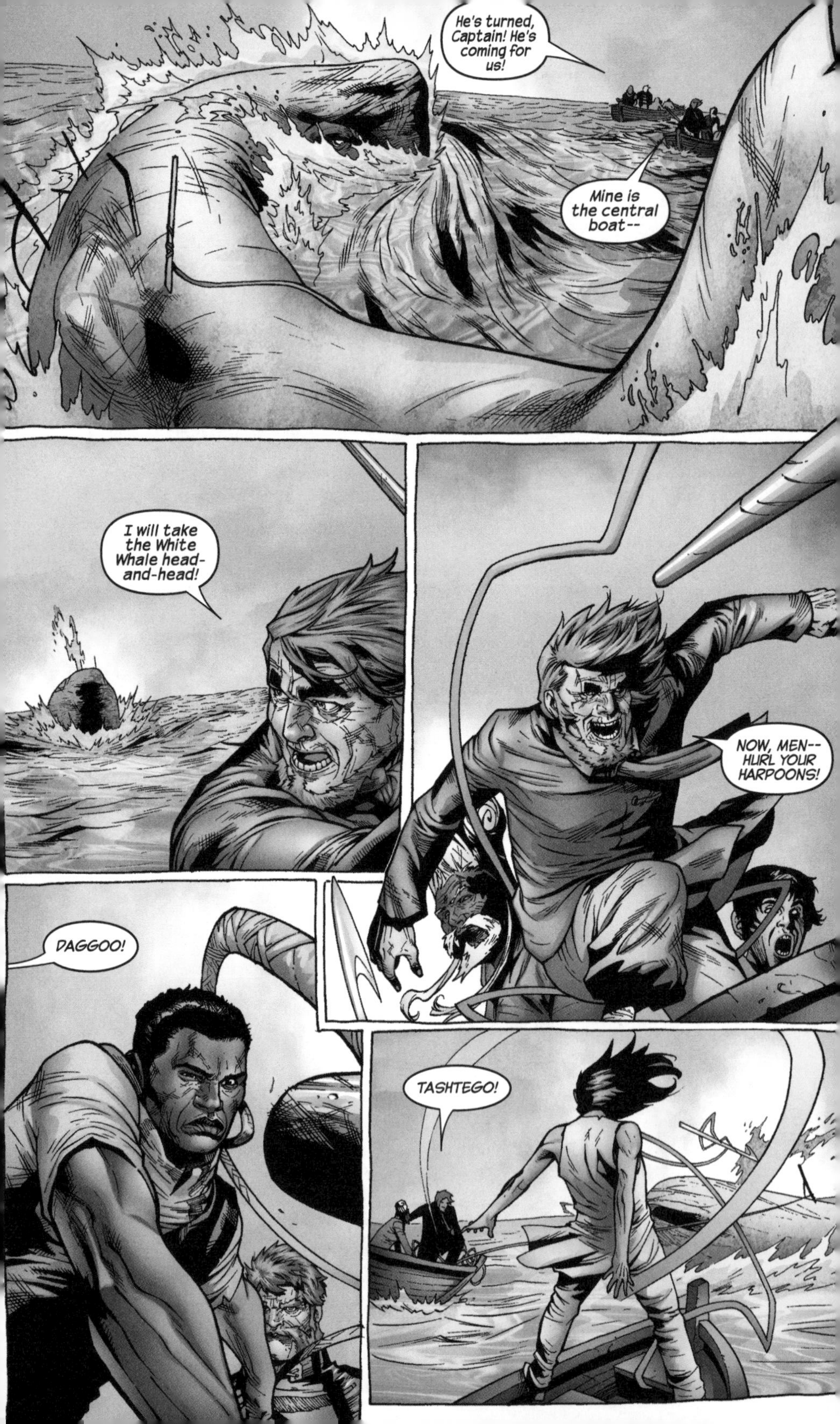
He's turned, Captain! He's coming for us!
Mine is the central boat--
I will take the White Whale head-and-head!
NOW, MEN--HURL YOUR HARPOONS!
DAGGOO!
TASHTEGO!

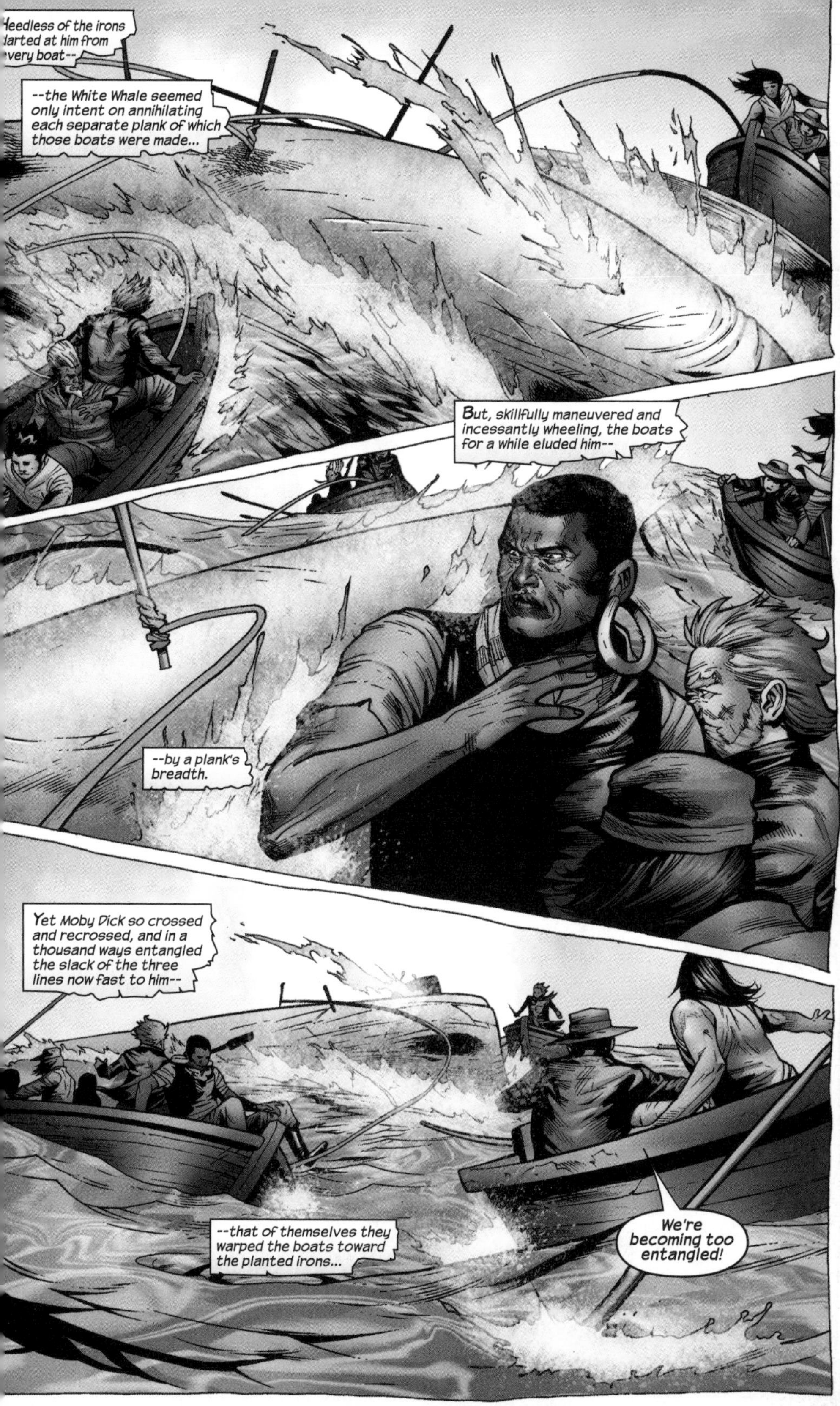
Heedless of the irons darted at him from every boat--
--the White Whale seemed only intent on annihilating each separate plank of which those boats were made...
But, skillfully maneuvered and incessantly wheeling, the boats for a while eluded him--
--by a plank's breadth.
Yet Moby Dick so crossed and recrossed, and in a thousand ways entangled the slack of the three lines now fast to him--
--that of themselves they warped the boats toward the planted irons...
We're becoming too entangled!

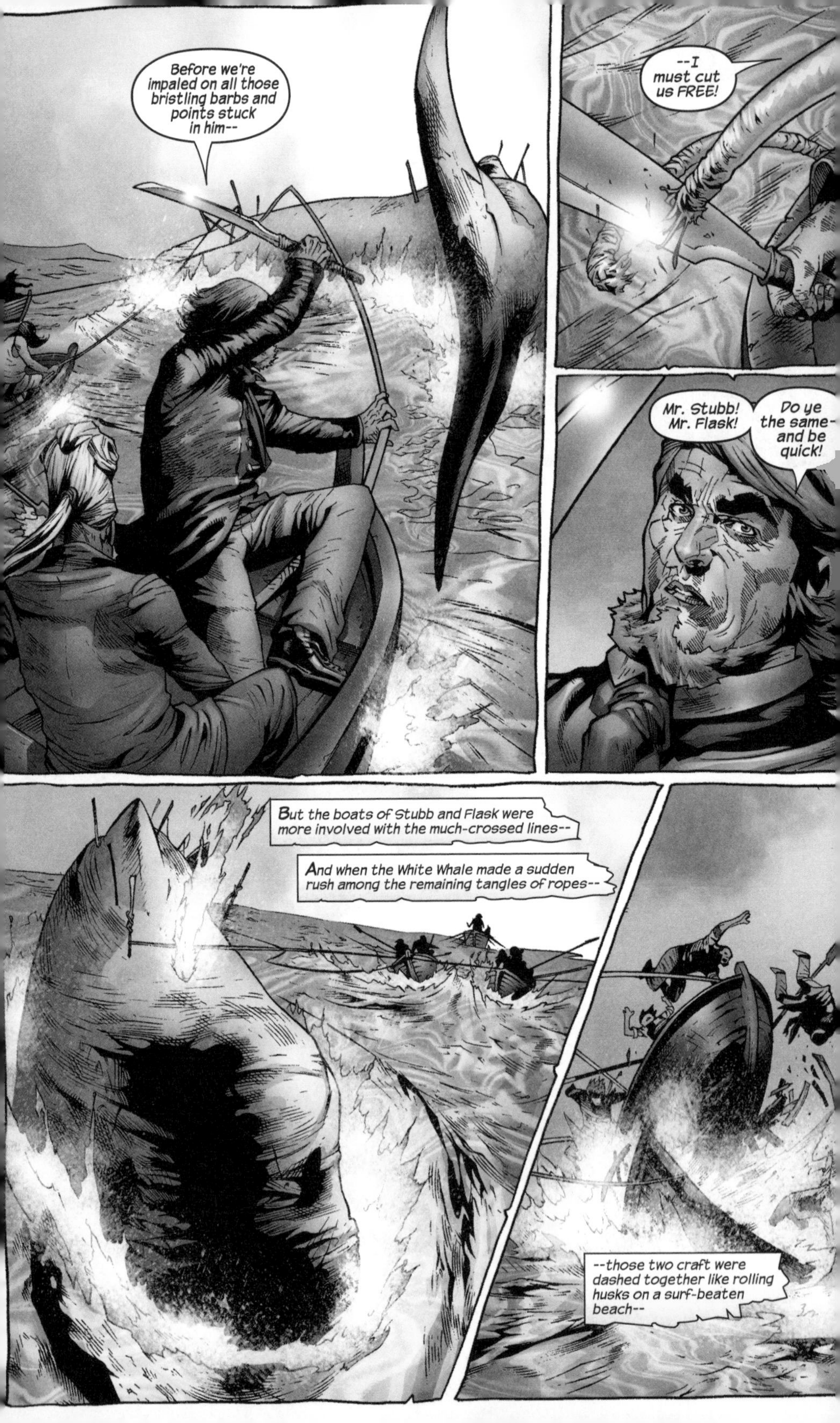
Before we're impaled on all those bristling barbs and points stuck in him--
--I must cut us FREE!
Mr. Stubb! Mr. Flask!
Do ye the same-and be quick!
But the boats of Stubb and Flask were more involved with the much-crossed lines--
And when the White Whale made a sudden rush among the remaining tangles of ropes--
--those two craft were dashed together like rolling husks on a surf-beaten beach--

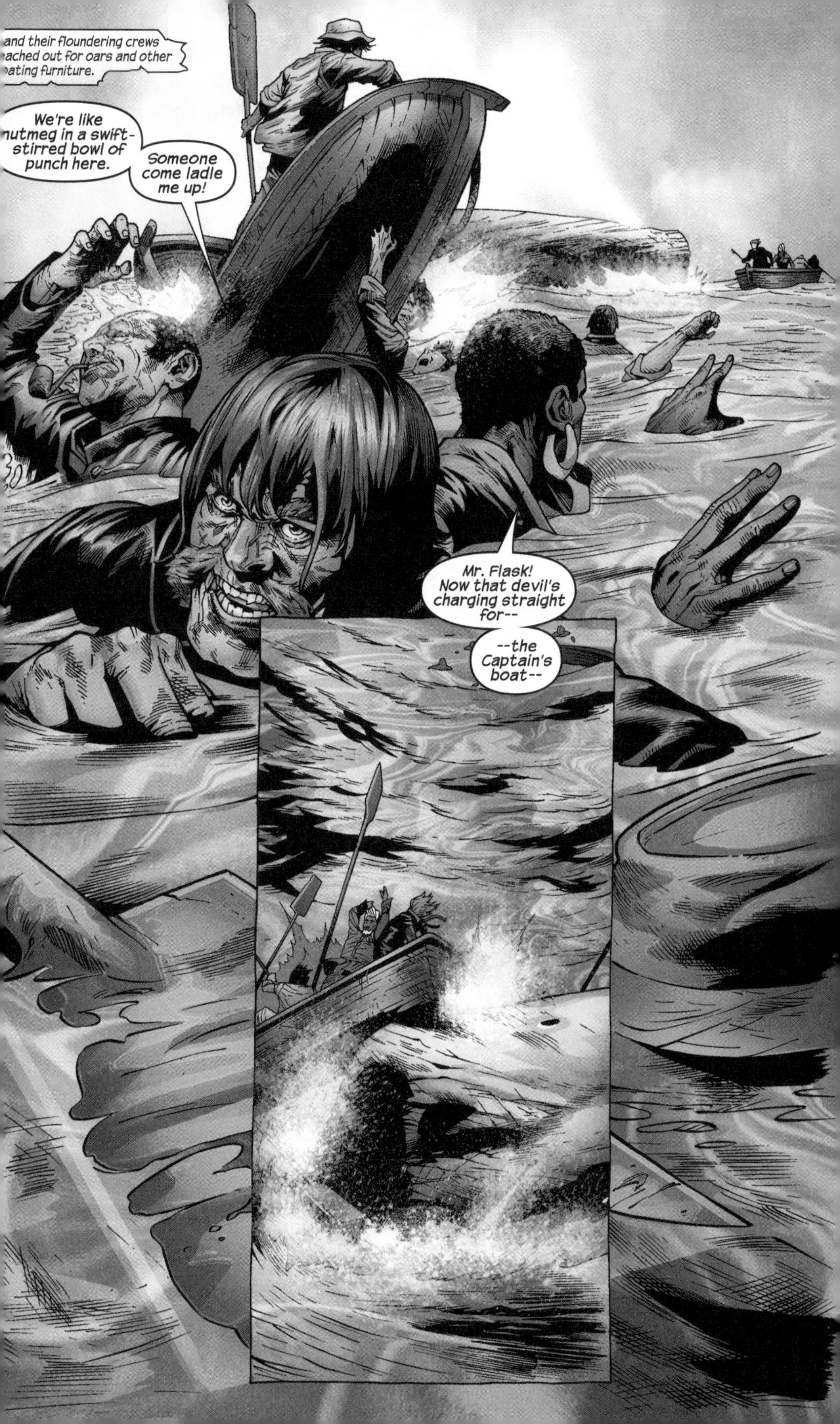
and their floundering crews eached out for oars and other oating furniture.
We're like nutmeg in a swift-stirred bowl of punch here.
Someone come ladle me up!
Mr. Flask! Now that devil's charging straight for--
--the Captain's boat--

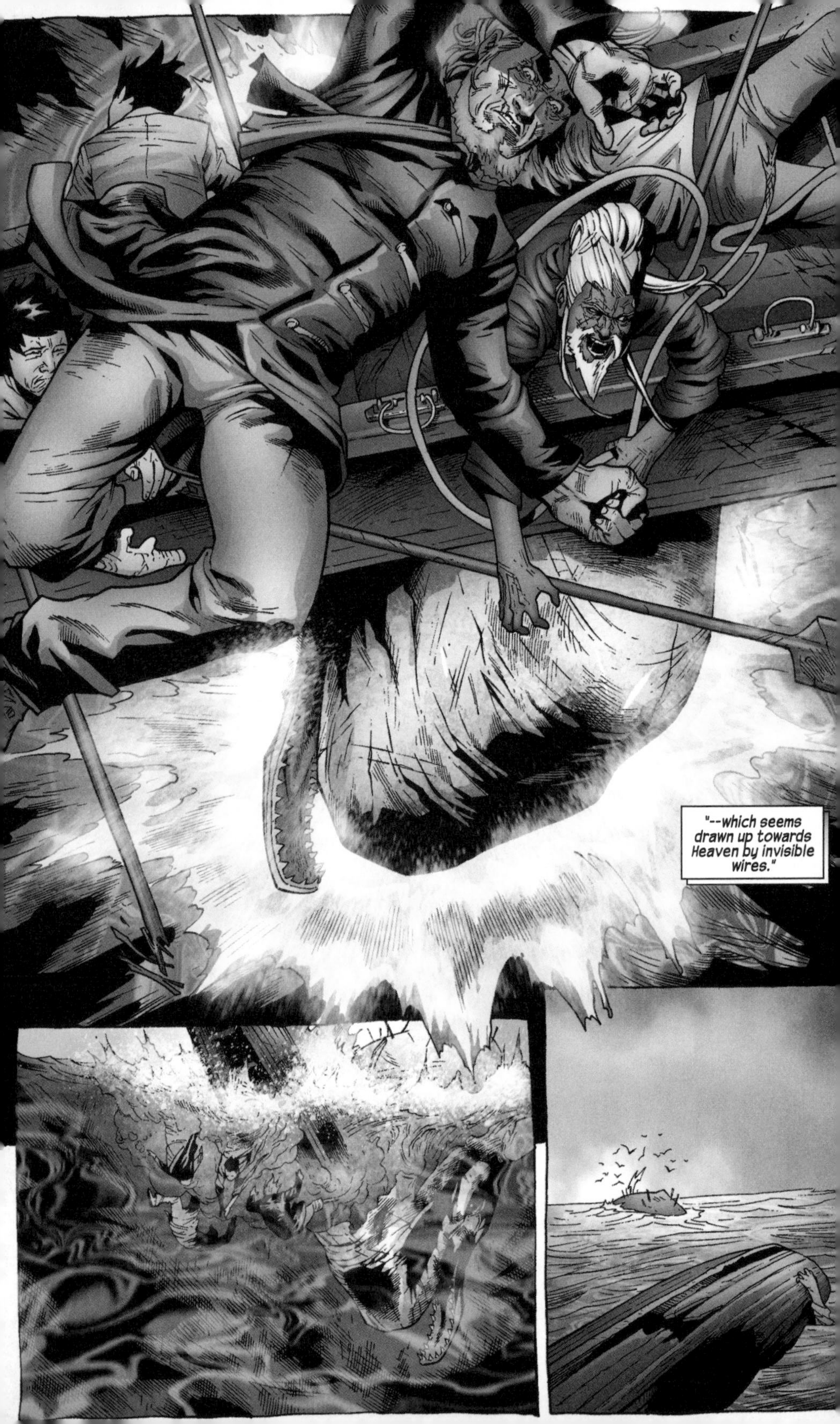
"--which seems drawn up towards Heaven by invisible wires."

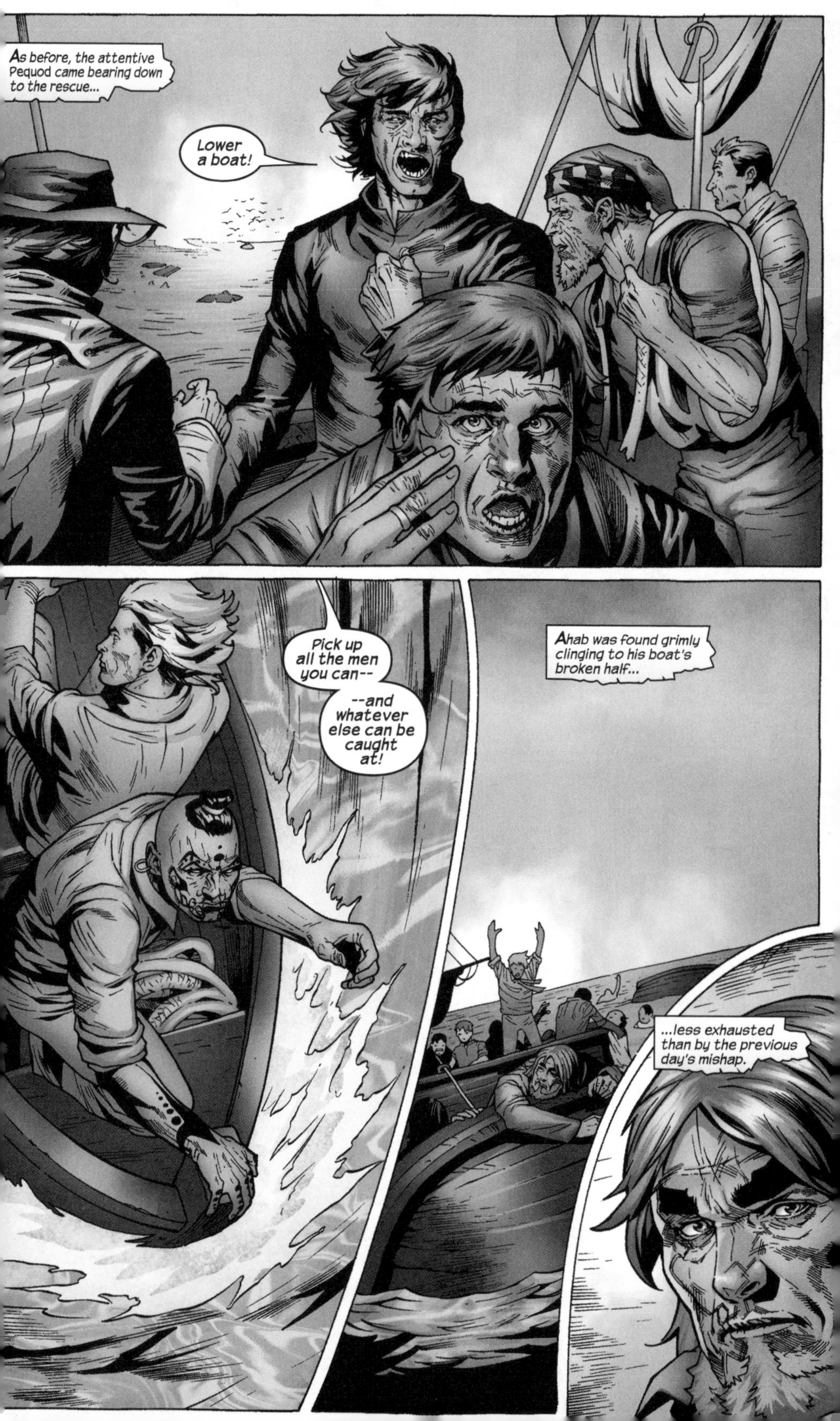
As before, the attentive Pequod came bearing down to the rescue...
Lower a boat!
Pick up all the men you can--
--and whatever else can be caught at!
Ahab was found grimly clinging to his boat's broken half...
...less exhausted than by the previous day's mishap.

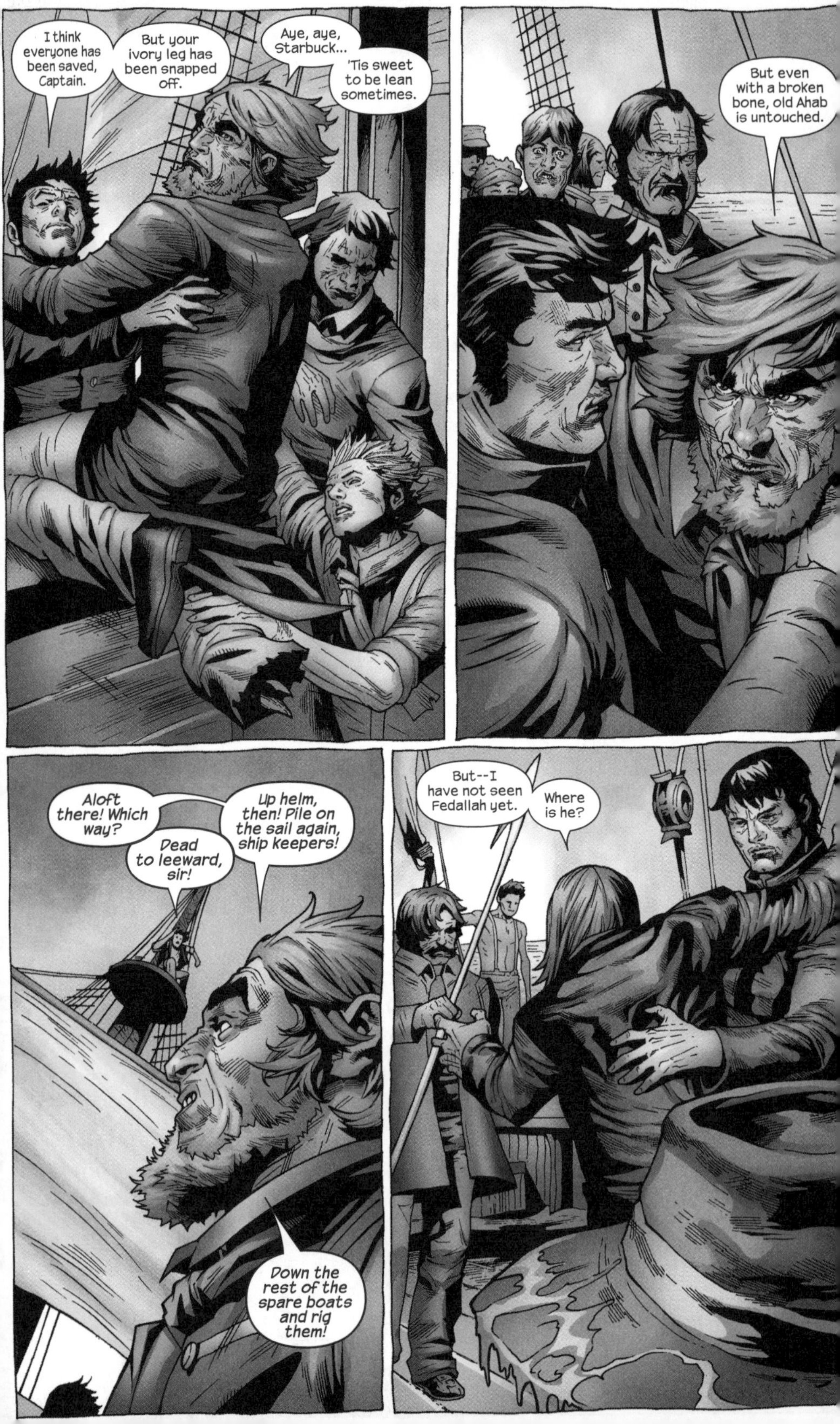
I think everyone has been saved, Captain.
But your ivory leg has been snapped off.
Aye, aye, Starbuck...
'Tis sweet to be lean sometimes.
But even with a broken bone, old Ahab is untouched.
Aloft there! Which way?
Dead to leeward, sir!
Up helm, then! Pile on the sail again, ship keepers!
Down the rest of the spare boats and rig them!
But--I have not seen Fedallah yet.
Where is he?

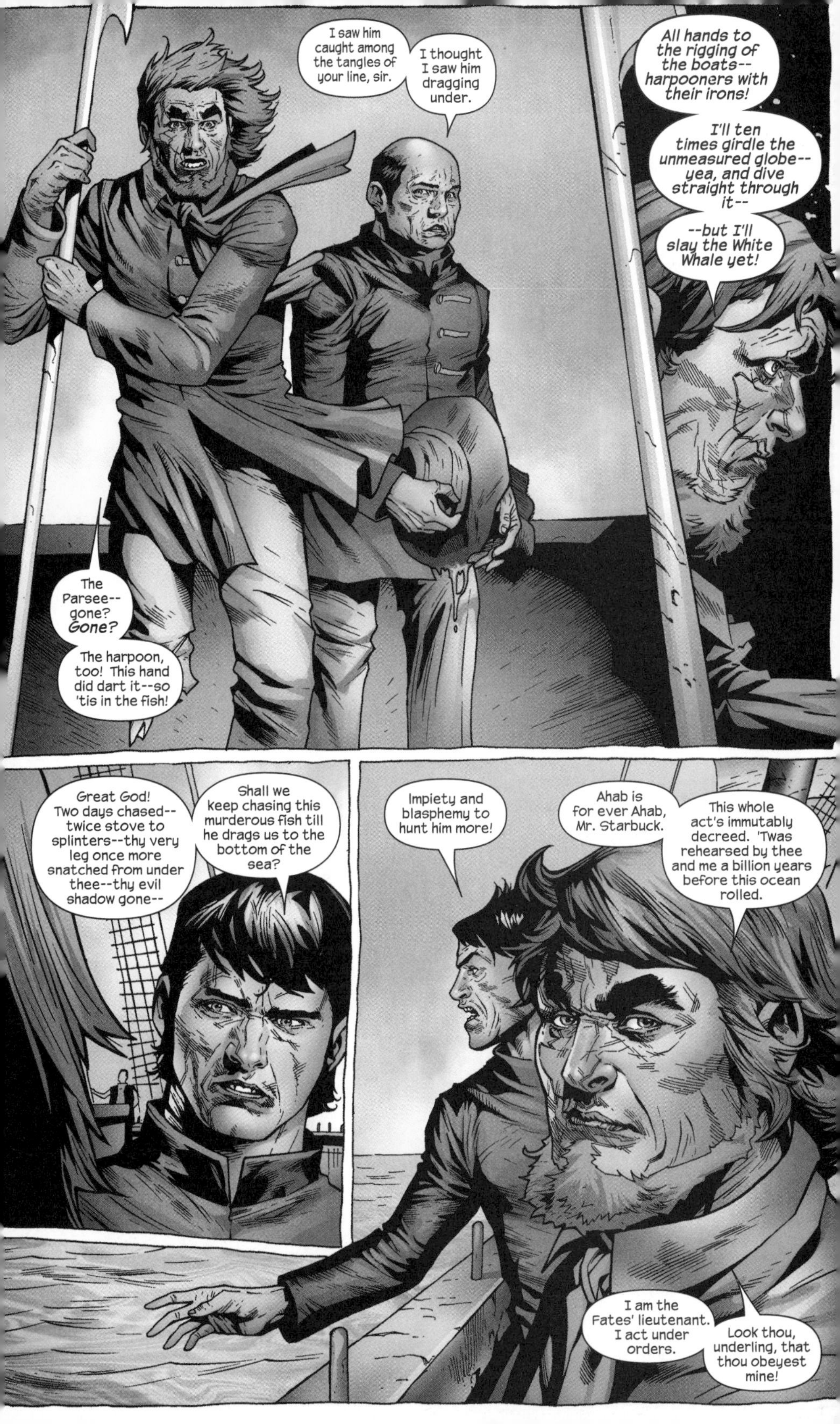

I saw him caught among the tangles of your line, sir.
I thought I saw him dragging under.
All hands to the rigging of the boats--harpooners with their irons!
I'll ten times girdle the unmeasured globe--yea, and dive straight through it--
--but I'll slay the White Whale yet!
The Parsee--gone? *Gone?*
The harpoon, too! This hand did dart it--so 'tis in the fish!
Great God! Two days chased--twice stove to splinters--thy very leg once more snatched from under thee--thy evil shadow gone--
Shall we keep chasing this murderous fish till he drags us to the bottom of the sea?
Impiety and blasphemy to hunt him more!
Ahab is for ever Ahab, Mr. Starbuck.
This whole act's immutably decreed. 'Twas rehearsed by thee and me a billion years before this ocean rolled.
I am the Fates' lieutenant. I act under orders.
Look thou, underling, that thou obeyest mine!

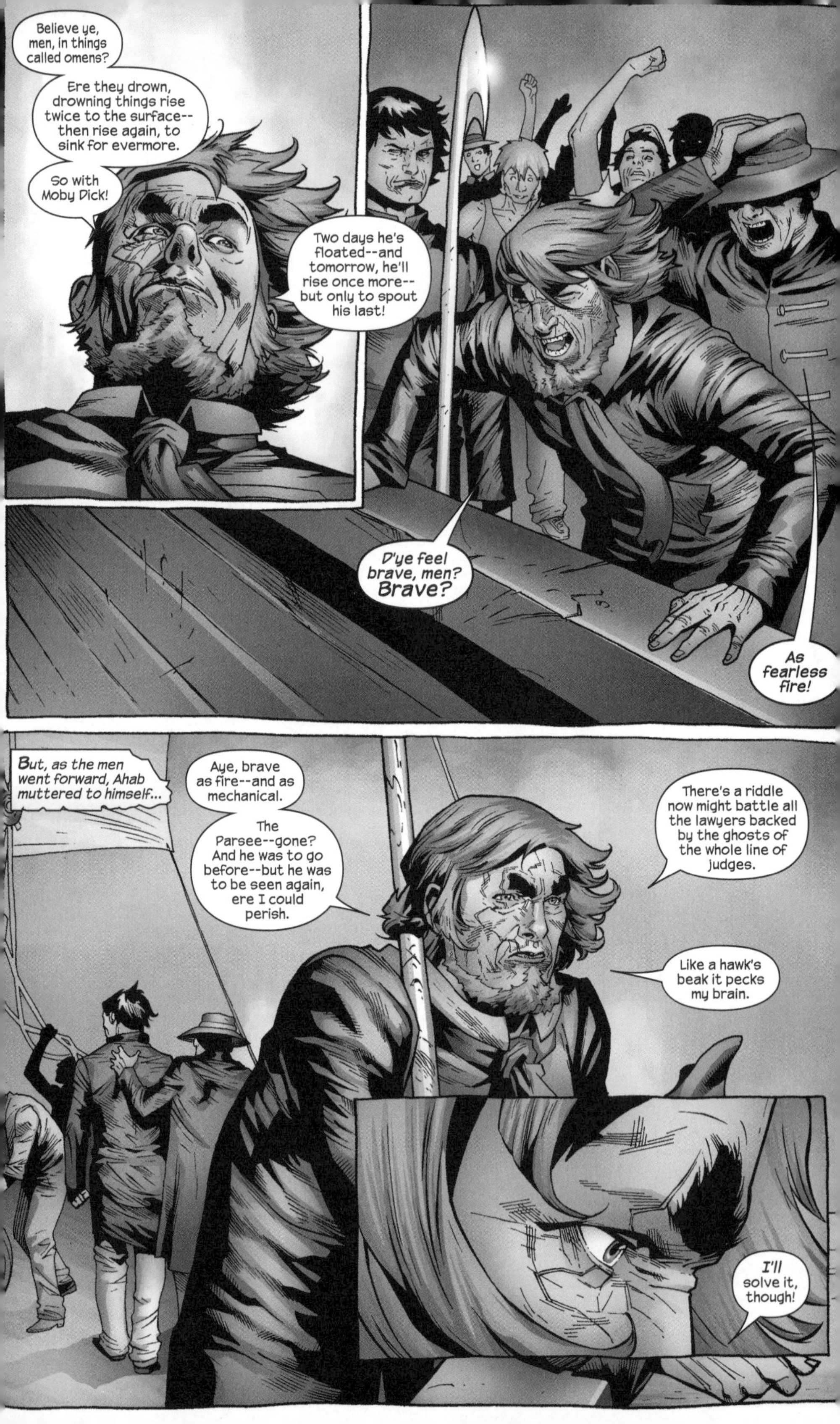
Believe ye, men, in things called omens?
Ere they drown, drowning things rise twice to the surface--then rise again, to sink for evermore.
So with Moby Dick!
Two days he's floated--and tomorrow, he'll rise once more--but only to spout his last!
D'ye feel brave, men? Brave?
As fearless fire!
But, as the men went forward, Ahab muttered to himself...
Aye, brave as fire--and as mechanical.
The Parsee--gone? And he was to go before--but he was to be seen again, ere I could perish.
There's a riddle now might battle all the lawyers backed by the ghosts of the whole line of judges.
Like a hawk's beak it pecks my brain.
I'll solve it, though!

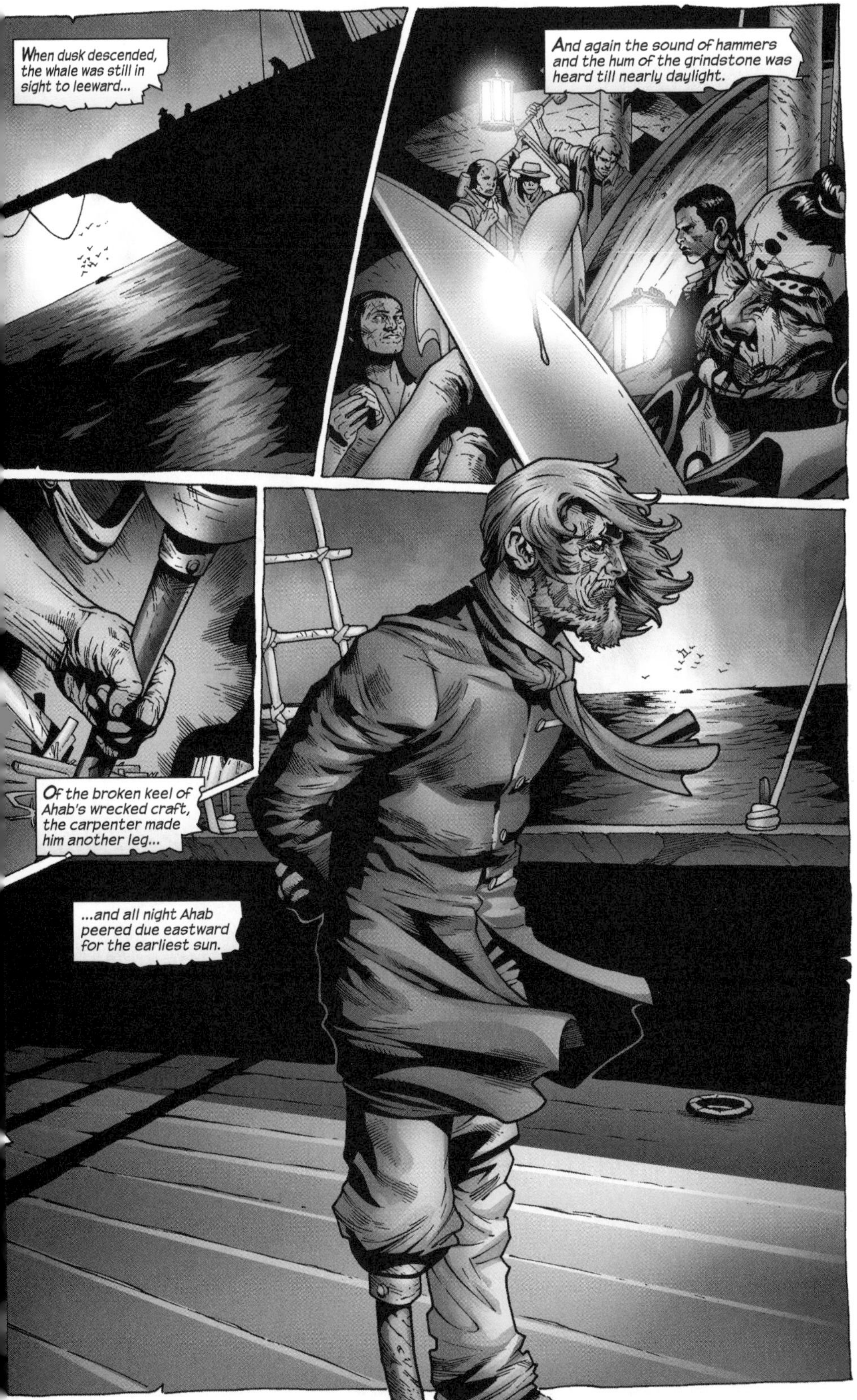
When dusk descended, the whale was still in sight to leeward...
And again the sound of hammers and the hum of the grindstone was heard till nearly daylight.
Of the broken keel of Ahab's wrecked craft, the carpenter made him another leg...
...and all night Ahab peered due eastward for the earliest sun.

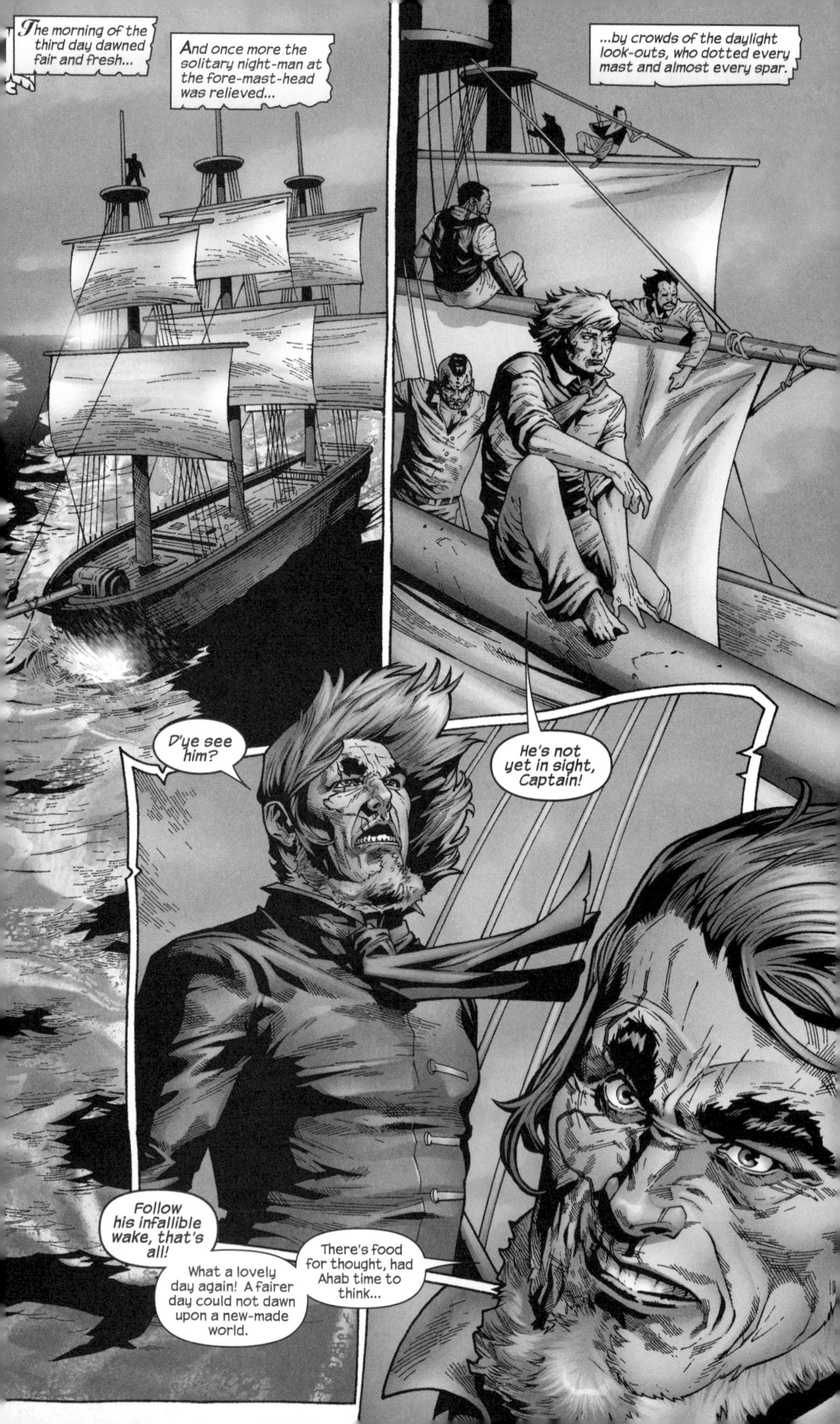

The morning of the third day dawned fair and fresh...
And once more the solitary night-man at the fore-mast-head was relieved...
...by crowds of the daylight look-outs, who dotted every mast and almost every spar.
D'ye see him?
He's not yet in sight, Captain!
Follow his infallible wake, that's all!
What a lovely day again! A fairer day could not dawn upon a new-made world.
There's food for thought, had Ahab time to think...

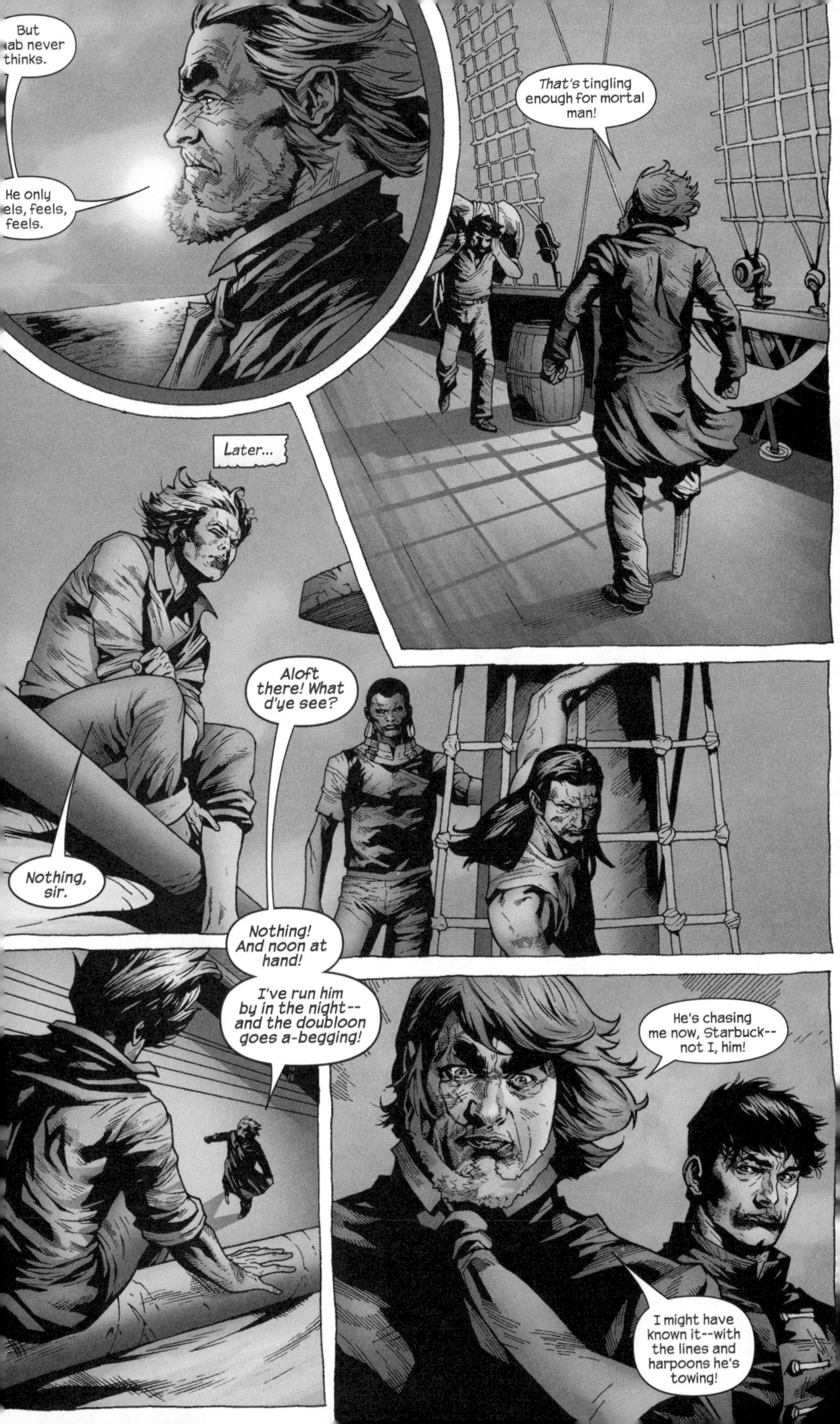
But
ab never
thinks.
He only
els, feels,
feels.
That's tingling enough for mortal man!
Later...
Aloft there! What d'ye see?
Nothing, sir.
Nothing! And noon at hand!
I've run him by in the night--and the doubloon goes a-begging!
He's chasing me now, Starbuck--not I, him!
I might have known it--with the lines and harpoons he's towing!

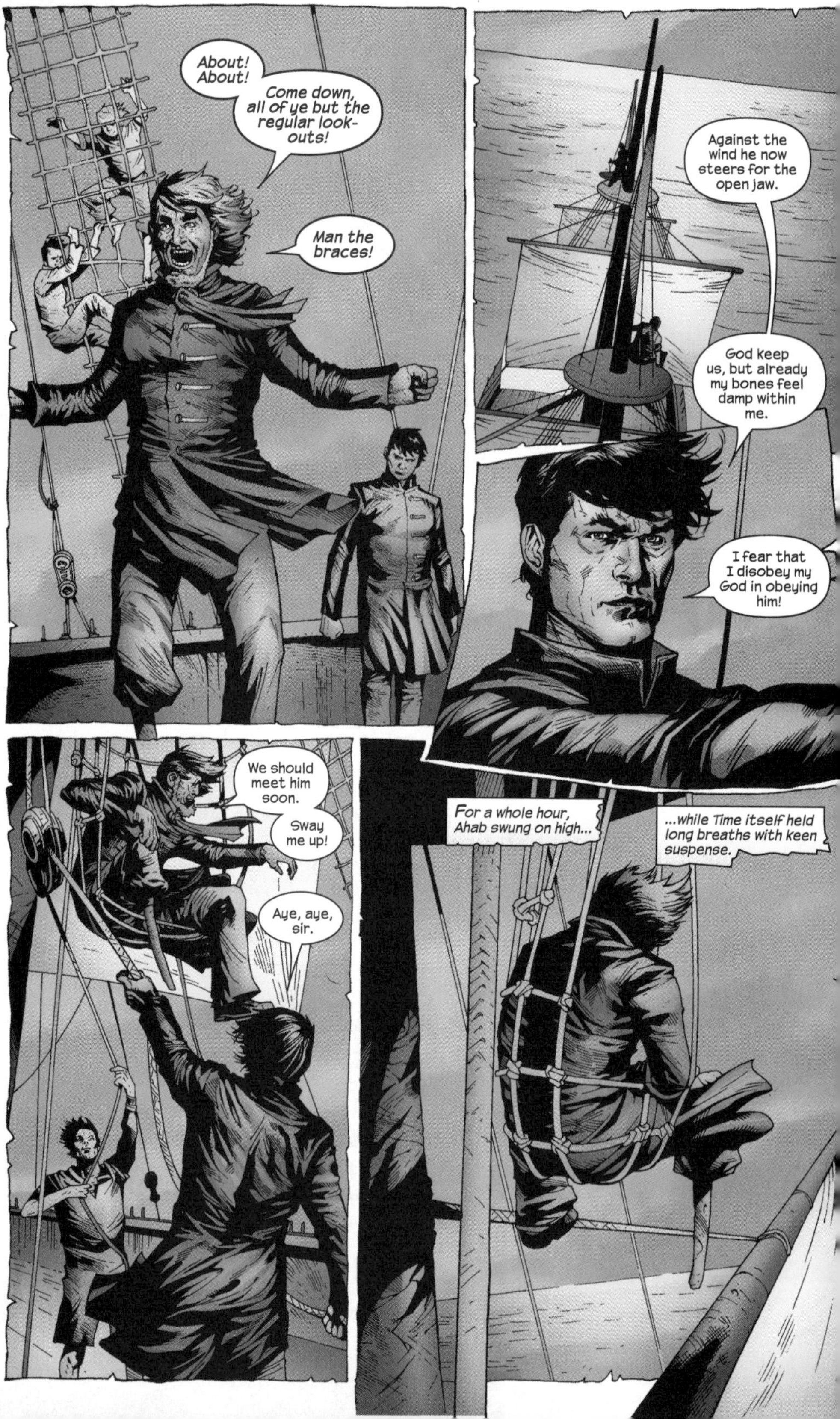
About! About!
Come down, all of ye but the regular look-outs!
Man the braces!
Against the wind he now steers for the open jaw.
God keep us, but already my bones feel damp within me.
I fear that I disobey my God in obeying him!
We should meet him soon.
Sway me up!
Aye, aye, sir.
For a whole hour, Ahab swung on high...
...while Time itself held long breaths with keen suspense.

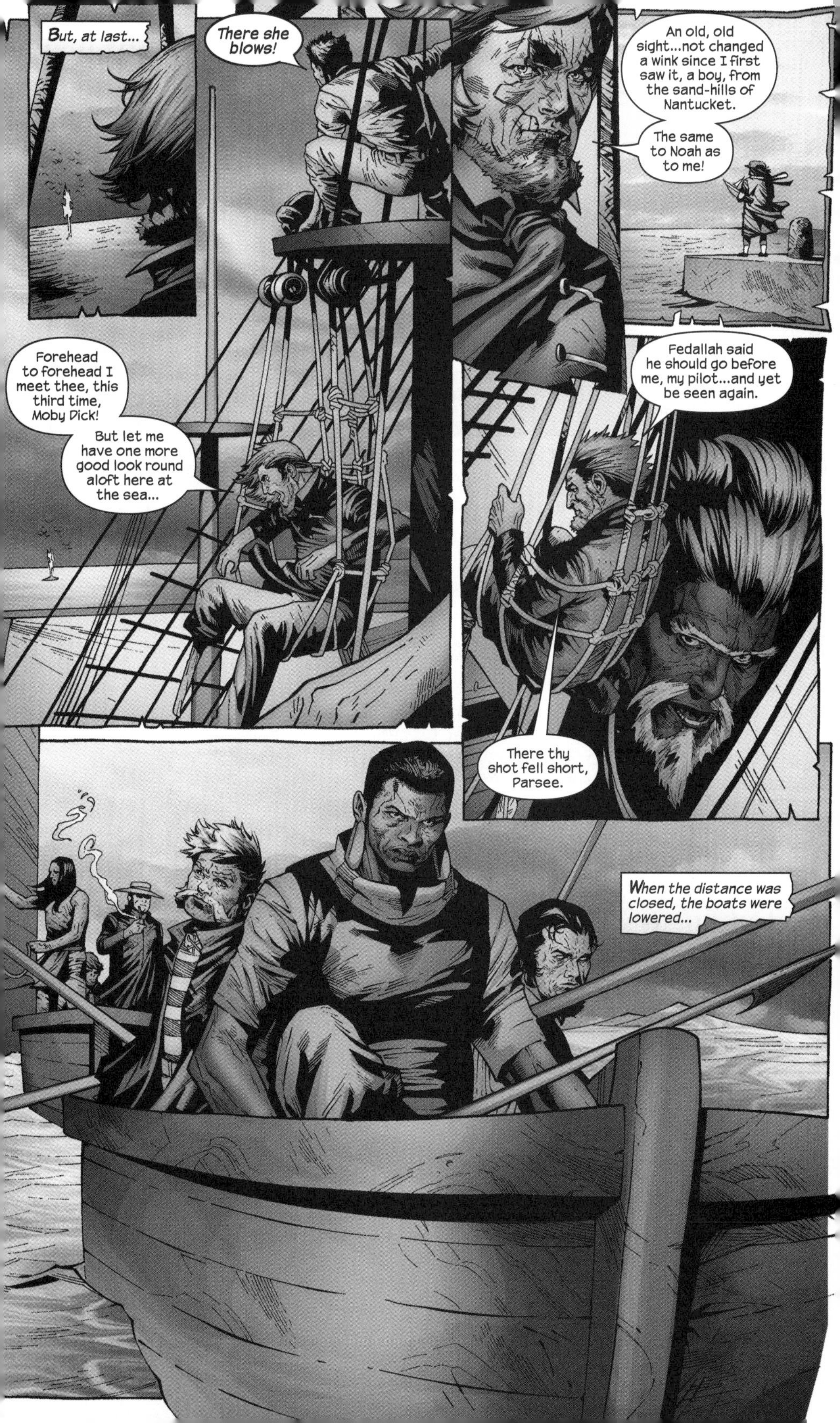
But, at last...
There she blows!
An old, old sight...not changed a wink since I first saw it, a boy, from the sand-hills of Nantucket.
The same to Noah as to me!
Forehead to forehead I meet thee, this third time, Moby Dick!
But let me have one more good look round aloft here at the sea...
Fedallah said he should go before me, my pilot...and yet be seen again.
There thy shot fell short, Parsee.
When the distance was closed, the boats were lowered...

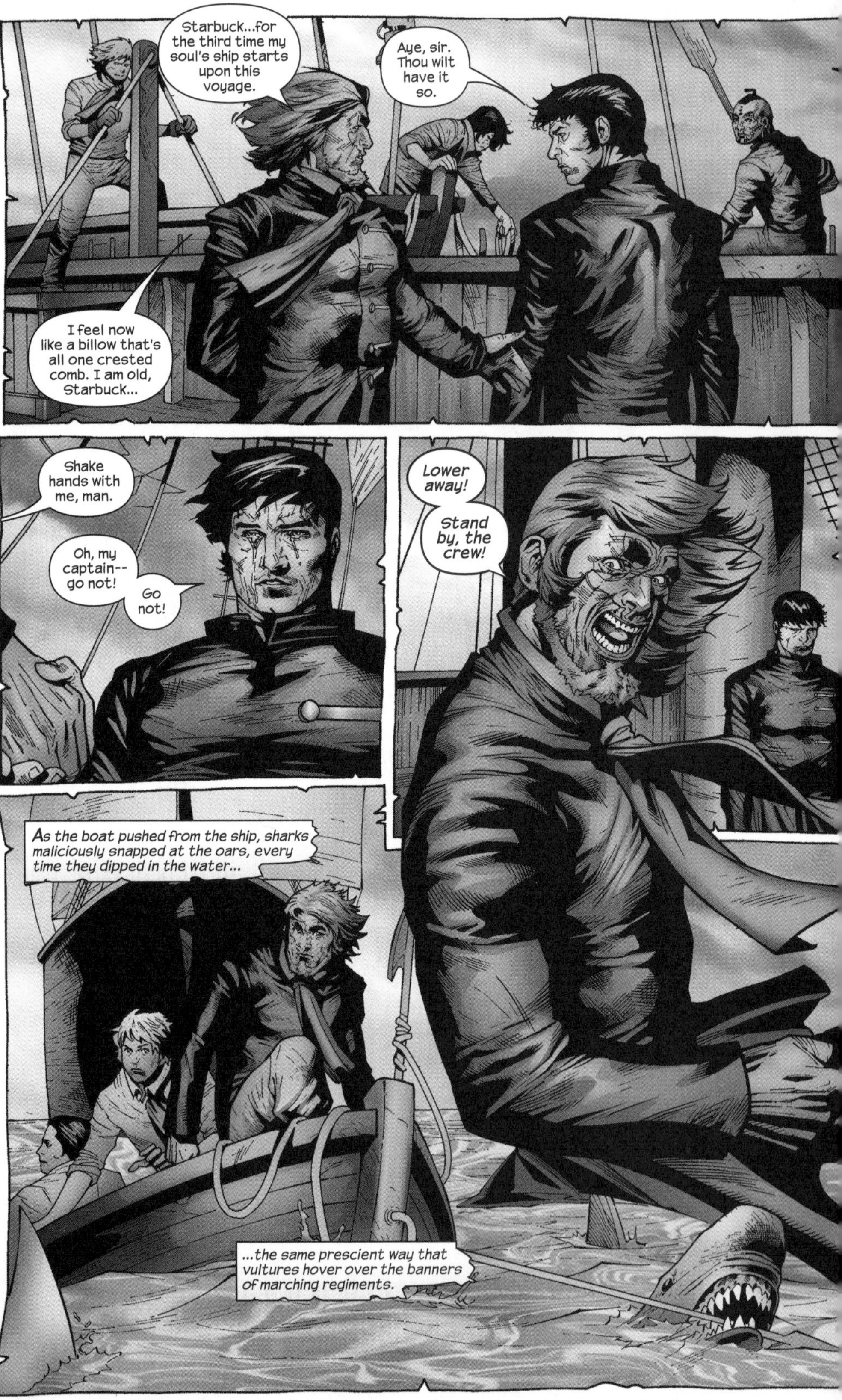
Starbuck...for the third time my soul's ship starts upon this voyage.
Aye, sir. Thou wilt have it so.
I feel now like a billow that's all one crested comb. I am old, Starbuck...
Shake hands with me, man.
Oh, my captain-- go not!
Go not!
Lower away!
Stand by, the crew!
As the boat pushed from the ship, sharks maliciously snapped at the oars, every time they dipped in the water...
...the same prescient way that vultures hover over the banners of marching regiments.

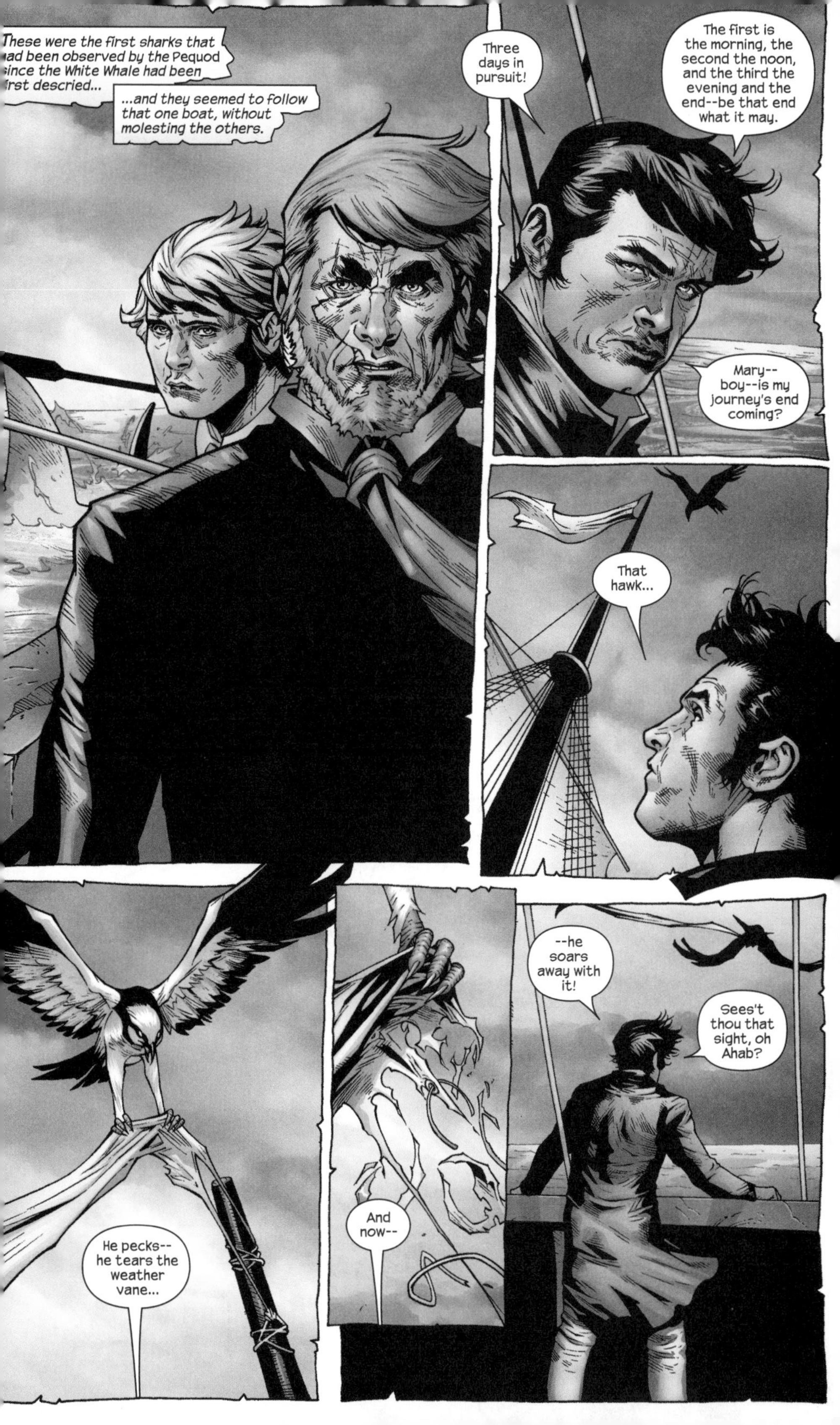
These were the first sharks that
had been observed by the Pequod
since the White Whale had been
first descried...
...and they seemed to follow
that one boat, without
molesting the others.
Three days in pursuit!
The first is the morning, the second the noon, and the third the evening and the end--be that end what it may.
Mary--boy--is my journey's end coming?
That hawk...
He pecks--he tears the weather vane...
And now--
--he soars away with it!
Sees't thou that sight, oh Ahab?

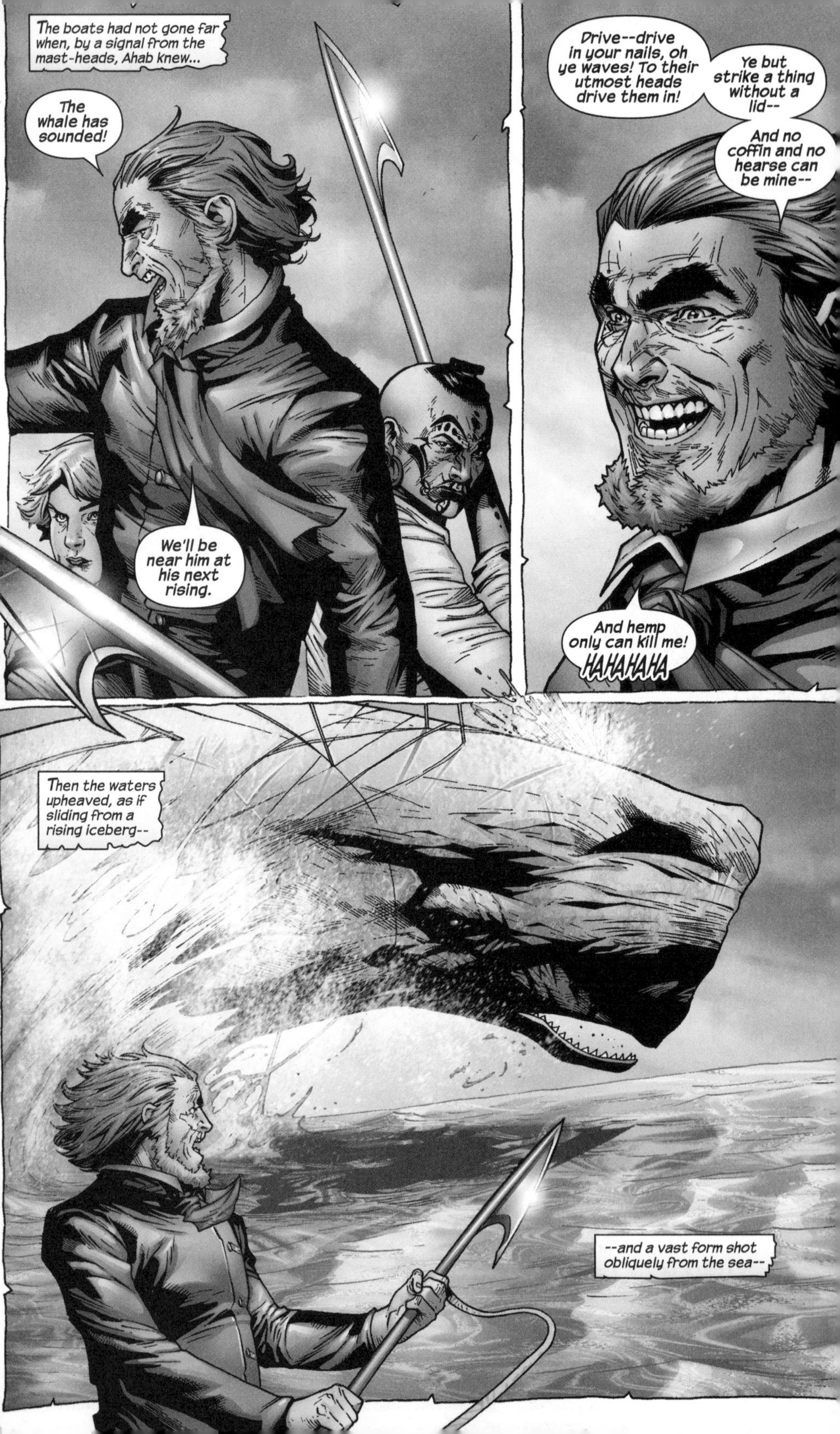
The boats had not gone far when, by a signal from the mast-heads, Ahab knew...
The whale has sounded!
We'll be near him at his next rising.
Drive--drive in your nails, oh ye waves! To their utmost heads drive them in!
Ye but strike a thing without a lid--
And no coffin and no hearse can be mine--
And hemp only can kill me!
HAHAHAHA
Then the waters upheaved, as if sliding from a rising iceberg--
--and a vast form shot obliquely from the sea--

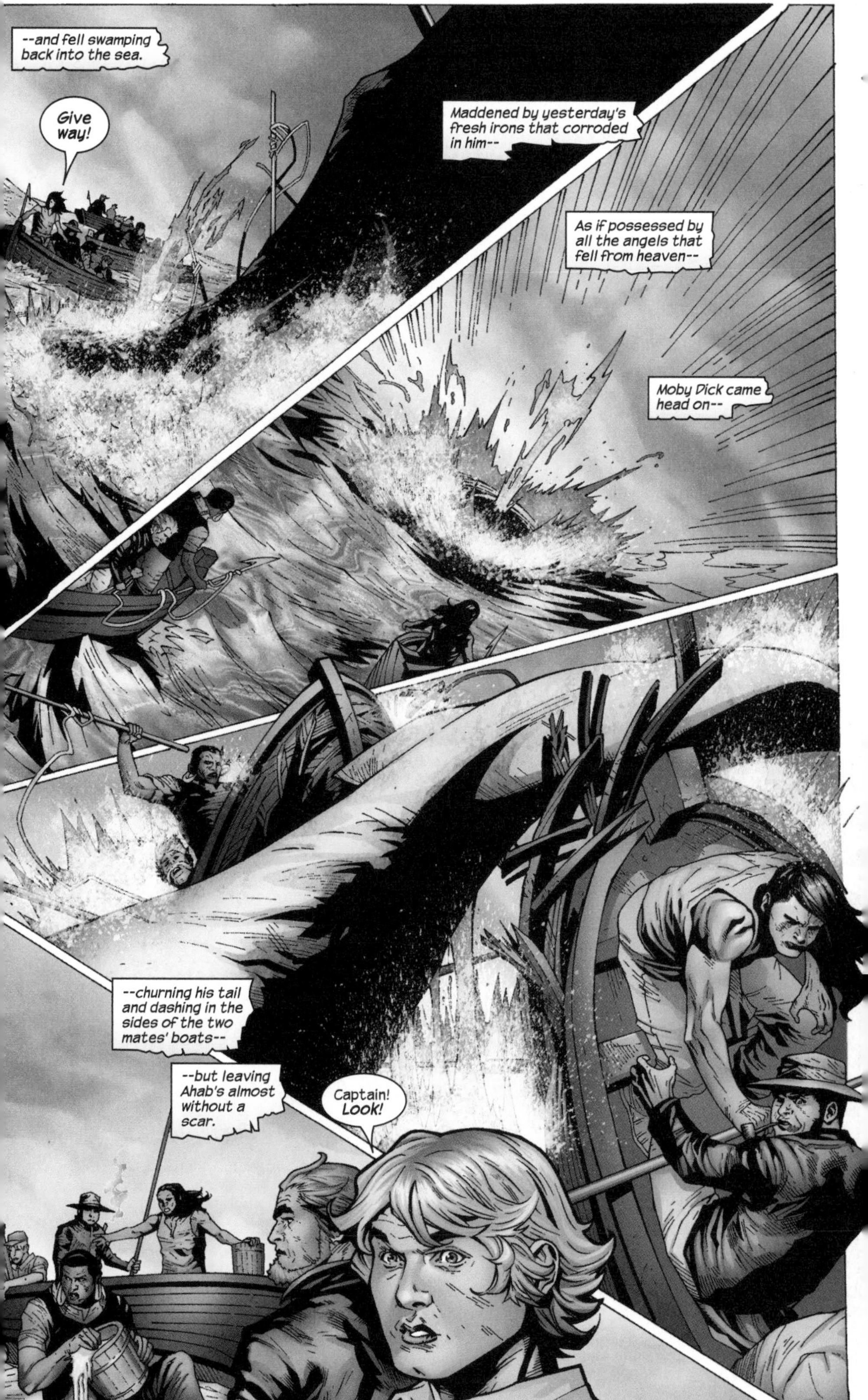
--and fell swamping back into the sea.
Give way!
Maddened by yesterday's fresh irons that corroded in him--
As if possessed by all the angels that fell from heaven--
Moby Dick came head on--
--churning his tail and dashing in the sides of the two mates' boats--
--but leaving Ahab's almost without a scar.
Captain! Look!

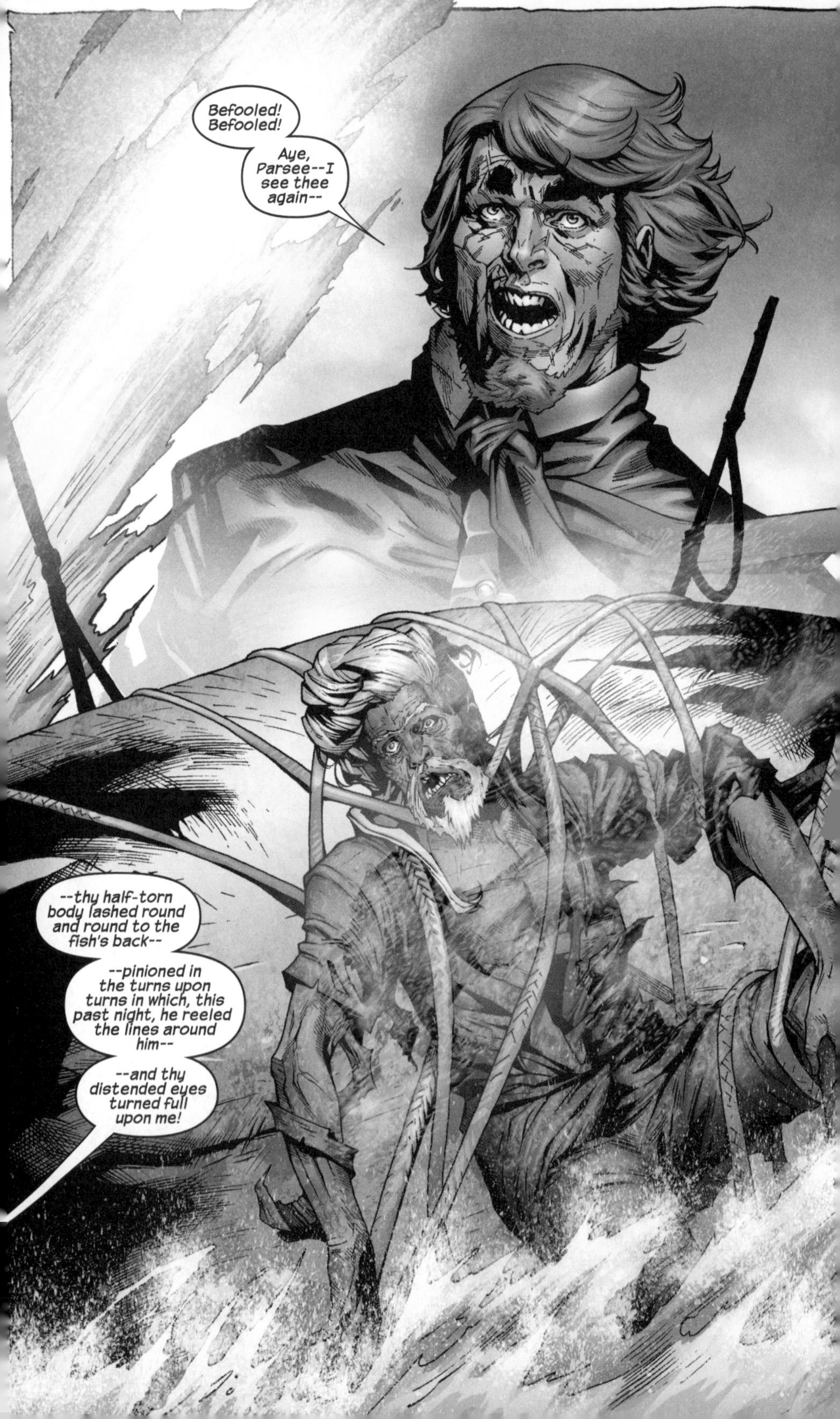
Befooled! Befooled!
Aye, Parsee--I see thee again--
--thy half-torn body lashed round and round to the fish's back--
--pinioned in the turns upon turns in which, this past night, he reeled the lines around him--
--and thy distended eyes turned full upon me!

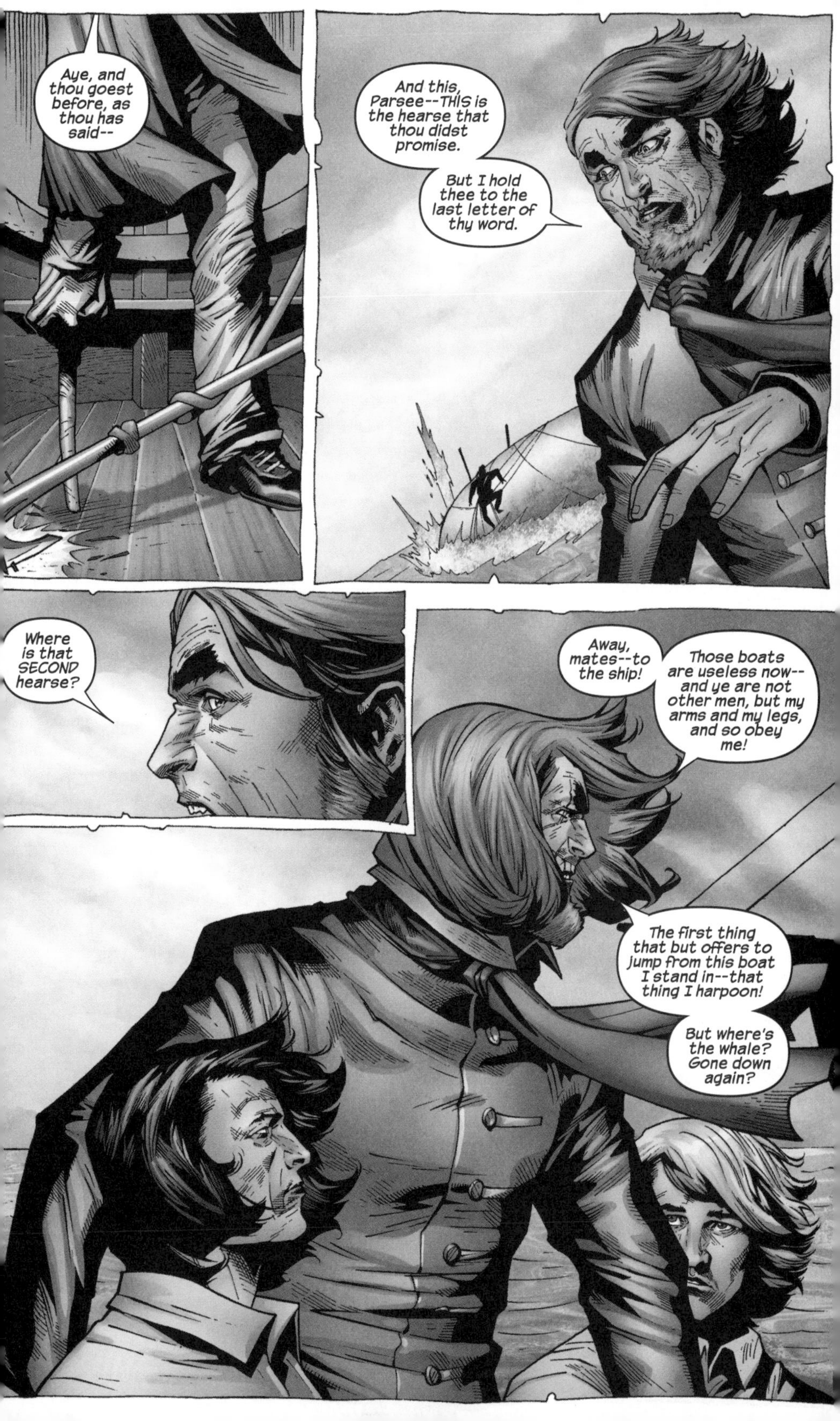
Aye, and thou goest before, as thou has said--
And this, Parsee--THIS is the hearse that thou didst promise.
But I hold thee to the last letter of thy word.
Where is that SECOND hearse?
Away, mates--to the ship!
Those boats are useless now--and ye are not other men, but my arms and my legs, and so obey me!
The first thing that but offers to jump from this boat I stand in--that thing I harpoon!
But where's the whale? Gone down again?

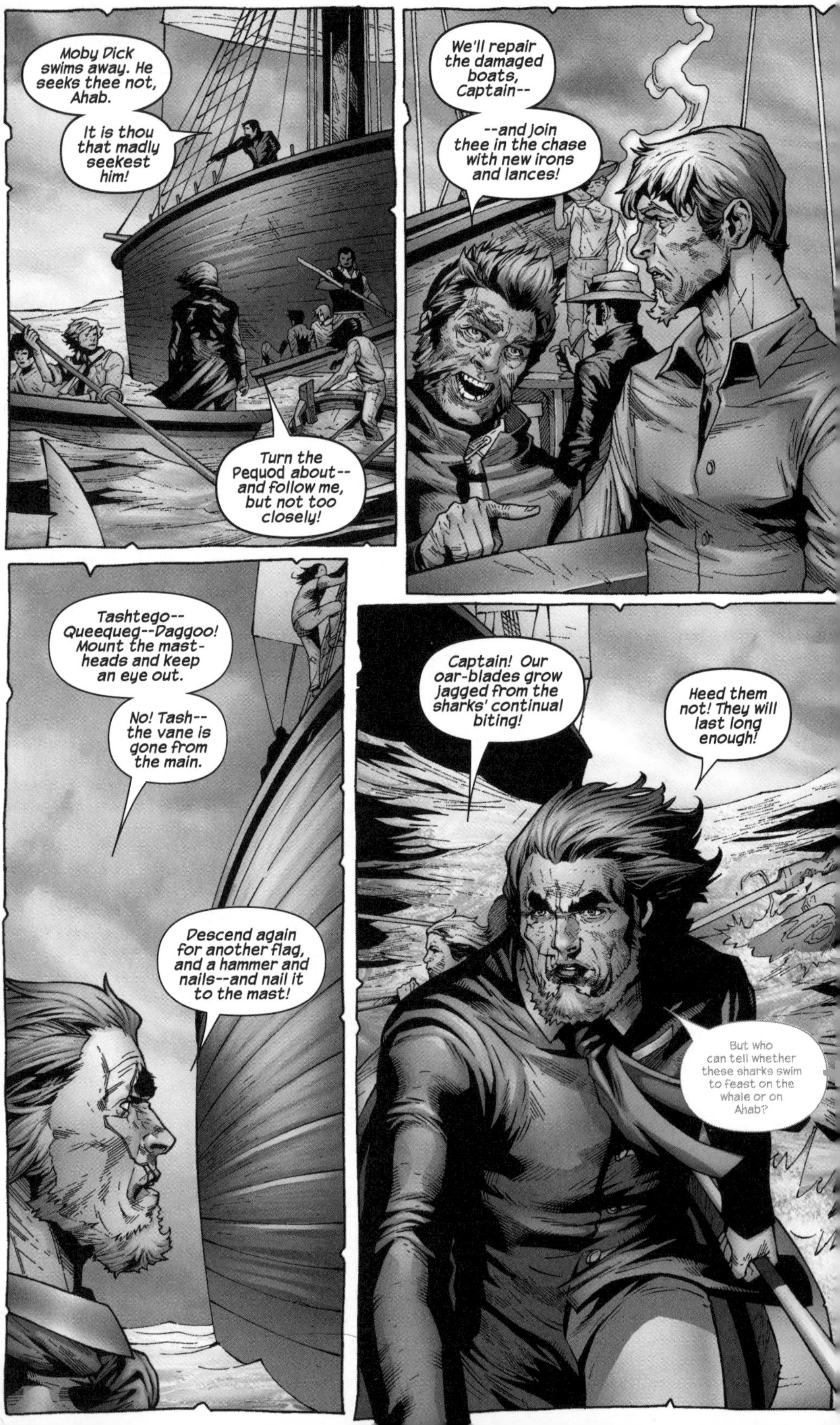

Moby Dick swims away. He seeks thee not, Ahab.
It is thou that madly seekest him!
Turn the Pequod about--and follow me, but not too closely!
We'll repair the damaged boats, Captain--
--and join thee in the chase with new irons and lances!
Tashtego--Queequeg--Daggoo! Mount the mast-heads and keep an eye out.
No! Tash--the vane is gone from the main.
Descend again for another flag, and a hammer and nails--and nail it to the mast!
Captain! Our oar-blades grow jagged from the sharks' continual biting!
Heed them not! They will last long enough!
But who can tell whether these sharks swim to feast on the whale or on Ahab?

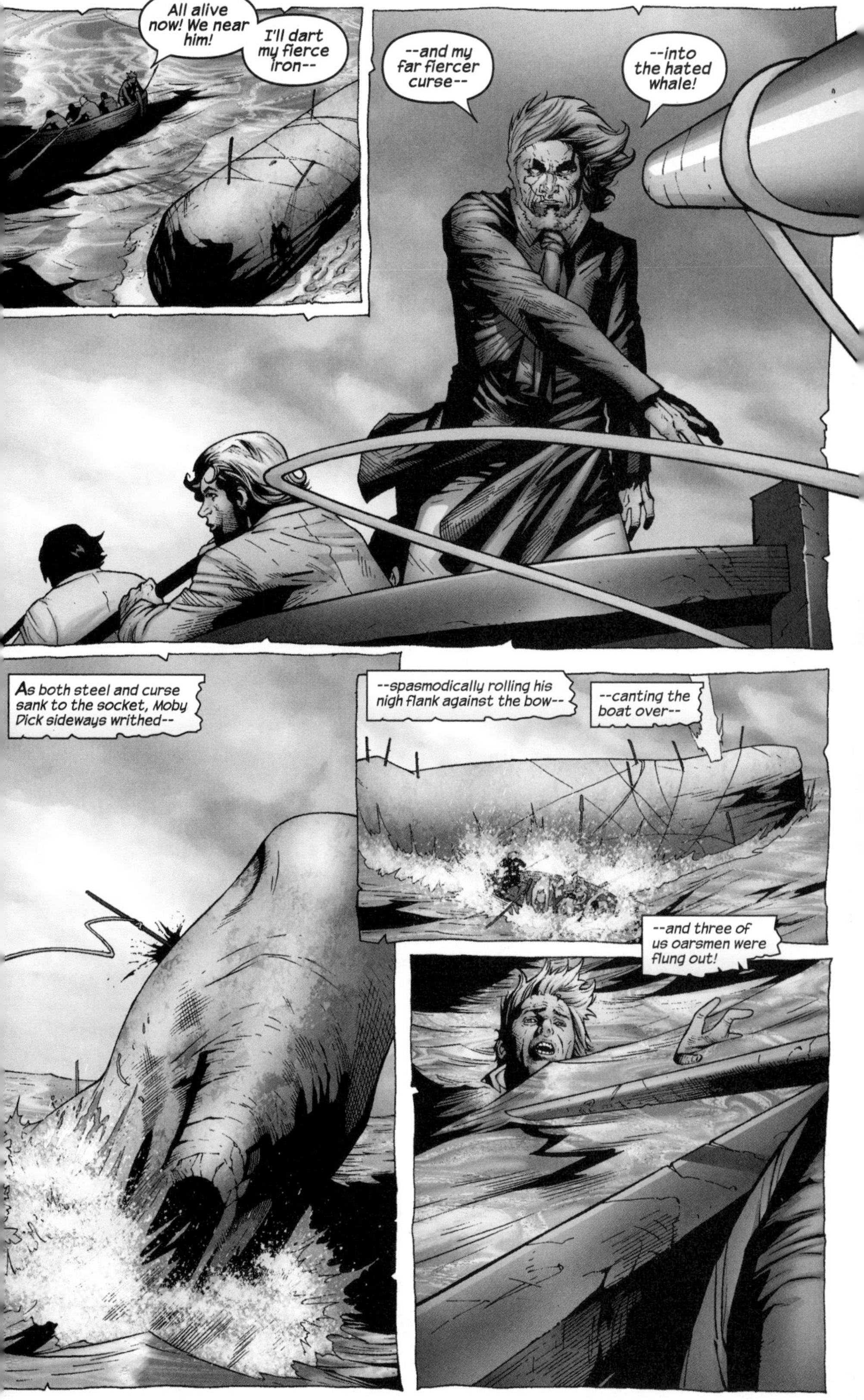
All alive now! We near him!
I'll dart my fierce iron--
--and my far fiercer curse--
--into the hated whale!
As both steel and curse sank to the socket, Moby Dick sideways writhed--
--spasmodically rolling his nigh flank against the bow--
--canting the boat over--
--and three of us oarsmen were flung out!

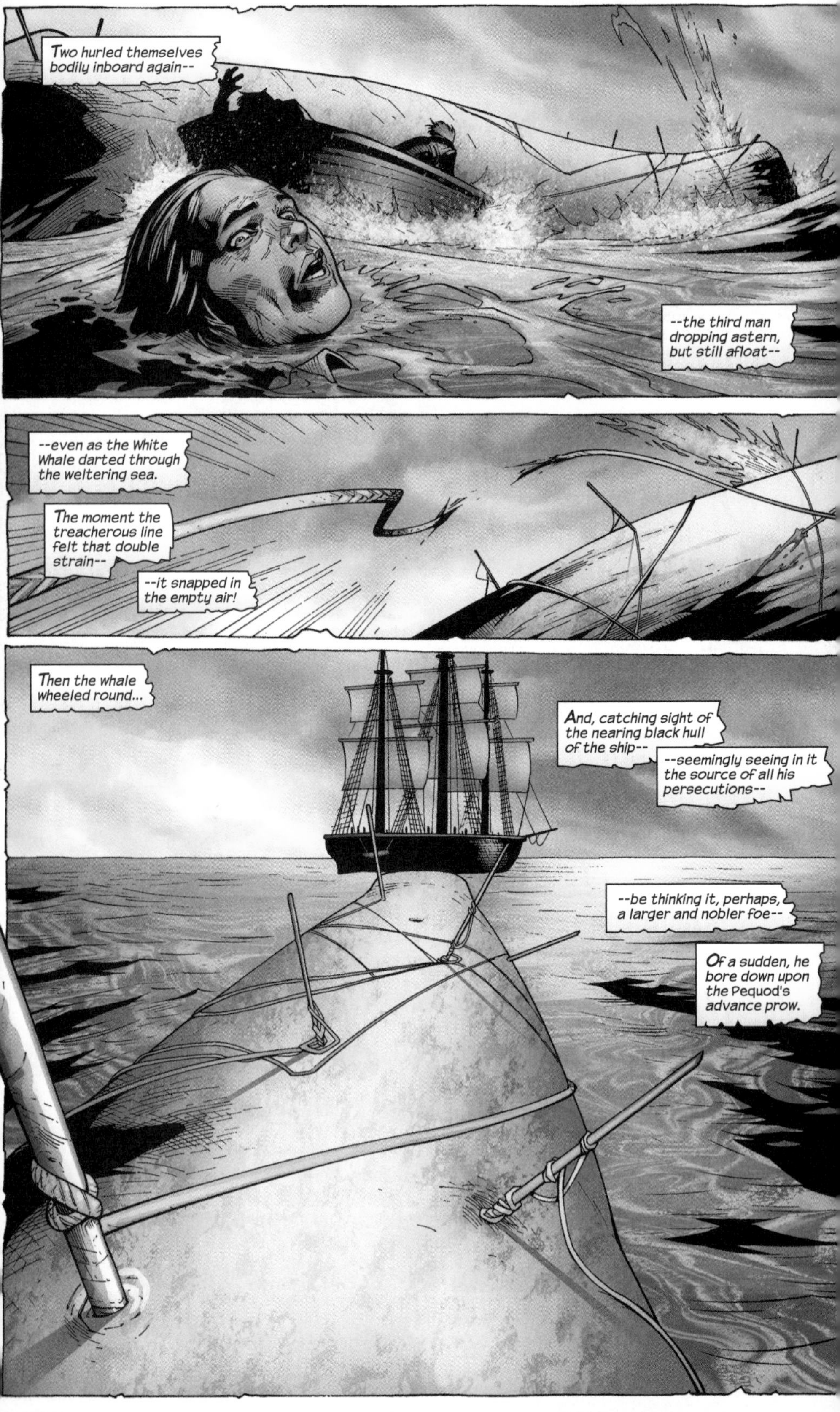
Two hurled themselves bodily inboard again--
--the third man dropping astern, but still afloat--
--even as the White Whale darted through the weltering sea.
The moment the treacherous line felt that double strain--
--it snapped in the empty air!
Then the whale wheeled round...
And, catching sight of the nearing black hull of the ship--
--seemingly seeing in it the source of all his persecutions--
--be thinking it, perhaps, a larger and nobler foe--
Of a sudden, he bore down upon the Pequod's advance prow.

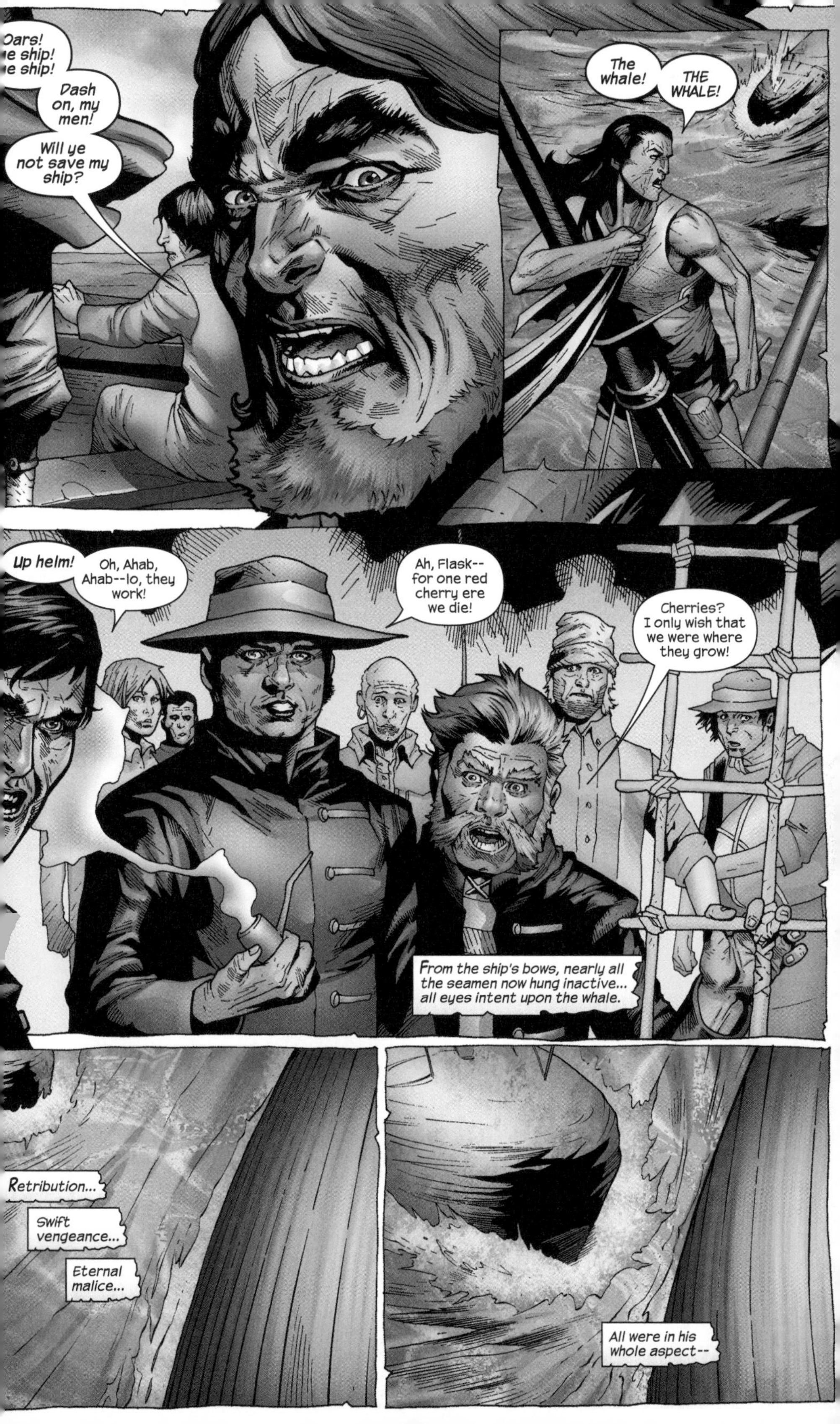

Oars!
e ship!
e ship!
Dash on, my men!
Will ye not save my ship?
The whale!
THE WHALE!
Up helm!
Oh, Ahab, Ahab--lo, they work!
Ah, Flask--for one red cherry ere we die!
Cherries? I only wish that we were where they grow!
From the ship's bows, nearly all the seamen now hung inactive... all eyes intent upon the whale.
Retribution...
Swift vengeance...
Eternal malice...
All were in his whole aspect--

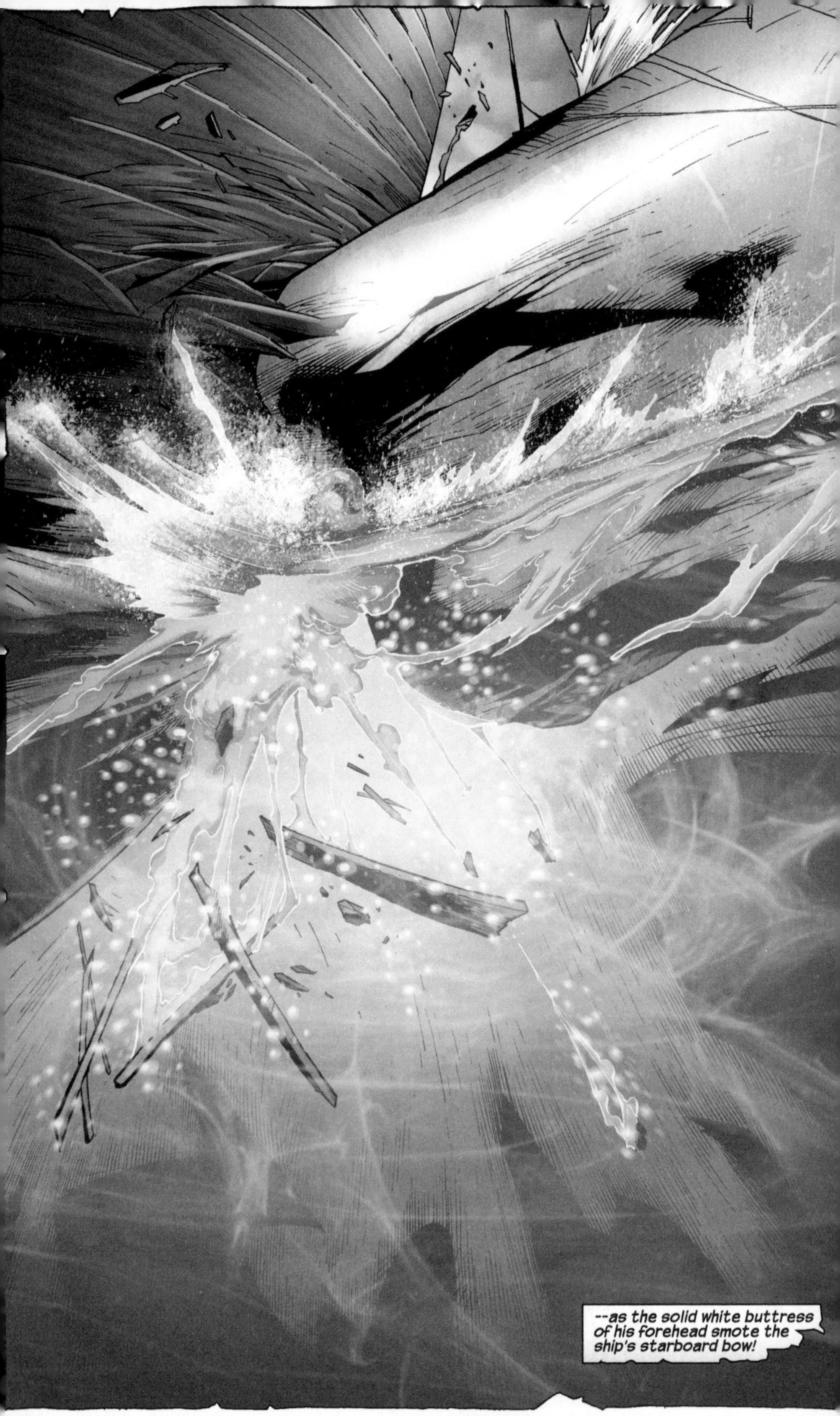
--as the solid white buttress of his forehead smote the ship's starboard bow!

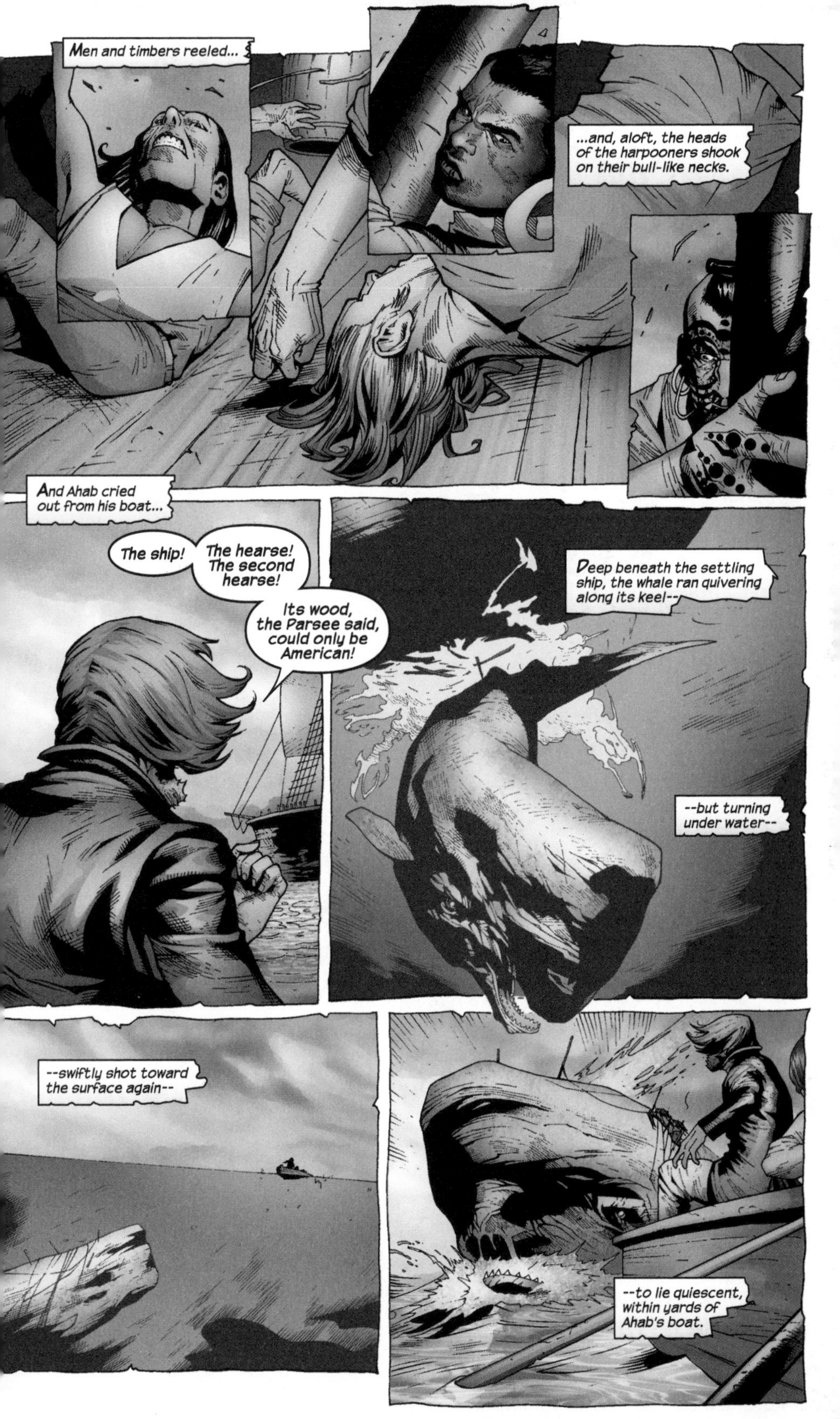
Men and timbers reeled...
...and, aloft, the heads of the harpooners shook on their bull-like necks.
And Ahab cried out from his boat...
The ship!
The hearse! The second hearse!
Its wood, the Parsee said, could only be American!
Deep beneath the settling ship, the whale ran quivering along its keel--
--but turning under water--
--swiftly shot toward the surface again--
--to lie quiescent, within yards of Ahab's boat.

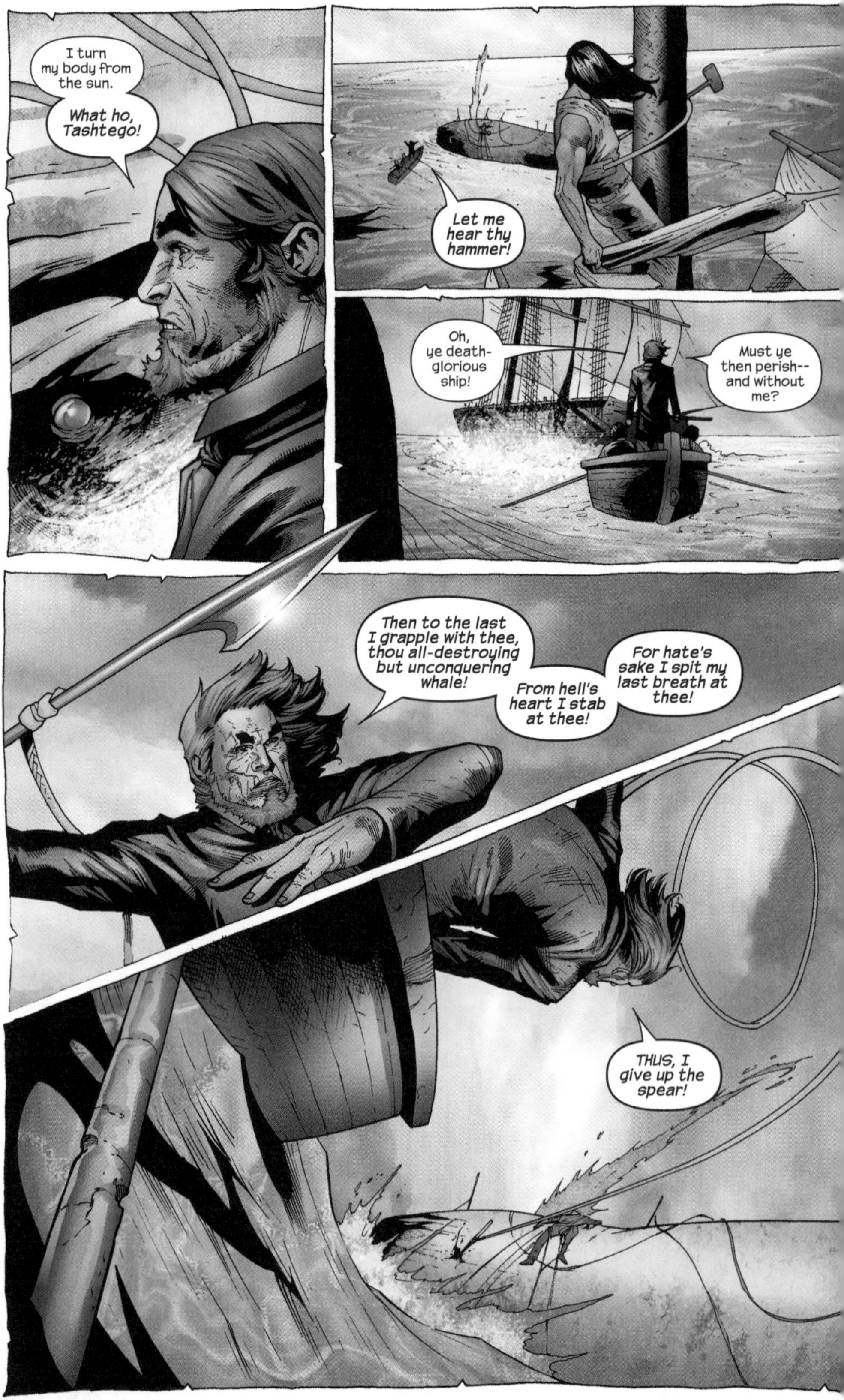
I turn my body from the sun.
What ho, Tashtego!
Let me hear thy hammer!
Oh, ye death-glorious ship!
Must ye then perish-- and without me?
Then to the last I grapple with thee, thou all-destroying but unconquering whale!
From hell's heart I stab at thee!
For hate's sake I spit my last breath at thee!
THUS, I give up the spear!

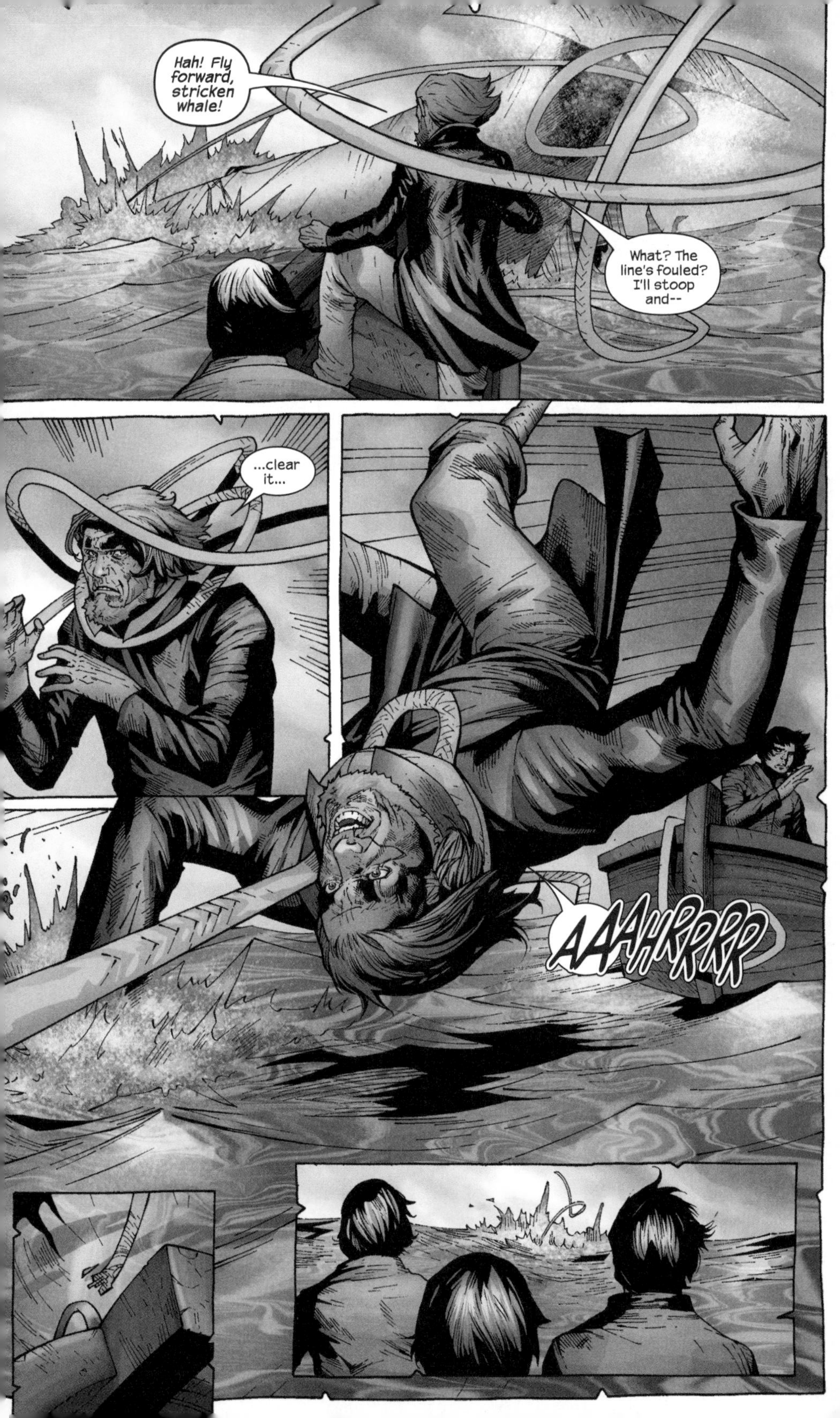
Hah! Fly forward, stricken whale!
What? The line's fouled? I'll stoop and--
...clear it...
AAAHRRRR

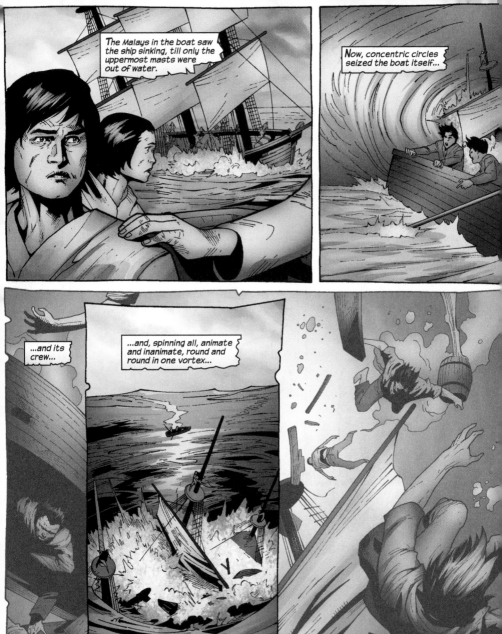

The Malays in the boat saw the ship sinking, till only the uppermost masts were out of water.

Now, concentric circles seized the boat itself...

...and its crew...

...and, spinning all, animate and inanimate, round and round in one vortex...

...carried the smallest chip of the Pequod out of sight.

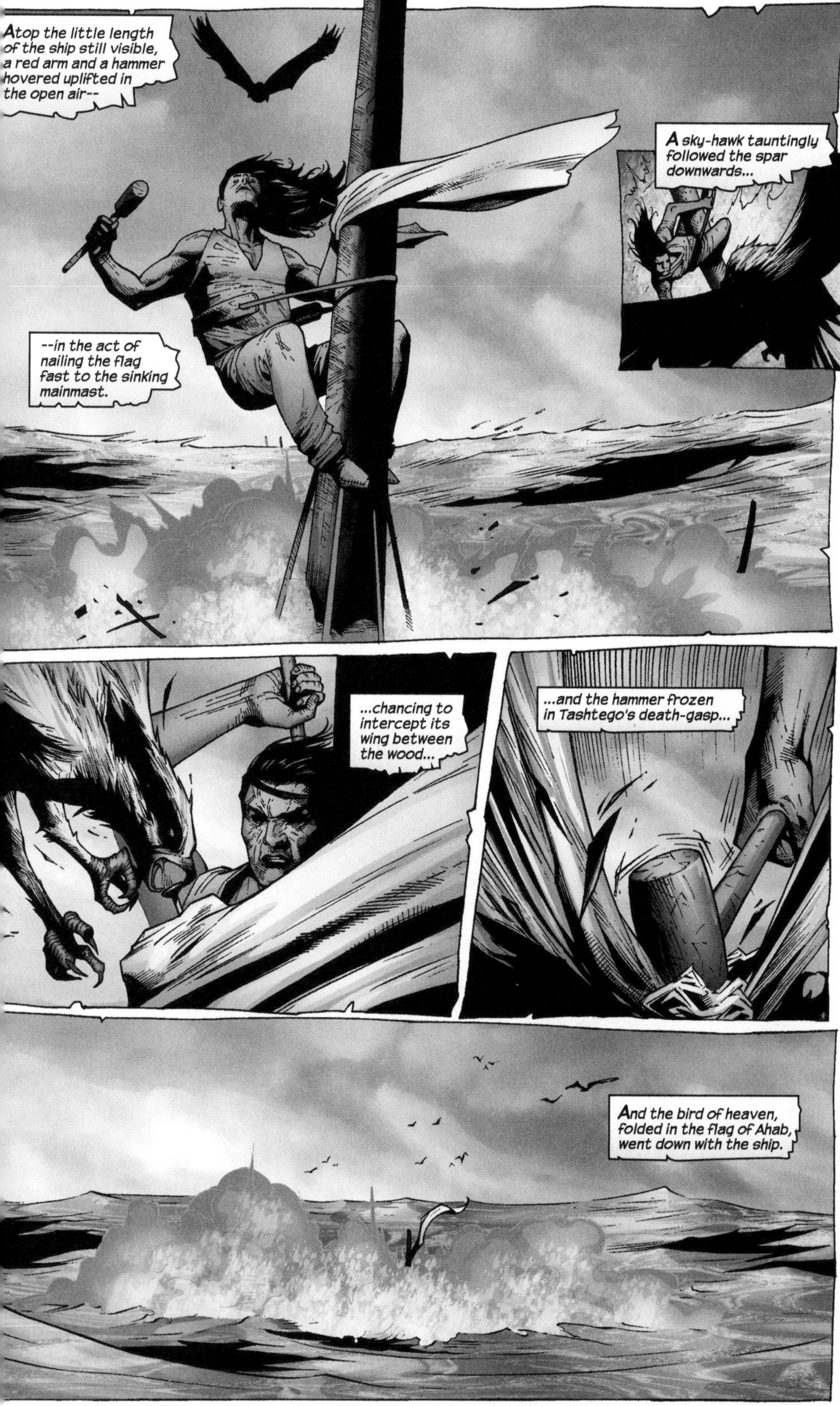
Atop the little length of the ship still visible, a red arm and a hammer hovered uplifted in the open air--
A sky-hawk tauntingly followed the spar downwards...
--in the act of nailing the flag fast to the sinking mainmast.
...chancing to intercept its wing between the wood...
...and the hammer frozen in Tashtego's death-gasp...
And the bird of heaven, folded in the flag of Ahab, went down with the ship.

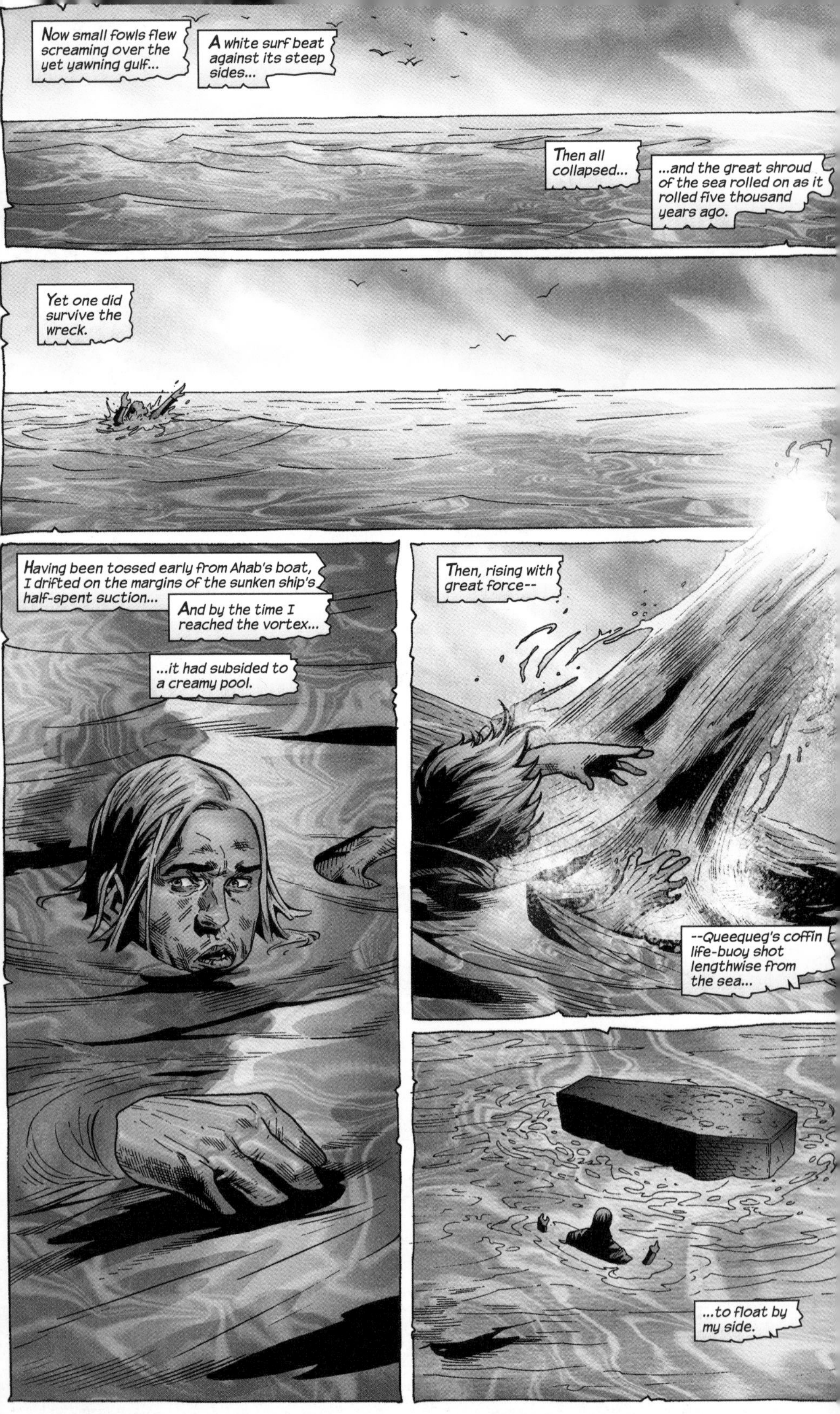
Now small fowls flew screaming over the yet yawning gulf...
A white surf beat against its steep sides...
Then all collapsed...
...and the great shroud of the sea rolled on as it rolled five thousand years ago.
Yet one did survive the wreck.
Having been tossed early from Ahab's boat, I drifted on the margins of the sunken ship's half-spent suction...
And by the time I reached the vortex...
...it had subsided to a creamy pool.
Then, rising with great force--
--Queequeg's coffin life-buoy shot lengthwise from the sea...
...to float by my side.

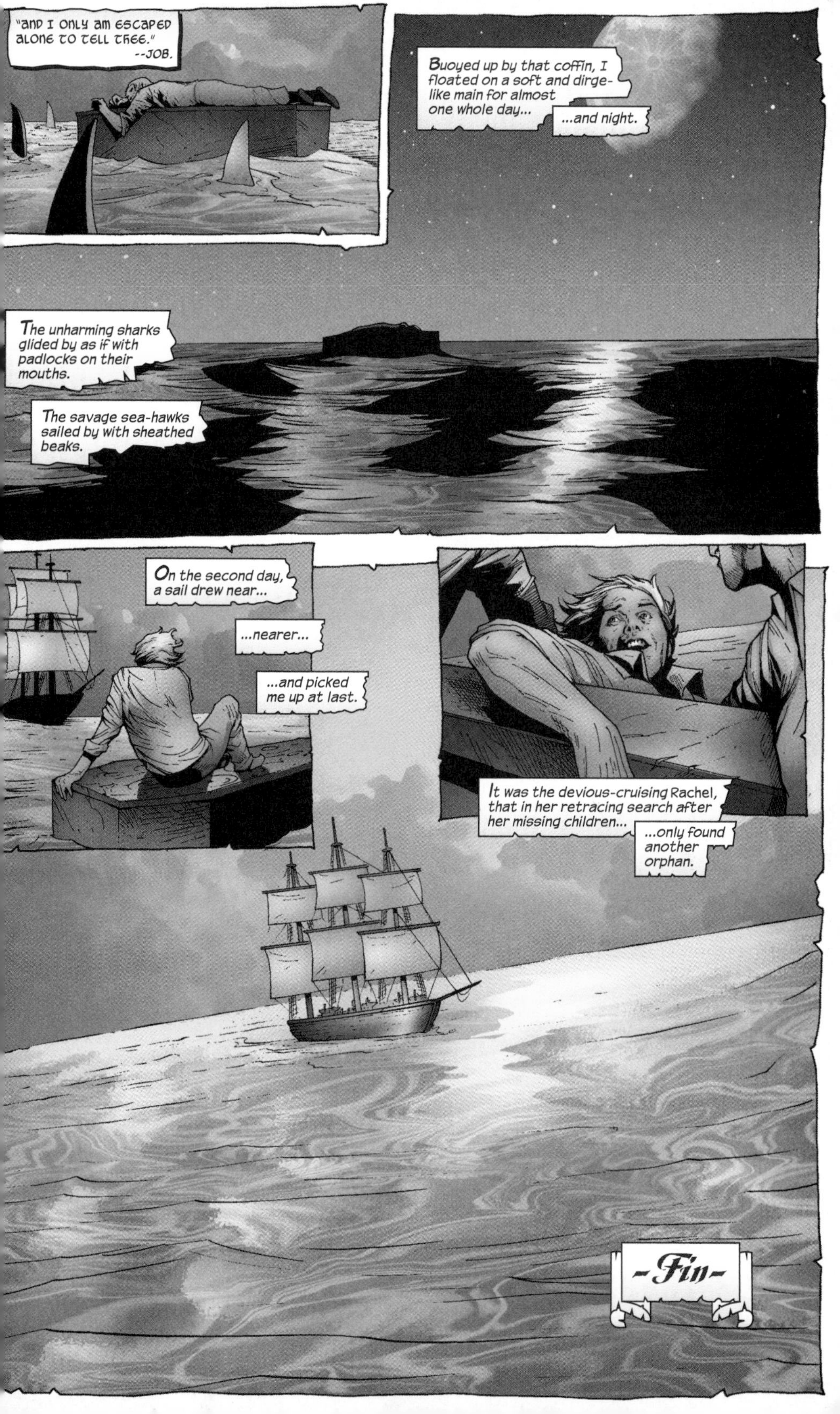
"AND I ONLY AM ESCAPED ALONE TO TELL THEE." --JOB.
Buoyed up by that coffin, I floated on a soft and dirge-like main for almost one whole day...
...and night.
The unharming sharks glided by as if with padlocks on their mouths.
The savage sea-hawks sailed by with sheathed beaks.
On the second day, a sail drew near...
...nearer...
...and picked me up at last.
It was the devious-cruising Rachel, that in her retracing search after her missing children...
...only found another orphan.
-Fin-

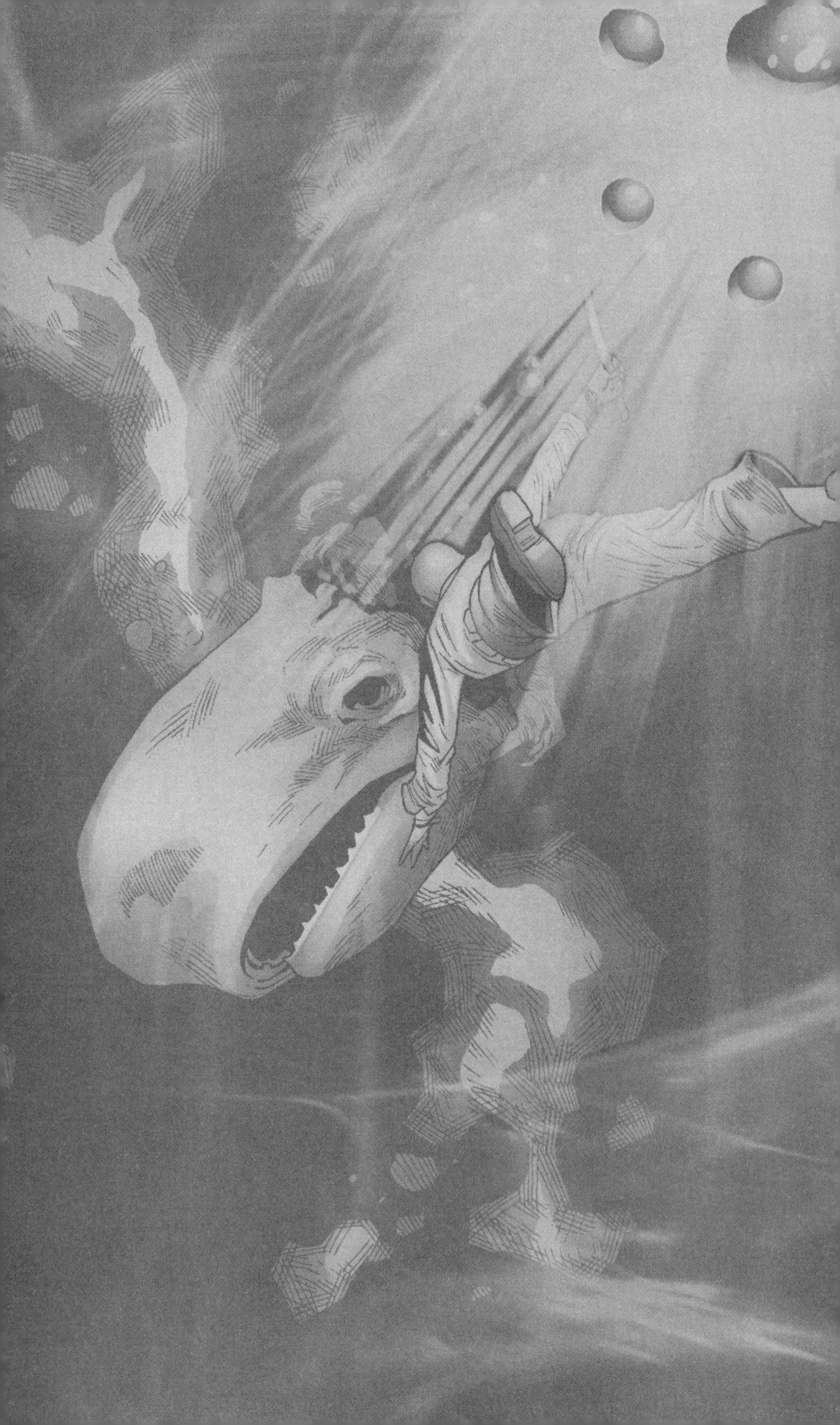

HERMAN MELVILLE
(1819 – 1891)

Short-story writer, novelist, poet, and essayist – one word cannot sum up the man, the myth, the legend...Herman Melville. Brought into this world on August 1, 1819 in New York City, Herman was the third child of Allan and Maria Gansevoort Melville. Belonging to a distinguished family, Herman Melville had all the makings to become an acclaimed writer whose most famous works are *Moby-Dick, The Confidence-Man: His Masquerade, Redburn,* and *White-Jacket.*

After a bout with scarlet fever in 1826, Melville was left with permanently weakened eyesight. In 1835 he attended the Albany Classical School for a year. After leaving the school he would often read Shakespeare and other historical and anthropological works. He then became a farmhand for his uncle in Pittsfield, Massachusetts.

In search of adventure, Melville travelled back to New York and became a cabin boy on a ship bound for Liverpool, England; he later joined the U.S. Navy and began several years of long voyages on ships, sailing the Atlantic and the South Seas.

On August 4, 1847, Melville married Elizabeth Shaw and they raised four children. After living for three years in New York, they bought a farm near Nathaniel Hawthorne's home in Pittsfield, Massachusetts where the two writers became close friends. Inspired by Hawthorne, Melville wrote his masterpiece, *Moby-Dick.* After the publication of *Moby-Dick* in 1851, Melville began to see positive reviews of his works both in England and America, captivating readers with his authentic gift for storytelling. In 1863, he and his family relocated to New York City.

In 1867, Melville's professional writing career was ending and his marriage was strained after his oldest son Malcolm accidentally shot himself. In hopes of pulling his life together, Melville found a job as customs inspector for New York City which he held for 19 years.

He died on September 28, 1891 and rests beside his wife Elizabeth in Woodlawn Cemetery in the Bronx, New York. By the time of his death, Herman Melville had slipped into obscurity as a writer. However, his work has stood the test of time and he now stands as one of the most successful writers of American literature.

MELVILLE'S MUST-READS

Billy Budd
Isle of the Cross
Israel Potter: His Fifty Years of Exile
Mardi: And a Voyage Thither
Moby-Dick
Omoo: A Narrative of the South Seas
Pierre: or, The Ambiguities
Redburn
The Confidence-Man
Typee
White-Jacket

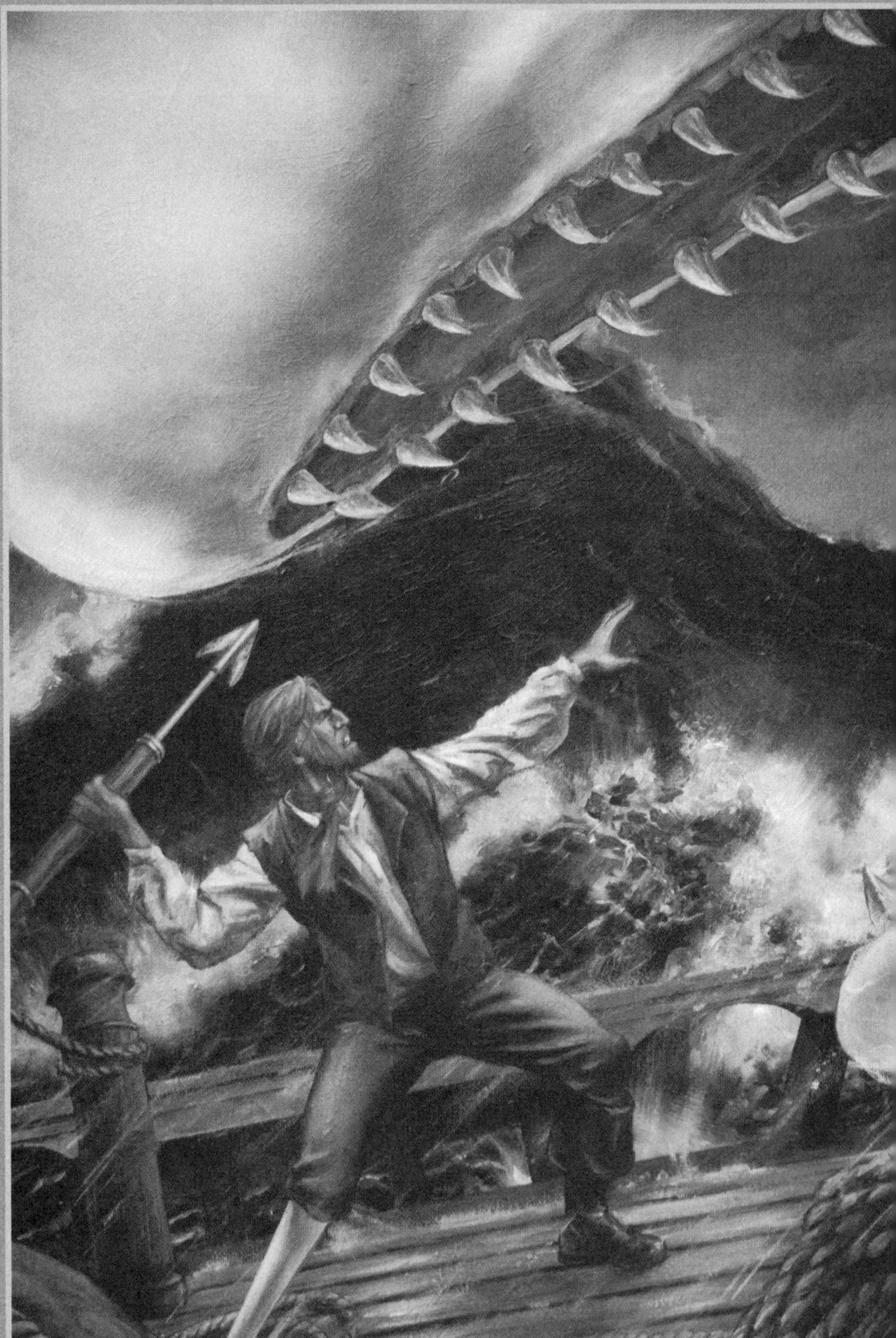

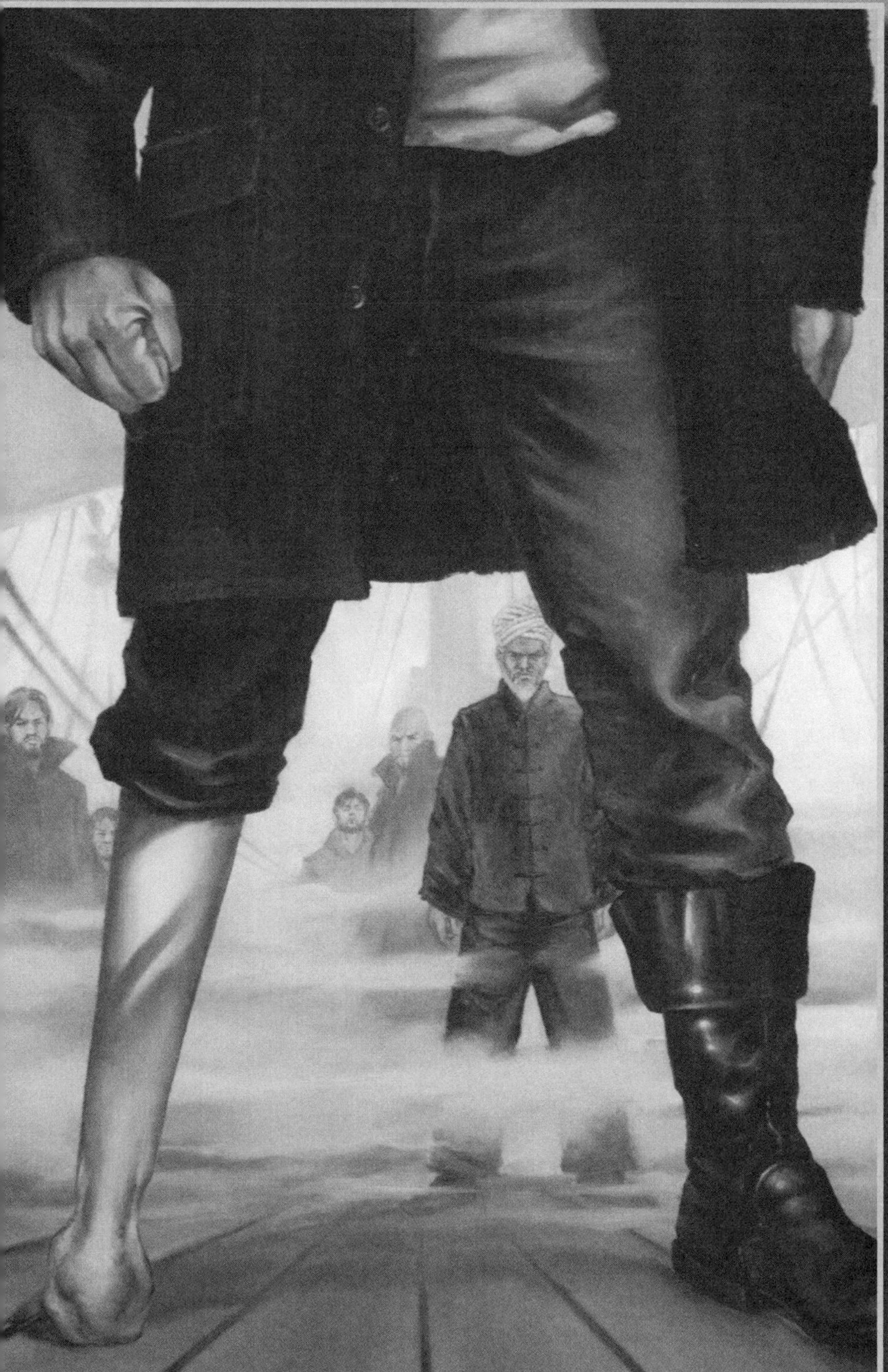

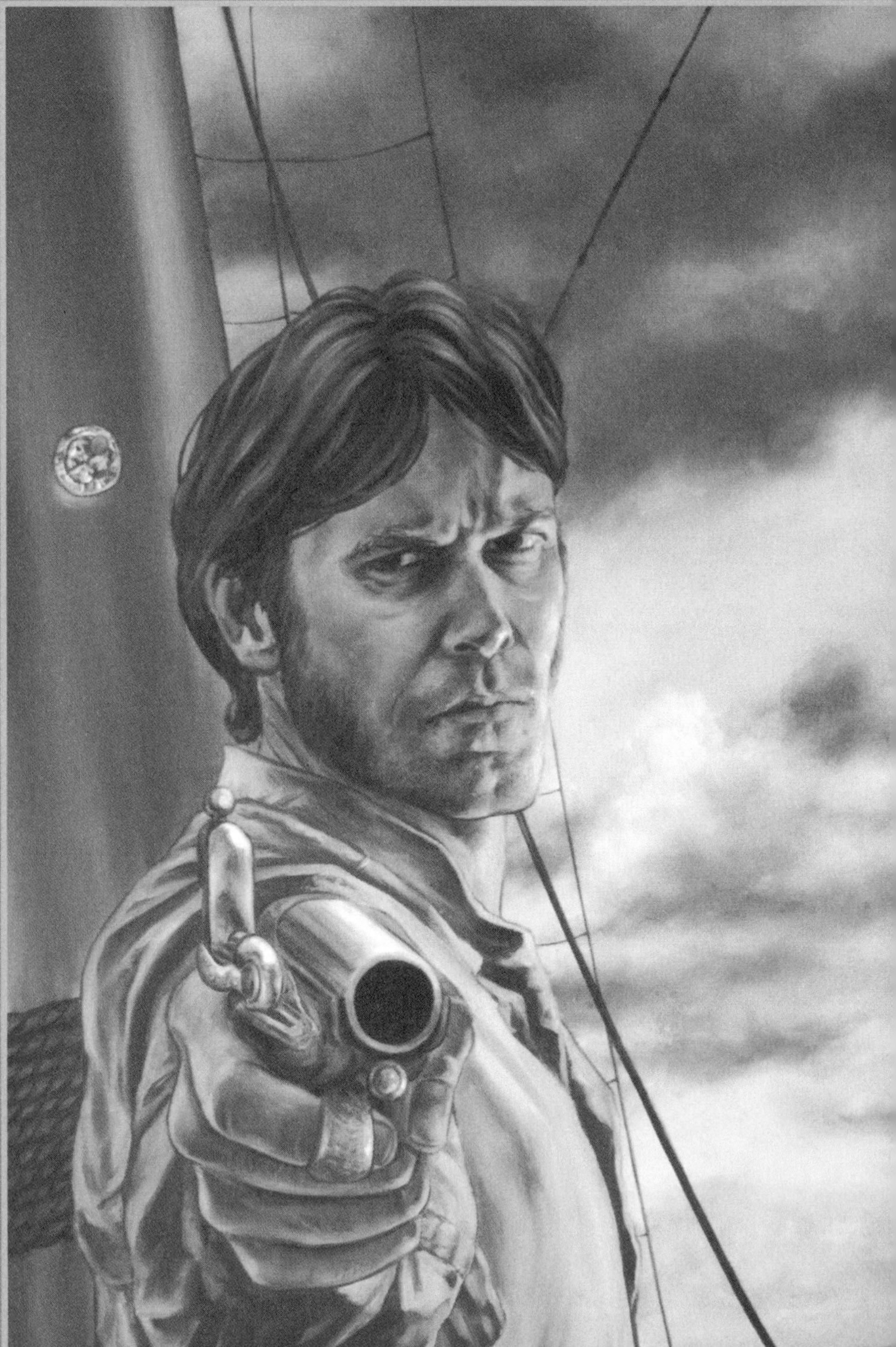

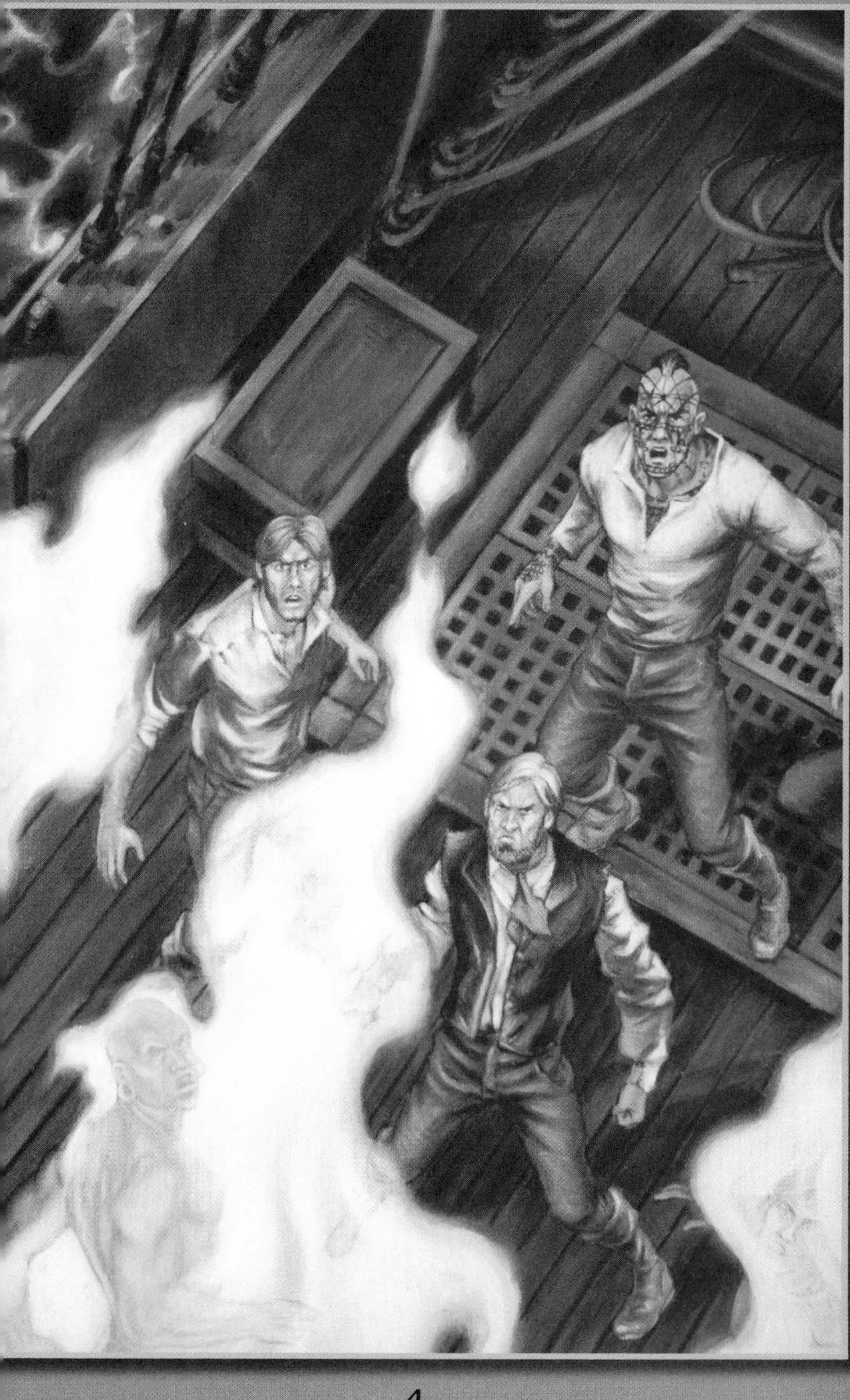

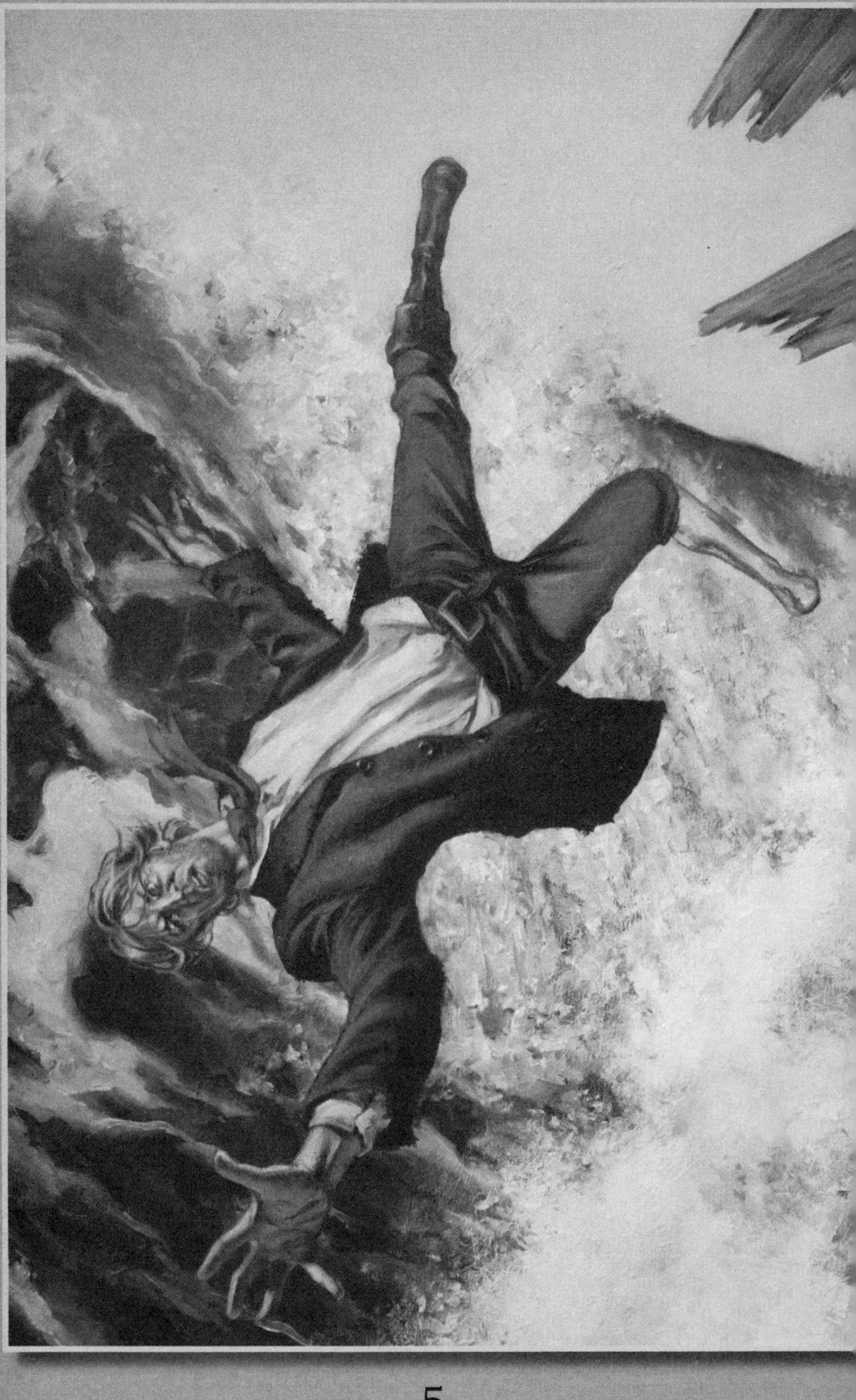

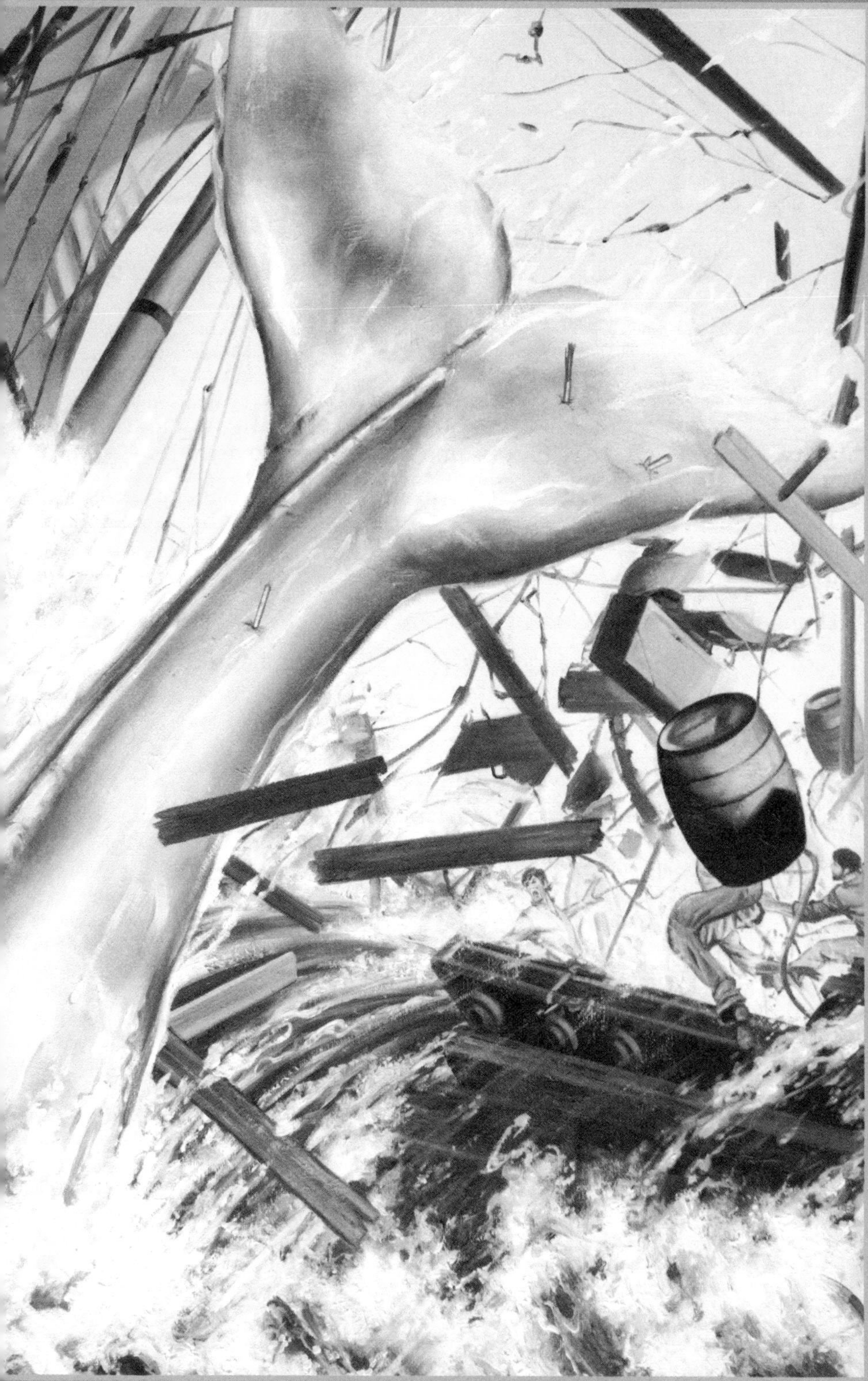

HERMAN MELVILLE
MOBY-DICK
GLOSSARY

abashed	ashamed or embarrassed
abate	to reduce in amount, degree, intensity
aft	at, close to or toward the stern or tail
aloft	on the masts; overhead
apprise	to give notice to, inform
archangel	a chief or high-ranking angel
astern	behind a vessel; in a position behind a specified vessel or aircraft
audacious	extremely bold or daring
auger-hole	a hole created by a boring tool
avast	a command to stop or cease
averted	turned away
banqueter	one who attends a ceremonious public dinner
barb	a sharp point projecting from a weapon or tool, as on a fishhook
befool	to hoodwink, deceive or trick
benediction	a blessing
billow	a great wave or surge of the sea
blacksmith	a person who produces objects of iron
blanch	to whiten by removing color with bleach or by other means
blaspheme	to speak impiously or irreverently of god or sacred things
blasphemous	grossly lacking respect toward what is held to be sacred
bulwarks	solid wall enclosing the perimeter of a weather or main deck for the protection of persons or objects on deck

bumpkin	awkward, unsophisticated person
buoy	a floating marker
comely	pleasing and wholesome in appearance; attractive
concernment	importance
corpusant (modern spelling: Corposant)	an electrical discharge accompanied by ionization of surrounding atmosphere; sometimes known as "st. elmo's fire."
corrode	to eat or wear away gradually, usually by chemical action
crockery	tableware
decree	a formal and authoritative order, esp. one having the force of law
deliriums	a temporary state of mental confusion
descry	to discover; perceive; detect
dirge	a funeral song or tune
dismast	to remove or break off the mast of
doubloon	a gold coin formerly used in spain and spanish america
engender	bring into existence
entreaty	earnest request or plea
epidemic	affecting many persons at the same time, usually in terms of a disease
ere	previous to; before
exulting	to rejoice greatly; be jubilant or triumphant
forge	a furnace or hearth where metals are heated or crafted
forlornness	of being lonely and sad; expressive of hopelessness
gallows	a wooden frame on which condemned persons are executed by hanging
genus	a class or group of individuals, or of species of individuals
green	new or inexperienced
grindstone	a revolving stone disk used for grinding, polishing, or sharpening tools
grotesque	odd or unnatural in shape, appearance
guttural	of or pertaining to the throat
handspike	a bar used as a lever
harpoon	a barbed, spear-like missile attached to a rope, and

	thrown by hand or shot from a gun, used for killing and capturing whales and large fish
head-and-head	straight up to the forehead
hearse	a vehicle for conveying a dead person to the place of burial
helter-skelter	in a haphazard manner; without regard for order
hemp	the tough fiber of the hemp plant, used for making rope or coarse fabric
hitherto	up to this time; until now
hogshead	any of various units of volume or capacity ranging from 63 to 140 gallons
hoist	to raise or lift
idolater	one who blindly or excessively admires or adores another
immitigable	not able to be lessened in force or intensity, as wrath, grief, harshness, or pain
immutable	not subject or susceptible to change or variation in form or quality or nature
impiety	lack of dutifulness or respect
infallible	trustworthy or sure
infidel	without religious faith
inscrutable	incapable of being seen through physical means
insular	detached; standing alone
intemperate	given to or characterized by excessive indulgence in alcoholic beverages
jeeringly	speaking or shouting in a taunting or mocking manner
keel	a structure in the hull of the ship that provides stability
kinsmen	men sharing the same racial, cultural, or national background as another
lance	a spear for killing a harpooned whale
larboard	on the port side
lay	a way of figuring wages, based on a percentage of the profits at the end of a whaling voyage
Lazarus	the person whom Jesus raised from the dead after four days in the tomb; this miracle caused the enemies of Jesus to begin the plan to put him to death
lee	the side or part that is sheltered or turned away from the wind

leeward	on or toward the side to which the wind is blowing
legatee	the inheritor of a legacy
leviathan	sea monster
line	the equator
lithe	limber, flexible
loom	an apparatus for weaving fabrics
maim	to cause a physical injury or impairment
make a clean breast	to confess something of guilt
malignant	tending to produce death
midships	at or near or toward the center of a ship
midwife	a person trained to assist women in childbirth
miser	a stingy, avaricious person who lives in wretched circumstances
mutinous	disposed to, engaged in, or involving revolt against authority
nondescripts	people of no particular or notable type or kind
pagan	pertaining to the worship of any religion that is neither Christian, Jewish, nor Muslim
palate	the sense of taste
pallid	pale; of faint color
pallbearer	person carrying or attending a coffin at a funeral
parcel	a small package or bundle
parmacetty	whale
Parsee	a member of the Zoroastrian religious sect in south Asia
perdition	place of final spiritual ruin; hell
perish	to pass away or disappear
pilot-cloth	a thick blue cloth used to make over-coats and coats for sailors
pinion	to bind quickly or hold down; shackle
pious	having or showing a dutiful spirit of reverence for god or an earnest wish to fulfill religious obligations
prow	the front end of a ship or boat
quadrant	an instrument for measuring angular distances between objects, especially useful for determining latitude and longitude
quarter-deck	part of the upper deck reserved for officers

queer	strange or odd, from a conventional viewpoint
Rachel	the wife of Jacob as described in the biblical book of Jeremiah, who is known for crying for an end to the sufferings of her descendants
resplendent	shining brilliantly; gleaming
retribution	something justly deserved
rouse	to stir or incite to strong indignation or anger
seaman	a person whose occupation is assisting in the handling, sailing, and navigating of a ship during a voyage
serene	calm or peaceful
smite	to strike down, injure, or slay
solemn	grave, sober or serious
soliloquy	the act of talking while or as if alone
solitary	alone; without companions
sound	to dive swiftly downward
spasmodically	given to or characterized by bursts of excitement
spermaceti	a pearly white, waxy, translucent solid, obtained from the oil in the head of the sperm whale used in cosmetics and candles
spout	the burst of spray from the blowhole of a whale
stern	the rear part of a ship or boat
stove	past tense of *stave*, meaning to crush or break inward
sullen	gloomy or somber in tone, color, or portent
squall	a sudden, violent gust of wind, often accompanied by rain, snow, or sleet
sulphurous	fiery or heated
sway	to move or swing to and fro
taper	to make thinner or narrower at one end
temper	to harden or strengthen
t'gallant	square-rigged sail above the topsail; also known as a topgallant sail
treadle	a pedal or lever operated by the foot for circular drive, as in a sewing machine
tumult	a violent and noisy commotion or disturbance
turban	a man's headdress worn chiefly by Muslims in southern Asia, consisting of a long cloth of silk, linen, cotton, etc., wound either about a cap or directly around the head

vortex	a whirling mass of water, where the suction creates a type of whirlpool
whimsy	something odd or fanciful
windlass	device for raising weights by winding a rope around a cylinder
woodcock	plump, short-legged migratory game bird of variegated brown plumage
wrought	produced or shaped
yore	of old; long ago

*notes from the text:

"Every whale-ship takes out a goodly number of letters for various ships, whose delivery…depends upon the mere chance of encountering them in the four oceans. thus, most letters never reach their mark; and many are only received after attaining an age of two or three years or more."

"Ego non baptizo te in nomine patris, sed in nomine diaboli" is translated from latin as "I baptize you not in the name of the father, but of the devil!"